PAPPY:
The Life of
JOHN FORD

Dan Ford

PRENTICE-HALL, Inc.
Englewood Cliffs, N.J.

Art Direction and Design by Hal Siegel

Printed in the United States of America

Prentice-Hall International, Inc., London
Prentice-Hall of Australia, Pty. Ltd., Sydney
Prentice-Hall of Canada, Ltd., Toronto
Prentice-Hall of India Private Ltd., New Delhi
Prentice-Hall of Japan, Inc., Tokyo
Prentice-Hall of Southeast Asia Pte. Ltd., Singapore
Whitehall Books Limited, Wellington, New Zealand

10   9   8   7   6   5   4   3   2

Library of Congress Cataloging in Publication Data

Ford, Dan.
  Pappy.

  Includes index.
  1. Ford, John, 1895-1973. 2. Moving-picture pro-
ducers and directors—United States—Biography.
I. Title.
PN1998.A3F566   791.43'0233'0924 [B]   79-14988
ISBN 0-13-648493-X

For Kelly and Little Kel

Acknowledgments

In the course of writing this book, I spoke to many of my grandfather's colleagues, a task made easier because most were also family friends. I would like to thank the following people for taking time from their busy schedules: Elizabeth Allen, Mark Armistead, James Warner Bellah, Bea Benjamin, Katherine Clifton Bryant, Harry Carey, Jr., Ollie Carey, Bill Clothier, Ken Curtis, Cecile DePrita, Joanne Dru, Philip Dunne, Alan Dwan, Josephine Feeney, Henry Fonda, Barbara Ford, Pat Ford, Phil Ford, Ben Goetz, Chuck Hayward, Katharine Hepburn, Winnie Hoch, Ace Holmes, Frank Hotaling, Lefty Hough, Ben Johnson, Nunnally Johnson, Michael Lord Killanin, John Lee Mahin, Lee Marvin, Roddy McDowall, Anna Lee Nathan, George O'Brien, Bob Parrish, Francis Rich, Wingate Smith, James Stewart, John Wayne, General A. C. Wedemeyer, and Terri Wilson.

I would like to thank particularly Katharine Hepburn, John Wayne, Lefty Hough, George O'Brien, and Harry Carey, Jr., each of whom gave me voluminous material without which this book couldn't have been written. I would also like to thank my typist, Adrienne McCorkle, my editor, Roy Winnick, for his patience, insight, and guidance, and my good friend Lindsay Anderson for his review–and criticism of the manuscript.

D.F.

Preface

Most students of the cinema consider my grandfather, John Ford, to have been Hollywood's greatest and most versatile director. In a career that spanned fifty-one years he directed 136 films and won Academy Awards for *The Informer, The Grapes of Wrath, How Green Was My Valley, The Quiet Man,* and two wartime documentaries: *The Battle of Midway* and *December 7th.* Although he made films on many subjects, he is probably best remembered for his westerns; indeed, the very name John Ford conjures up images of the American West.

Yet my grandfather was an enigma, a complicated man of many sides. Born John Feeney, the son of an immigrant saloonkeeper, he alternately embraced and rejected his Irish origins all his life. Famous for his cantankerous disposition and his heavy-handed treatment of actors, he was also a sentimentalist with a marvelous (and mischievous) sense of humor. He was a great film maker, a consummate craftsman, but he also had a notion of himself as a man of action, a Byronic figure, that accounts for his lifelong fascination with the military. He served with great distinction in World War II and was eventually awarded an admiral's star. After the war he became obsessed with the American military tradition, and in the minds of his liberal critics he became the American Kipling.

My granddad was as difficult as he was complicated. A driven "workaholic," he was not a good family man. Although his marriage to my grandmother lasted for fifty-four years, it was a less than ideal union. He was close to his daughter, Barbara, but his relationship with his son, Pat–my father–was less than it might have been. Pat toiled unhappily on John's pictures until 1965, when they had a bitter falling-out.

While my father loathed Hollywood, I loved it. Perhaps I was more inclined to embrace the traditions that my grandfather stood for. When I graduated from college I joined the Army, became an officer, was sent to Vietnam, and spent a year with a rifle company. My radio call sign was, fittingly enough, "Lost Empire 44." In retrospect, I realize that, left to my own inclinations, I would never have ended up as a combat soldier. I was only there because I felt compelled to live out what I thought were my grandfather's expectations of me.

After I came home from Vietnam my grandfather often bragged about my military record. Three years after my return he was still introducing me as "my grandson Lieutenant Ford, who just got back from Vietnam." Several times I tried to tell him how I felt about the war, how it had rubbed against the grain and how agonizing it had been. After talking for a while I'd stop and look into his eyes, and he'd be staring at me with an unnerving intensity. Only now, after studying his life, do I know what that look meant: he knew the agony I had gone through, and he knew why I had done it. It was his way of saying that he understood.

Being John Ford's grandson was rough at times, but it also had its advantages. It opened certain doors for me. In 1969 I began a career in television and worked in the production departments of CBS and later NBC. In 1971 I co-produced "The American West of John Ford," a television special based on his work. Although this program was well received, its real importance to me was that it gave me a chance to study my granddad's films, particularly the early silents that I wasn't familiar with.

In his later years he would never talk about those films, and would typically dismiss them as just another "job of work." I realized that if I ever wanted to get past the blarney—and I did—I'd have to dig through some pretty hard ground. In March 1973 I took the first tentative steps that led to this book. Climbing through dusty attics, going through old trunks and filing cabinets, I assembled my granddad's personal and professional papers, which, after they were painstakingly arranged and ordered, filled thirty-six folio-sized loose-leaf binders. When I got them together I saw arrayed before me the skeletal story of the man's life. Not being a professional writer, I was overawed by the subject and the task that lay ahead. But I began to work, and the more material I gathered and the more of my grandfather's friends and colleagues I talked to, the more I began to get a grasp on his life.

One of the problems I faced in writing about him was the sheer quantity of his professional output, which, if I had tried to describe it completely, would have filled one or more very long volumes and have often been thematically redundant. I decided, therefore, to limit my discussion to those films which were most important or most representative. Some of the more important ones that I did not discuss are: *The Plough and the Stars* (1936), *Wee Winnie Winkie* (1937), *Tobacco Road* (1941), *When Willie Comes Marching Home* (1950), *What Price Glory* (1952), *The Last Hurrah* (1958), the Civil War interlude in *How the West Was Won* (1962), and *Donovan's Reef* (1962). With a few exceptions, I also steered clear of film reviews, because if there's anything duller than reading an old review, it's reading 136 of them. Scholarly assessments of my grandfather's career I leave to more qualified students of film history. From the outset, it was my intention to concentrate on the personal, family, and professional aspects of the life of John Ford.

—*Dan Ford*

March 1973–December 1978
Hollywood, California

NOTE: As this book was going to press, John Wayne passed away. Since it was too late to change the text, references to "the Duke" originally written in the present tense remain in that form.

Contents

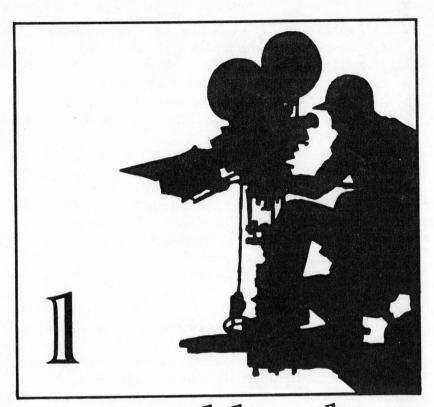

1

Beachhead in a Better Land

In 1872 a ship rounded up in Galway Bay, dropped anchor, and a jaunty Irishman named Michael Connelly stepped ashore. He had just come home from America.

News of his return spread. Neighbors gathered in a cottage perched above the sea; they pushed in the doorway, jostled for a position beside the peat fire, and bickered for a taste of the whiskey being passed around.

Michael Connelly said he had bought a ticket for Quebec fourteen years ago on a leaky hulk with rotten rigging and an inept master. Space was cramped, food scarce, and the water cut with vinegar. Sanitary facilities were nonexistent. During rough weather the passengers were locked below in the dark steerage. Nerves rubbed raw and men exploded into violent fights.

In Quebec he was approached by a stranger who talked reassuringly of the old country and took him to a saloon. The next day he woke with a blinding headache to find himself in a jolting wagon stacked with the bodies of twenty other men. They were taken to a nearby lake, shackled in chains, and put to work digging a canal. Three months later, Connelly escaped into the forest and was picked up by a band of Blackfoot Indians. They put him to work scraping buffalo hides and smoking meat. Nights, he slept with the dogs. At a place called Duluth a French trapper befriended him and bought him his freedom.

Then came the great Civil War in America. A man named Purvis T. Earl paid Michael Connelly two hundred dollars to enlist in his name. He was with the Army of the Potomac when it crossed the Rappahannock River at Fredericksburg and advanced toward a line of trees—until withering Rebel fire dropped the blue-clad soldiers of the Union Army by hundreds in the field. That night Michael Connelly decided to let Mr. Earl fight for himself, and in the darkness he sneaked past the watchfires of a hundred circling camps. He deserted.

After the war he signed on as a tracklayer with the Union Pacific Railroad and helped lay the ribbons of steel that brought the Iron Horse to the remote outposts of America.

After years of adventuring and roaming in the New World, good fortune at last came his way. He met a widow who owned a rooming house in the city of Portland, in the state of Maine. He married her and settled down to the good life of a man of property. Now, fourteen years later, he had come back to visit Ireland to share his adventures with old friends and kinfolk.

Sitting in the cottage listening to Connelly was a tall, thin, big-boned young man with a shock of red hair. His name was John Feeney, and he was Michael Connelly's nephew. He would later remember that the bigger the crowd and the more whiskey that was drunk, the better his uncle's stories about America became.

In the next few days John Feeney and Michael Connelly spent a lot of time together walking in the fields and talking about the New World. There was little opportunity in Ireland. Jobs were hard to find, rents were high, and land scarce as freedom under the Union Jack. When his uncle offered to sponsor him in America, John Feeney jumped at the chance.

In the summer of 1872 he kissed his mother good-bye, received the blessing of his parish priest, and left the cottage where he was born. He walked down the narrow dirt track toward the sea with his uncle. They boarded a Cunard ship bound for Boston, and when they stepped ashore in Boston Harbor, they kept on walking—past the rows and rows of cheap boardinghouses that lined the waterfront, and headed up the Old Post Road to Portland.

Portland, Maine, is a city of hills beside the sea, of wood frame houses shaded by elm trees, and of red brick warehouses along the waterfront. in the 1870s it was bustling, thriving and growing. There was timber to be cut and milled, ships to be loaded, and roads to be built. The brute push of the Irish was needed, and they flocked there.

As in other cities on the Eastern Seaboard, two distinct cultures had grown up: the native Yankee and the immigrant Irish. The Yankees had their Protestant church, with its steeple pointing straight up to heaven; the Irish had their saloon, with its swinging doors leading straight down to hell. The Yankees lived in the east end and ran the lumber industry, the shipping, and the counting houses, while the Irish huddled together in slums near the docks. There was little contact between the two cultures. Generations of Yankees grew up thinking of the Irish as rowdy ne'er-do-wells, quarrelsome, drunken, and threadbare. They would remember a hundred childhood fights with the "Mick" gangs from across the tracks.

In 1850 the Yankees had gathered their forces and passed Prohibition—to "protect" the Irish from themselves. To Michael Connelly this had been the opportunity of a lifetime: he had become a bootlegger. Now young John Feeney set out to learn the bootlegger's trade. Operating out of his uncle's boardinghouse, he sold pints of whiskey to Portland's dockworkers, who needed something to fend off the morning cold. Business boomed and a few years later he opened an illegal saloon, a speakeasy, in the back room of a red brick building on Center Street along Portland's waterfront. He named it Feeney's.

An impeccable dresser, with a bow tie, elastic armbands, and a handlebar mustache, John Feeney was an impressive man standing behind his bar. He was warm and sentimental, ever ready to shed a tear when a good tenor sang of the Auld Sod. But Feeney was also solid, dependable, hard-working, and seldom drank—ideal qualities for a saloonkeeper. The bar became a runaway success, a local gathering spot, a "must" among Portland's Irish dockworkers. For John Feeney it was a liquid gold mine.

Since talk was the cheapest diversion of the Irish poor, and Irishmen always talk most where they won't perish of thirst, they clustered in Feeney's Saloon to talk about the county societies, the lodges, and the militia companies. Sooner or later, the talk of an Irishman always turns to politics. The promise of a steady job, plus a natural animosity toward the Yankee Republicans, drew the Irish to the Democratic Party. A saloonkeeper in a Prohibition state had to be active in politics; bribes had to be arranged and politicians recruited. A man who could keep a good, noisy saloon open commanded respect. As the years went by, John Feeney became a kingpin of the local Democratic machine: party caucuses were held in his saloon, important municipal decisions affecting schools, transit, and the general welfare were made amid the cigar smoke and the spilt beer. John Feeney's advice was widely sought, and his opinions carried weight. When an Irishman stepped off the boat, John Feeney helped get him a job on the docks, and saw that he had a bucket of coal on a cold day and a free beer on a hot one. He helped the newcomer file his naturalization papers and registered him in the Democratic Party. Then he told him who to vote for and how many times.

In 1878 John Feeney met Barbara Curran; with her blonde hair and flashing green eyes, she was perhaps the prettiest Irish girl in Maine. She had a flair for the creative, an instinct for style. Although Barbara could neither read nor write, she was a woman of perception and uncanny intuition. Two months after they met, she and John were married.

At first they lived over the Center Street saloon, but Barbara soon tired of the singing, the guffaws, and the fistfights that lasted late into the night. They moved into a succession of flats around the city, each bigger than the one before, and began having children. The first was Mary Agnes, nicknamed Maime, in 1879. Then came Patrick the following year, followed by Bridget, who died in infancy.

In 1883 Michael Connelly retired and left John to run Feeney's Saloon. In that same year John opened a "restaurant." Sawdust covered the floor, the honky-tonk piano never stopped playing, and all the meals were liquid. Then he opened a second bar, and, finally, as an insurance against Yankee politicians and their Prohibition laws, a package store at the railway station in Portsmouth, New Hampshire.

In the new decade, John prospered and his family increased. In 1883 Francis was born; Eddie followed in 1885; a girl, Dorothy, was born in 1886 but died two years later of scarlet fever; Josephine came in 1892; then in 1893 a boy, who died at birth. In 1894 the family moved to a white New England house on Cape Elizabeth, south of Portland, with forty acres of land that sloped down toward the sea. A quiet haven away from the city, Cape Elizabeth's most famous resident was Winslow Homer, the great American artist who immortalized its rugged coastline in his work. There, on February 1, 1895, John Feeney, Jr. was born.

The family enjoyed their suburban house for only four years, though; in 1898 they moved back into Portland so John could be closer to his saloons. He set up his family in a green-shingled triplex at 93 Sheridan Street, close to downtown. Two other large Irish families, the Myers and the Mahoneys, partners in a construction firm, already lived there. Each had five children, and the addition of the Feeneys' made it sixteen children under a single roof. The three families grew very close and developed a loose communal relationship.

Four of young John's brothers and sisters were adults while he was still a child. Maime, sixteen years older, had married young, was widowed, and moved back in with her family, where she became an assistant mother to the younger children. Pat married late and also helped raise his younger brothers and sisters. Freed from some of the more mundane, authoritative chores of child rearing, John's parents were left with the affectionate, fun-loving aspects, and they became more like grandparents than parents to the boy.

But while John was having an exceptionally happy childhood, his older brother Francis was not. A creative child and a loner, Francis was chafing at the bit in Portland. When the Spanish-American War broke out in 1898, he ran away from home and joined the army.

The Army soon discovered that he was only fifteen and sent him home. Back in Portland, his problems went from bad to worse when he had an affair with a young woman named Dell Cole. She became pregnant, they got married, and Francis went to work in one of his father's saloons. But he was unhappy. He dreamed of things that didn't exist in Portland: highly polished shoes, fancy cravats, fashionable derbies, and cologne that smelled of lilac vegetal. There were bright lights, beautiful women, and a finer life out there, and Francis shuddered at the thought of spending the rest of his life mopping up beer in a workingman's saloon. So Francis Feeney did what he had done before—he disappeared.

Adrift from his family, he wandered to New York and before long discovered the theater. In 1900 there were over two thousand legitimate theaters in the country, offering a variety of entertainment from plays to vaudeville acts to slapstick and folksy humor. In this shadow world there was plenty of opportunity for a bright, good-looking young man like Francis Feeney, and for the next ten years he immersed himself in it, working his way from stagehand to makeup artist to stage manager, understudy, and finally actor. He was one of those mysterious, glamorous showmen drifting in and out of railway depots accompanied by worn trunks plastered with stickers from faraway places. But while it was a glamorous life, it was also one of constant travel on cindery, lurching night coaches, of sleeping in fleabag hotels, of eating tasteless meals in the dirty lunchrooms of a hundred nameless towns and cities. There were outbursts of temperament, and occasional unscrupulous theater managers, but Francis made a success of his new life and in time became an accomplished actor. He took a stage name, a simple one that people would remember. He became Francis Ford.

Francis may have been successful in his new life but he couldn't entirely escape his past. He was plagued by Victorian, Puritan, Catholic "thou shalt nots." He felt guilty about leaving his wife, guilty about being a failure at small-town life. He was ashamed that he had changed his name, and was sure that his family would disapprove of his new life in the theater. Francis had no contact with his family. It was easier that way—at least on him.

His first work in films was for Gaston Méliès, a maker of western serials based in Nepara Park, New York. Méliès moved to California in 1909. Francis went with him and became part of a brand-new industry.

Educated people looked down on "the Flickers," as films were called. The middle and upper classes went to vaudeville or to the theater. Films were aimed at the lower classes and the immigrants, most of whom couldn't speak English. Certain clichés emerged early and lasted all through the silent era: there was the villain, ruthless and mustachioed, in a black cape and a stovepipe hat; there was the heroine, always a poor but noble working girl; and there was the hero, a clean-cut Jack Armstrong type. The settings and decor—red and white checkered tablecloths and lace curtains—were designed to appeal to working-class tastes. Acting, such as it was, consisted of highly exaggerated gestures that expressed fear, love, hatred, or horror.

Back in Portland, Barbara Curran Feeney was a great fan of the flickers and never missed a new picture when it came to town. She did not know that her son Francis was already part of this world.

Meanwhile, young John was growing up with only the dimmest childhood memory of his absent brother, whom his mother and father spoke of with lowered voices and an air of sadness.

When he was eight years old, John came down with diphtheria and for months he lay in bed at home while his sister Maime nursed him. She swabbed his throat with alcohol and fed him cool ices. She read to him until her voice cracked: Robert Louis Stevenson, Grimms' *Fairy Tales*, Mark Twain's *Tom Sawyer*, *Huckleberry Finn*, and *A Connecticut Yankee in King Arthur's Court*. John fell a year behind in school but picked up five years' worth of education in the process, developing a sensitivity and an awareness that, combined with his rough-and-tumble competitive spirit, made him a very special young man.

In 1905, completely recovered, John returned to the Emerson Grammar School in Portland. A year older than his fourth-grade classmates, a year bigger, and a year wiser, he became a class leader.

Through the sixth, seventh, and eighth grades, John's marks were in the high seventies and low eighties and his best subjects were the "talking subjects"—history, geography, and English. All his life he would remember the image of Lyman's Historical Chart, a formidable visual aid that showed the entire march of world events coded in different colors. Schools at that time put a great deal of emphasis on elocution, and students were taught such classic orations as Mark Anthony's "Friends, Romans, Countrymen" and Patrick Henry's "Give me liberty or give me death." John was blessed with a facile memory and easily absorbed pages of these orations. He was relaxed and poised standing up in front of others.

John entered Portland High School in 1910, and there he found a new outlet for his energy—football. To this immigrant's son, football was more than a game, it was a symbol of his assimilation, a mark of his moral worth. With the wild enthusiasm that was becoming his trademark, he set out to master the game and to become a running back.

Football meant endless practice; it meant wind sprints, calisthenics, and laps around the track. Football also meant bruises, sprains, torn ligaments, and pulled hamstrings, but it didn't matter: John was proud to be a part of football's brotherhood of pain.

Football changed him. It toughened him and increased his competitive spirit. Because he thought it was a better name for a football player he began calling himself Jack instead of John. Jack Feeney: blunt, tough, to the point. His teammates did him one better. They called him Bull Feeney.

"Bull Feeney, the human battering ram" was frequently mentioned in the local press as Portland High rolled over the rival Bangor, Deering, and Westbrook teams to become state champion in 1913 and 1914.

John earned three football letters in high school. Twice he won Honorable Mention for the all-state team, and coaches from the University of Maine, Holy Cross, and Boston College came to visit his father.

There were other lessons in those days that were more important, if less dramatic. In high school, John came to the attention of two men who greatly influenced him. One was an English teacher named Lucian Libby, who saw a fine mind and a potential talent behind John's Bull Feeney pose. He taught John to write in simple, straightforward sentences, and encouraged him to read and expand his mental horizons beyond the insular limits of Portland, Maine. The second man was the principal of Portland High, William Jack, a popular New England schoolmaster whose talks about America, its history and its Constitution, stimulated John and other students enough to keep them lingering after class to continue the discussion. Mr. Jack saw a fire burning deep inside young John Feeney and was the first one to tell him that he could really do something with his life. He urged John to go to college and think about getting out of Maine.

Then there were the lessons learned outside of school. Evenings John worked as an usher in Portland's Jefferson Theater, a prime stop for every road company playing on the eastern circuit. There he saw most of the famous actors of his day: Carter DeHaven, Ina Fagan, Sidney Toler, Roscoe Arbuckle, the great Barrymore, along with the old Wild West shows. He saw the life backstage, the road-weary touring companies, the scenery, the footlights, the backstage construction. There was glitter, glamour, and excitement in this world, and like his brother before him, John was fascinated by it.

Hoping to pick up a bit part, John made it a practice to hang around backstage. Once he was selected to play a messenger boy in a play with Sidney Toler. His part called for him to walk in and hand a telegram to Toler. John was terrified as he walked out into the lights.

"What's this?" Toler demanded with a glare.

"A telegram, sir," John whispered.

"A telegram. You mean a wire, don't you?" Toler improvised, clearly enjoying John's discomfort.

"A wire, yes sir, a wire, sir." John shifted his feet.

"What does it say?"

"I don't know."

"Well, why don't you know?"

"Because I haven't read it."

"Why haven't you read it?"

"Well, I . . ."

"You delivered it, didn't you?"

In the spring of 1914, young John Feeney graduated from Portland

High School. His family looked ahead to a university education for him. They wanted him to be more than another saloonkeeper; their hopes were that he would move into some respectable position, become a man who would be looked up to—a lawyer perhaps—and maybe someday run for office. John applied to the University of Maine, but he never made it to Orono. Instead, something happened that would determine the course of his life: one afternoon his mother went to the local Empire Theater to watch a flicker and saw a familiar face on the screen. "No, it couldn't be," she thought. "It's impossible." It was Francis!

John Feeney, Sr. wrote to the makers of the film, the Universal Film Manufacturing Company of Hollywood, California, who put him in touch with his son. In the spring of 1914, at his father's urging, Francis Ford made a triumphant return to Portland. Dressed in a cashmere coat and a wide-brimmed fedora, he drove up from Boston in a gleaming Stutz Bearcat with big fenders and a hand brake on the running board. He talked about a place just outside Los Angeles called Hollywood, and the wide-open new industry that was booming there.

John sat and listened to his brother, just as his father had listened to Michael Connelly thirty years before. And he knew right away that Hollywood was where he belonged.

2

Success

John stepped off the train in Los Angeles on a July day in 1914, and as he rode out Sunset Boulevard in his brother's big open car, he smelled scrub oak, sweet eucalyptus, and dusty pepper trees for the first time. Pastels blurred by the periphery of his vision, faded red Spanish tiles, white stucco walls with bougainvilleas spilling over. Los Angeles in 1914 was a place of bright sun, strong shadows, dry heat, and a sense of the desert just over the hills.

The car rattled over the dirt roads and dust boiled up behind it. Francis, wearing riding breeches, jodhpur boots, and a shirt open to the waist, drove expertly and fast. He carried a riding crop and smoked cigarettes and seemed the very epitome of sophistication to his younger brother. Sitting beside Francis was a handsome woman in her early thirties. She had quick blue eyes, a wide sensual mouth, and was dressed in an efficient brown suit. Her name was Grace Cunard; she was Francis' friend, business partner, and lover.

In 1914 Francis Ford was beginning to make his mark as an actor-director of western shorts. John went to work for his brother as an all-around assistant, and the experience and training he got is difficult to imagine in the Hollywood of today. In those pre-union days, John was able to work in every area of film production. He played bits, did stunts, and learned about cameras, smoke pots, explosives, and how to do horse falls with running W's. He learned about timing, cues, breakdowns, and budgets. By 1916 he was an assistant director at Universal Studios, owned by Carl Laemmle, the diminutive German-born tycoon. To take advantage of his brother's well-known name, he started calling himself Jack Ford. He was in on the ground floor of a budding new industry.

During his first years in Hollywood, John shared a room at the Virginia Apartments, located at 6369½ Hollywood Boulevard, with Hoot Gibson. A former drifter, rodeo cowboy, and veteran of the Wild West shows, Gibson was now a bit player at Universal.

On March 15, 1915, accompanied by much fanfare, Carl Laemmle moved Universal to its present site in the San Fernando Valley. Every employee, including the entire Francis Ford Serial Company, stood by as Laemmle cut the ribbon and walked onto the lot.

The new studio was called Universal City. With its western, New York, and Hong Kong "streets," it was the first truly modern studio. There was one enormous stage that could accommodate thirty-six film companies. Because there was no sound, they could all work at the same time; a comedy scene would be shooting on one set, a barroom brawl on the one next to it.

R. L. "Lefty" Hough is a crusty, colorful man whose trademarks include a baseball cap cocked back on his head and four-letter words spewing out the side of his mouth. He began in motion pictures in 1915 as a carpenter with the Francis Ford Serial Company, stayed with John as a prop man and assistant director, and eventually became a production head at Fox, a job his son holds today. He remembers the heady atmosphere of Universal City in 1915.

"It was a very exciting place in those days—something was always going on. An elephant would get loose or a tiger would get out and everybody would run for cover. At one time there were forty companies shooting at Universal, and there were five thousand people on the lot. Whenever one of the other companies would hire a lot of extras, Francis, Jack, myself, and a cameraman named Harry Grant would sneak out and photograph their crowd scenes. Then Francis would go back and write a picture around what we had photographed. If it was a group of Civil War soldiers, then he would write a Civil War picture. If he'd photographed a crowd of Indians, then he'd write a western.

"In those days there were so many companies working at Universal that the sets were all built back to back. One time we were working on a western street and there was a colonial home built behind it. There was an actor by the name of Phil Small, one of those guys who used to lay around on a pillow. He had a woman director named Lois Webber. They were doing a Southern story with girls in big crinoline skirts. They were the first outfit ever to have music on the set: violins, organs and all that sort of stuff. The Ford outfit was making a western on the other side. One day we blew up a bank that was attached to Small's colonial home. There was a huge explosion and this colonial house came down on their laps, musicians, organs, big hooped skirts and all. It's a wonder we didn't kill somebody. Oh, it was a hell of a mess."

Although Jack often worked as an actor with the Francis Ford Serial Company, he showed little promise in that area, being neither expressive nor handsome. He did, however, show some promise as a writer and was constantly submitting scripts to his brother.

But it was the men with the megaphones—the directors—that

Jack Ford admired most. In 1916 the big names were Thomas Ince, Sidney Franklin, Alan Dwan, Tod Browning, and the master of them all, D. W. Griffith. Griffith was then breaking up the static narrative of the stage play with the close-up, the dolly shot, the fade, and the dissolve. He was inventing the new language of film.

From the very beginning, Jack Ford showed an aptitude for directing. By 1916 he was an assistant director in charge of large groups of extras and cowboys. He took control naturally and with ease. Most of the early movie cowboys were veterans of the Wild West shows. Just barely removed from the real thing, as a group they were mean, stupid, and cruel, respecting only rattlesnakes and live ammunition. These were the men Jack Ford had to keep sober and get to the set on time. Then he had to run them through their scenes. Alan Dwan, who by then was already a prominent director, recalls how Jack Ford did it.

"Jack Ford was a leader and he could handle men. He used his own language when he lined the cowboys up. There wasn't any 'Please step over this way.' It was, 'Come on, you bastards, get in line and shut up.' He was only twenty years old, but there was no doubt about who the boss was.

"He was a natural director. He wouldn't just say to a bunch of cowboys, 'Come over the hill and yell.' He'd give them all specific pieces of business. He'd say, 'You there, when you ride over the hill, throw your hat up in the air; you over there, get shot and fall, and you, I want you to get shot at the top of the hill but make it all the way down before you keel over.' He'd pick those things out for himself. He directed the crowd scenes and he was starting to make a name for himself. He wasn't directing principals, but he was directing."

Throughout 1916 and 1917, Francis ground out two-reel serials. Their plots were primitive by today's standards, but they were the usual fare for their time. There was *The Broken Coin*, a 15-episode serial in which Francis and Grace Cunard search for two halves of a coin because it has a map to a buried treasure on it. There was *The Lumber Yard Gang*, in which detective Phil Kelley (Francis Ford) chases Dan McLean (Jack Ford). There was *Peg o' the Ring*, *The Bandit's Wager*, and *The Purple Mask*.

Francis was a man of many talents. He was an excellent actor, a sure-handed director, and a fluid, graceful writer. But Francis wanted to be his own boss, to have full control of his pictures, and in 1917 he left Universal to go into independent production. He opened his own studio, The Francis Ford Serial Company, on Beachwood Drive, between Sunset and Santa Monica boulevards. The day he moved in, Francis posed for photographers, straight-backed and proud, his arms crossed in front of him. He was a man at the peak of his powers.

Francis found his new freedom intoxicating and worked from sunup to midnight, grinding out serials of every description. He wrote them, directed them, and starred in them. But he was a creative man, not a factory manager; an artist, not a businessman. The added responsibility of running a studio proved too much for him; he spread himself too thin, and the quality of his work suffered. Within a year he was back at Universal as an actor-director under contract.

Because it divided the European market in two, World War I gave a tremendous boost to the American motion picture industry. British films could not be seen in Germany, and the varied and excellent German films couldn't be seen in the Allied countries. American films, however, were distributed throughout Europe, and during World War I Hollywood became the world center for motion picture production, a position it never relinquished. But America's isolation ended in April 1917, when the country entered the war. Everyone John had grown up with seemed to be getting involved, as suggested by a 1917 letter to John from his sister Josephine: "The old crowd seems pretty much broken up. There was no draft in Portland. The enlistments were so large and above the quota that they took no one. Fat Riley from the West end is in France with Jimmy Walsh and have already been fired on. Bet they wish they were back 'doing' Congress Street...."

Unlike many of his contemporaries, John never served in World War I. Because of their propaganda value, motion pictures were declared an essential industry, and he was given a deferment.

The expansion of the American movie industry during the war gave John the opportunity he was looking for. In 1917 he directed his first film, a two-reel short called *The Tornado*. He wrote it, directed it, and worked in it as an actor. Then, with the breakneck speed with which he would lead his entire life, he followed it with another two-reeler called *The Scrapper*. Jack Ford had made it—he was now a director. In September 1917, he signed a contract with Universal that called for "The Universal Film Manufacturing Company" to "employ the employee as director in and about the business of producing plays and scenes for moving picture films." His pay was $75.00 a week.

Along with his contract he received a memo from the Universal front office containing the following list of things not wanted in the company's pictures:

"Stories dealing with the ruin of young girls. Black jacking. Excessive smoking. Fake wallops in fight scenes. Cowboy stories which get over the idea that cowboys are either always drunk, getting drunk, drunk fighting, or looking for a fight. Stories requiring inserts and long explanatory titles. Maudlin displays of patriotism. Insanity. Hunchbacks. Mugging in close ups. Rats. Snakes. Kittens. Pie slinging contests. Preachments. Propaganda. Drinking scenes. Bar room brawls. Sissies. Heavy dames. Men, especially policemen and detectives who are constitutionally incapable of removing their hats when entering a room in the presence of ladies or in any other way showing the least sign of impoliteness."

In three hectic years John Feeney, a lace-curtain Irishman from the State of Maine, son of a saloonkeeper, had become Jack Ford of Hollywood, California, director of action-packed western films.

He was twenty-two years old.

Francis Ford was John's first great teacher and his first great professional influence, but it was John's teaming with silent star Harry Carey that paved the way to his eventual success. Ford and Carey made twenty-three films together, and when their partnership ended John Ford was a first-rate action director.

Harry Carey's widow, Olive Golden Carey, is one of the senior members of the old "John Ford stock company." I've known her all my life and look on her as part of my family. Crusty, outspoken, and profane, a genuine character with plenty of salt, she is part gypsy, part circus, part carnival, and all Hollywood. In her own inimitable way, she remembers how Harry got started in motion pictures and how he got teamed up with John Ford:

"Harry was from New York, and his father was a judge in White Plains. He wanted to follow in his father's footsteps and went to law school at N.Y.U. In those days there was a whorehouse down in the village called Madam Moran's, and one day Harry got stiff and stole Madam Moran's picnic drawers, those big things with ruffles and lace, and put them up on a flag pole. They expelled him from school for that.

"Harry drifted around for a while then, playing semi-pro baseball and working here and there. Then he went back to law school and graduated in the same class as Jimmy Walker, but he got pneumonia and never did take the bar examination. While recuperating, Harry started reading a lot of western history and became an absolute nut on the subject. He read someplace that no play that actually had a live horse on stage had ever failed, so he decided to write a western melodrama with a horse. It was called *Montana*. He got some dough together, took it out on the road, and it cleaned up. After touring the country, Harry joined D. W. Griffith's American-Biograph when it was still in New York and came to California with Griffith in 1913. I met Harry two years later when I went up to San Francisco to make a movie for O.A.C. Lund. Harry was the leading man, and I fell for him like a ton of bricks. We got married right away. After that, he came down to Universal and signed a contract for $150.00 a week.

"Harry was working with a director named Fred Kelsey and they weren't getting along. Jack Ford was on the lot working for Francis, and one day he came over to the set. Harry and Jack got to talking. Jack was so responsive that they just clicked, that's all. That started the whole damned thing. Harry went to Laemmle and said he wanted Jack to be his director."

Jack Ford and Harry Carey went to work grinding out two-reel, or twenty-minute, western shorts. Most of the shooting was off-the-cuff, often as not, with no script, only a rough continuity that John had blocked out. Then in July 1917, they wrote a feature-length script called *Straight Shooting*. They presented the idea to Universal,

17

but the studio told Carey and Ford to stick to their two-reel format. The two men had nothing to lose but their shirts, so they went ahead and made the picture as a feature without Universal's knowledge. To get enough raw stock John claimed that he had accidentally dropped his film in a stream and needed another 4,000 feet. When they finished, they presented Universal with a ninety-minute feature, a *fait accompli*. Incensed at their insubordination, the studio wanted to cut *Straight Shooting* back and release it as a two-reel short, but Irving Thalberg, Carl Laemmle's executive assistant, intervened. In August 1917, it was released as a feature-length film and was an immediate hit.

In 1965, a print of *Straight Shooting* was uncovered in Prague. It is the oldest John Ford film known to exist.

Straight Shooting was surprisingly sophisticated for 1917, with its strongly defined plot, real rhythm, and subtle bits of characterization. Many aspects of the film suggest that John had carefully studied the work of D. W. Griffith. There is one sequence where the cattlemen assemble their forces, salute their leader, and ride into ranks that exactly copies a parallel scene, the assembly of the Klansmen, in *The Birth of a Nation*.

With the success of *Straight Shooting*, Universal scheduled a whole series of Harry Carey features, and the Ford-Carey team went to work turning out a feature-length western every six weeks. Billed by Universal as "Harry Carey's and Jack Ford's Just Plain Westerns," they had titles like *The Secret Man, Three Mounted Men, A Woman's Fool, The Phantom Riders, A Scarlet Drop, Hell Bent, Roped, Riders of Vengeance*, and *Bare Fists*. They used all the basic dime-novel western plots: sin towns with corrupt sheriffs, stories about gold or silver mines, railroad right-of-ways, and gun runners or whiskey peddlers stirring up the Indians. There were family feuds, range wars, cattlemen vs. sheepmen, and cattlemen vs. farmers. If all else failed, there was always the classic standby: a hero's search for his father's murderer.

For young Jack Ford this was a time of hard work and of growth. Working twelve hours a day, seven days a week, he learned invaluable lessons about story, construction, exposition, and plot. Every day there was a new light effect or camera angle to try, and with every picture his characteristic style emerged. The Harry

Carey westerns, made with small budgets and under great pressure, forced John to shoot quickly with a minimum number of setups, to keep the camera stationary, and to use simple shots rather than opt for intricate compositions. Working under this kind of pressure taught him the greatest lesson of all: to find the beauty in simplicity. In the dry alkaline canyons around Newhall, where most of these films were made, John was drawing the blueprints for an entire career.

Even during these early years John showed an inclination for working with familiar and congenial collaborators. On the Harry Carey pictures, he formed bonds with actors J. Farrell McDonald and Mollie Malone, cowboys Vester Pegg, Cap Anderson, and Duke Lee, and cameramen Jack Brown and George Schneiderman.

Perhaps the most fascinating character in this group was a thickset man with a handlebar mustache named Edward Zachariah "Pardner" Jones, a great marksman and trick-shot expert who, as one of Wyatt Earp's deputies, had helped his "pardner" Earp sweep the pimps, dicemen, and gamblers out of Tombstone.

But of all John's professional and personal relationships, the one with Harry Carey was by far the most important. Carey was a boss, a teacher, and a Dutch uncle. Ollie Carey remembers them together.

"They were working in Newhall, around Placerita Canyon, and we were spending so much time out there that we decided to move to Newhall. We rented a little joint and all lived together. There were six of us: Jack, Harry, myself, George McConigal, Pardner Jones, and Teddy Brooks. We had this funny little three-room house, but Harry and Jack wanted to be pioneers, so we had to sleep in the alfalfa patch in bed rolls.

"At night they would sit around this little tiny kitchen with a wood fire going in the stove and drink Mellow Wood. They would talk, talk, talk, late into the night and Jack would take notes. They molded the whole thing between them and the next day they'd go out and shoot it. Every once in a while Universal would decide they needed a story department so they'd hire some writers and send us these *terrible* scripts. Harry and Jack would take one look at them and say, 'Christ, that's horrible,' then throw them away and go back to their own stuff. They had a strange and funny relationship. Harry was eighteen years older than Jack, had graduated from law school and had been in pictures for about ten years, but Jack still held his own. Harry started out as the dominant one, but Jack was catching up awfully fast."

The Harry Carey pictures established John as a first-rate action director and gave his career a dramatic upward turn. His salary went from $75 a week in 1917 to $150 in 1918 and $300 in 1919. Adopting the *de rigueur* life-style of a Hollywood director, he bought a 1916 peacock blue Stutz with a long hood, high fenders, enormous wheels, and a canvas top. He dressed in jodhpur boots, khaki twill riding breeches, and hunting jackets that he bleached white with gasoline.

But if John's salary had doubled and doubled again, it was nothing alongside Harry Carey's, which went from $150 a week in 1917 to $1,250 in 1918 and a staggering $2,250 in 1919. The discrepancy between John's $300 and Carey's $2,250 became a point of real tension between the two men, since John couldn't help but feel that he was entitled to more of the spoils of their success.

With his new affluence Harry Carey adopted one of the most flamboyant life-styles in Hollywood. He bought a 3,000-acre ranch near Newhall and built an adobe ranch house with walls three feet thick, high beamed ceilings, a tile roof, and massive fireplaces. Carey's ranch was like the backlot of a movie studio. There were chuckwagons, covered wagons, stagecoaches, and corrals filled with Appaloosa ponies. He even brought sixty Navajo Indians from their Arizona reservation and had them live on his ranch. They built hogans, raised sheep, and brought their life-style intact to California. On Sundays, in a small canyon near his ranch house, Carey staged Wild West shows and invited his friends to come out, sit in the shade, sip warm whiskey, and watch the trick roping, the bronc riding, and the bulldogging. The Carey ranch was a western showcase, a place where Harry Carey, western actor, could live out his fantasies, bridging the gap to the "real" West. But Carey's life-style, like his salary, aggravated the tensions between him and his young director.

In the summer of 1919 John and Carey undertook their most ambitious film together, an adaptation of Bret Harte's "The Outcasts of Poker Flat." Then, in November 1919, they made *Marked Men*, based on a Peter B. Kyne short story called "Three Godfathers." It was their last picture together.

The following month John was loaned to the William Fox studios to direct two Buck Jones westerns, *Just Pals* and *The Big Punch*. This was exactly the opportunity that he had been looking for. Fox was a bigger studio than Universal and made a more sophisticated product. When John's contract at Universal expired a few months later, he became a contract director at Fox, at a salary of $600 a week.

Since stepping off the train in 1914, John's rise had been nothing short of meteoric. In six years he had risen from his brother's stunt double to a leading action director, and although he was still a long way from realizing his future greatness, by 1920 Jack Ford was a prominent man in the Hollywood community.

But success is sometimes more difficult to deal with than failure, and if there were a recurring problem, a dominant theme, weaving through this period, it was John's difficulty in dealing with success. Jealousy, competition for money and recognition, had undermined the Ford-Carey relationship. Most important of all, it brought on an identity crisis as John began to molt his Irish skin and replace it with an American coat. For the first time in his life John felt rootless and lost.

On Saint Patrick's Day, 1920, at a party given by director Rex Ingram, Jack met a woman with long dark hair, delicate bone structure, and fine classical features. Her name was Mary McBride Smith. John was completely taken with her elegance, style, and natural good humor.

It was a wild, hot-blooded time for courtship. The Volstead Act had been passed in October 1919, and America was discovering just how thirsty it really was. No longer afraid of being branded with Nathaniel Hawthorne's scarlet letter, women were throwing off their corsets, smoking cigarettes, and dancing the Hesitation Waltz. It was the era of speakeasies, hip flasks, tin lizzies, white mule, bathtub gin, Al Capone, Bugs Moran, Valentino, and Theda Bara. From radios and victrolas came the sultry sounds and jungle rhythms of a hot new music called "jazz."

John and Mary had a whirlwind romance. They went for long drives out to the beach in his open Stutz and ate quiet dinners at the Ship's Café on the Venice pier. They went to all the speakeasies: the Clover Club on Sunset, Lucy's on Melrose, and the Little Mill down in Watts. On July 3, 1920, John and Mary were married. Their first home was a bungalow at 2253 Beachwood Drive in

Hollywood. The following October they moved to a stucco house perched precariously on the side of a hill, at 6860 Odin Street, in the "Majestic Heights" section of Hollywood. They paid $14,000 for it, and Mary furnished it with conservative wooden furniture. In April 1921, Mary gave birth to an eight-pound, ten-ounce son whom they named Patrick, after John's older brother. It was an unabashedly Irish name, chosen as though to reaffirm John's roots, to implant the future with the seeds of the past.

On the surface, it looked like an ideal match. Mary was bright, sharp, cynical, strong enough to stand up to John and to live with his boundless energy, while still being supportive of his career. But deeper down, there were some very basic differences between the two. Mary had North Carolina Presbyterian blue-blood roots. She was a direct linear descendent of Sir Thomas More and traced her family in America back to the seventeenth century. A number of Mary's uncles and cousins had gone to Annapolis and West Point; an uncle, Rupert Blue, was the Surgeon General of the United States; and Mary's father was a wealthy Wall Street speculator. Mary had money and family, and John was very much aware of both. Although he wouldn't have admitted it, he had married above himself.

While class consciousness continued to be a problem for John, rootlessness did not. During these years a bloody revolution was being fought in Ireland, as Irish nationalists, the Sinn Fein, largely financed and encouraged by the Irish community in the United States, struggled to break away from British rule. "The Troubles," as they were called, were of great interest to John, who studied the papers for news of the Dail Eireann, of Patrick Pearse and De Valera. John's father was a generous backer of the Sinn Fein, and the cause of Irish nationalism brought the two back into contact. The Troubles gave father and son things in common that they hadn't had in years.

John became so caught up in the Irish Revolution that in the fall of 1921 he decided to go to Ireland and get a firsthand look at the war. On November 19, 1921, he boarded the S.S. *Baltic* in New York and sailed for Liverpool. During the trip he wrote Mary a chatty account of his travels. It reads in part:

"Dear Old Fruit, on board S.S. Balls-tic. I am going to keep a sort of diarrhea for you about happenings on board—(with the proviso, of course, that I am able). We are just leaving. I am glad you are not on the wharf with that throng of handkerchief waving maniacs ... We are approaching the Statue of Liberty. What a sight. It recalls the old saying of the cheapskate who would not pay a nickel to see the old gal piss over the Brooklyn Bridge. Will write more later. Adios.

"5:30 PM: Darling, I am sorry to say that I am slightly skunked. Yes Sir! Burned! I also have hiccups. Mary, how I wish you were with me. Gosh, we would have had such a wonderful trip. It's really wonderful on our boat. I have spent the entire afternoon in the *BAR* drinking Bass' Ale and feel quite wonderful (except for the hiccups). Honey, the first opportunity we get you and I and Pat shall take a sea trip because every night I think how Mary would love this. I think that after Emmett [Fox Director Emmett Flynn] and I finish our contracts, I shall persuade him to take Jean and then we all can take a trip around the world. How I wish you were with me...

"As soon as I landed in Liverpool I left for Ireland. The boat I travelled in across the Irish Sea carried Michael Collins and Arthur Griffith, the returning Sinn Fein delegates with Lloyd George's proposals to Dail Eireann. We were only twenty minutes from Holyhead when we cut a fishing schooner in two and sank her. Three of the crew were drowned and although we cruised around for an hour we found no bodies. The shock of the impact was terrible. When we struck, the boat shivered and rocked for quite a while before she straightened out...

"At Galway I got a jaunting car and rode to Spiddal and had a deuce of a time finding Dad's folks. There are so many Feeney's out there that to find our part of the family was a problem. At last I found them...

"Spiddal is all shot to pieces. Most of the houses have been burned down by the Black and Tans and all the young men had been hiding in the hills ... Cousin Martin Feeney (Dad's nephew) had been hiding in the Connemara Mountains with the Thornton boys. I naturally was followed about and watched by the Black and Tan Fraternity. Tell Dad that the Thornton house is entirely burned down and old Mrs. Thornton was living with Uncle Ned's widow while his sons were away..."

The trip to Galway was one of the most important experiences in John Ford's life. Its significance goes far beyond the making of contact with relatives. The Martin Feeney to whom John's account refers was an IRA cell leader with a price on his head, hiding from the Black and Tans, the British military police. Martin Feeney is still alive today, a man in his mid-eighties with reddish cheeks, wispy white hair, and a farmer's rough hands. He recalled for me how his cousin John sought him out in the hills to give him food and money. The British, he says, knew who John was and were hoping he'd leave the country before he got involved in any "incidents." He also says that his cousin was repeatedly stopped and questioned by the Black and Tans and was at one point "roughed up pretty well" by them. After two weeks in Galway John was picked up by the British, put on a boat bound for England, and told that if he ever returned to Ireland he would be imprisoned.

This trip helped resolve the identity crisis that had grown out of John's success and his marriage. John had found a facet of himself that he would never forget—his Irishness. In Martin Feeney's words, "He has been back many times since then, and although he was rich and famous he never felt he was above us. He felt that we were his people and this is where he really belonged."

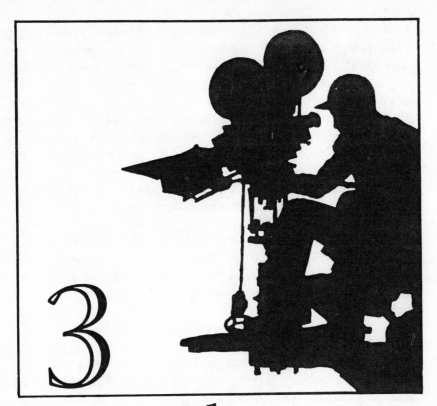

3

The
Iron Horse

O ne of the great first-generation movie moguls, William Fox was a Jewish immigrant's son who had grown up in poverty on New York's Lower East Side. A gambler, a speculator, a player of long shots, he had parlayed a penny arcade into a string of nickelodeons, a distribution network, and finally into his own studio. But Fox had none of the four-lettered flamboyance of some of the other picture pioneers. He was a self-educated businessman with a conservative style, a money man more at home sitting before a ledger sheet or an annual report than in a projection room. Tall, gaunt, and elegant, Fox disliked Hollywood's show business affectations and ran his company from its New York headquarters. His California production facility, located on the corner of Sunset Boulevard and Western Avenue in Hollywood, was run by Sol Wurtzel and Winnie Sheehan. Wurtzel, with close-cropped gray hair and thick glasses, looked like the principal of a good boy's school. Sheehan, on the other hand, was a dapper Irishman with dark features and baby-blue eyes. Charming and gregarious, he was a womanizer whose parties were famous in Hollywood.

In 1921 the William Fox Studios had three principal assets: the best distribution organization in motion pictures; a stable of directors that included David Butler, Alan Dwan, Howard Hawks, William Wellman, Raoul Walsh, and John Ford; and, most important of all, Tom Mix—the hottest western star in Hollywood.

John made two pictures with Tom Mix in 1922 and 1923; *Three Jumps Ahead* and *North of Hudson Bay*. Although neither has survived to the present day, the reviews of the time suggest that they were pretty much formula pictures. Tom Mix was a very different kind of western hero from Harry Carey. While Carey had played a dusty working cowboy, Mix was a dandy who wore tight white pants, silk neckerchiefs, and embroidered shirts. His films, aimed at the juvenile trade, had strong comedic elements, plenty of action, and daring stunts which Mix, a gifted athlete, often did himself. Tom Mix was a children's hero who never entered a saloon unless it was to punish a villain. In the early 1920s, with Prohibition in force, his clean-cut character had enormous popular appeal. Perhaps the most interesting thing about Tom Mix was the contrast between his on-screen image and the real man. In his pictures he was the all-American idol of the anti-saloon league, but in actuality he lived a life of opulence and excess. His Beverly Hills home had a seven-car garage and his brand, the T Bar M, was emblazoned on the roof in neon. Mix was a womanizer who went through five wives and had countless affairs. He had more guns than a banana republic and was always armed to the teeth. A heavy drinker, only the resiliency of his athletic body kept him from destroying himself.

Fox was always careful to hide the dark side of Mix's personal life. Having been rocked by a series of scandals involving Roscoe "Fatty" Arbuckle, William Taylor Desmond, and Wally Reid, Hollywood was on a vigorous campaign to clean up its image, if not its act.

John's early pictures at Fox weren't limited to Buck Jones and Tom Mix westerns. His new studio made a diverse product, and before long John was making fairly sophisticated films. His first really interesting film at Fox was made in the summer of 1923. Based on a Harry Leon-Booth Tarkington play called *Cameo Kirby*, it was the story of a chivalrous riverboat gambler. This film still exists today, and I was fortunate enough to screen a print of it. Photographed with great dramatic flair, the river scenes seem to leap out of the pages of Mark Twain. *Cameo Kirby* was John's first truly mature film, the first to receive real critical acclaim, and the first to carry the name by which he would henceforth be billed: not Jack, but the more dignified John Ford.

As John was growing professionally during his early years at Fox, he was also growing financially. In 1921 his income was over $27,000, in 1922 it was over $37,000, and in 1923 it was almost $45,000.

Boom was in the air in the mid-twenties, and America was in the midst of the gaudiest spree in its history. Hemlines were rising above the knee, and the Dow Jones Industrials were climbing with them. Like everybody else, John got into the market. In 1922 he bought 500 shares of the Western Costume Company, 500 shares of Fox Theaters, and 500 shares of U.S. Steel. But John wasn't particularly good with money. He was too busy, too preoccupied with his work, and he just couldn't manage his personal business affairs. So in 1922 he hired a full-time business manager, a kindly, quiet man named Fred Totman. While Totman was competent, he was no genius. For someone with such an astute eye for creative talent, John had little appreciation for business ability.

On December 16, 1922, Mary gave birth to a second child, a

daughter they named Barbara Nugent. To help Mary with the children they hired a governess, a warm, kind-hearted woman named Maude Stevenson, whom the children called Mama Steve. As the family grew, John and Mary expanded their Odin Street home, first adding a bedroom, which they used as a nursery for Barbara, then two dens. One, located off the living room, was called "the new room." John lined it with books and used it as a study. The other, located off the dining room, expressed another side of John's personality. It had an entrance hidden by a sliding door, and secret compartments that were used to store cases of liquor. Coping with Prohibition was no problem for this Irish saloonkeeper's son.

Even in his twenties liquor was starting to become a problem for John. He went on long destructive binges from which it took him days to recover. When he sobered up, he often signed pledges, witnessed by his parish priest, resolving to abstain from all alcoholic beverages. John would hold to these pledges until the next time his drinking cronies got together.

In 1923 director James Cruze made an epic-scale western for Paramount called *The Covered Wagon*. Although crudely made, it offered sheer size and spectacle and was enormously popular with audiences. The success of *The Covered Wagon* was not lost on Sol Wurtzel and Winnie Sheehan. Working with a writer named John Russell, they put together a script about the building of the first transcontinental railroad and called their story *The Iron Horse*. To direct it, they selected John Ford, who, on the verge of his twenty-ninth birthday, had already made fifty pictures—thirty-six of them westerns.

From its inception *The Iron Horse* was designed as an epic. With a then enormous budget of $450,000, it was to be the biggest picture ever made at Fox. To raise the money, William Fox stretched his line of credit to the limit, mortgaging everything on the back lot: the props, the trucks, the tools in the shops, and, finally, the lot itself. Then, to hold the line on further costs, the studio decided to cast an unknown instead of a high-priced actor in the starring role. John suggested testing a young assistant camera-man who had been working in George Schneiderman's crew. His name was George O'Brien, and he was the son of Dan O'Brien, San

Francisco's Chief of Police. With his sleek dark hair, Roman nose, and a physique that rippled with muscles, he looked like an Irish Valentino.

Today George O'Brien, veteran actor, producer, and a lifelong friend of John Ford's, is approaching his eightieth birthday. Still fit, energetic, and alert, he recently recalled his beginnings as an actor. Because he was an unknown, everyone knew it would take a remarkable test for him to land the part. John set up a scene between O'Brien and Gertrude Olmstead in which O'Brien played a soldier saying farewell to his sweetheart. After embracing her, he turned to leave, and as he did so, John whispered to Olmstead, "Grab George's sleeve." She did, and the inexperienced O'Brien, not knowing what to do, gave her a look of pained surprise. This was exactly what John wanted; it added a dimension of feeling to an otherwise ho-hum test, and the studio decided to take another look at O'Brien.

This time, deciding to go for broke, John dressed O'Brien in buckskins, put him on horseback, and told him to "Pony Express" —that is, to gallop along, vaulting over the horse from side to side. The secret of this stunt is to ride fast, since the rider needs a lot of spring to get over the horse. To make sure O'Brien was going fast enough, John hit O'Brien's horse across the backside with a leather strap just as he shouted "Action!" The horse took off like a rocket, O'Brien vaulted like a veteran rodeo hand, and John got a sensational test. The studio was so impressed with O'Brien's athletic ability that they gave him the part.

With O'Brien set in the lead role, Francis Powers, J. Farrell McDonald, and James Welsh were cast as the three comic section hands. Madge Bellamy, at the time under contract to Thomas Ince, was cast as the heroine; George Schneiderman was director of photography, Lefty Hough the propman, and Pardner Jones the head wrangler.

The first assistant director was John's older brother Eddie, who had come to California in 1917 and had become John's assistant at Universal. To assert his independence from his two famous brothers, Francis and John, Eddie reverted to the Gaelic form of the family name, calling himself Eddie O'Fearna. The relationship of John and Eddie was strange, to say the least. While Eddie was generally warm, funny, and open, he could also be cantankerous, abrasive, and independent-minded. He resented working for his younger brother, whom he thought was getting too much attention and publicity. The two brothers argued constantly, but while John would have preferred to use other assistants, a combination of magnanimity and family loyalty made him stick with Eddie, who had always been their mother's favorite.

Because *The Covered Wagon* had been made there, Fox selected Wadsworth, Nevada, near Reno, as a location site. There was no housing in the area, so Sol Wurtzel hired a circus train to transport the company and house it at the location as well. After arrangements were made with the A. G. Barnes Circus, a major circus of the time, the two-hundred-man *Iron Horse* troupe began loading on New Year's Eve, 1923.

From the day the company left Los Angeles, *The Iron Horse* was plagued by problems: intolerable living conditions, bitter cold winter weather, blizzards, and deep snow drifts. Propman Lefty Hough remembers a potpourri of impressions from *The Iron Horse* location:

"The Barnes circus train was a broken-down filthy mess. The food was stored in a boxcar that had been used to carry the elephants and no amount of cleaning would ever get the smell out. The sleeping cars had wooden bunks three deep. Some were built for midgets, some for giants. There were no mattresses and few blankets. George O'Brien didn't have a bunk at all—and he was the leading man!

"The company arrived in Wadsworth the next day. Most of the people were wearing white linen knickers and stood around shivering in the snow. Ford passed out wardrobe and everybody put buckskins and Union Army uniforms on over their knickers.

"I had fifty thousand pieces of property on *The Iron Horse*. I took over one of the buildings that had been built for the Western street and made a prop room out of it. We put a pot-bellied stove in there and built six bunks for me and my crew. I'd been smart enough to bring blankets and we really had a pretty good setup. We could make our own coffee in the morning and had frying skillets and could cook breakfast.

"One of the biggest problems up there was getting a bath, which mostly bothered the women. Well, the railroad tracks ran right behind my prop room so I got one of those big metal tubs and got the engineer to pull the locomotive up and fill the tub with hot water right from the engine. Pretty soon everybody got wise to this and was wanting to take a bath.

"Most of the extras were locals—Piute Indians and the Chinese and Irish tracklayers who still worked for the railroads up there. The Chinese lived quietly with their families in boxcars along the railbed, but the Irish, they were something else. All single, all drunks. Oh, they were great! Full of flit all the time, and fight? They'd fight a buzz saw!

"We picked up a priest named Father Brady. He was about thirty years old, and hanging around the location he got to be a pal of the Old Man's. Pappy wanted him to say Mass in the mess tent so he told me to dress the altar for him. I'm not a Catholic and didn't know what went on the altar, so I asked Eddie, and he told me everything I needed. But I couldn't get hold of a bell. I told Eddie, and he said, 'Oh Christ, you don't need a goddamn bell! Just get him a hammer.' So Father Brady said Mass—with a hammer.

"We had everything we needed up there: bootleggers who sold us booze, and all the hookers from Reno, who'd come out on Sundays. There was one cathouse down the track a ways that was owned by a woman named Blossom. She had been a socialite in the East somewhere and had apparently gotten involved with some domestic problem and wound up out in Nevada. She picked up four or five girls and set up a cathouse in a place the railroad used to stop for water. The funny part of it was that for five bucks you could go there, get your clothes washed, get a bath, a haircut, and a dame for a night. Five bucks! What a location!"

Almost as soon as *The Iron Horse* began shooting, a severe blizzard hit Wadsworth followed by a second and a third, and after nearly a month John was badly behind schedule. The studio began getting nervous, and the telegraph wires between Wadsworth and Hollywood sang with heated words. William Fox began to get nervous and was considering cancelling the picture. He sent Sol Wurtzel to Nevada to find out what was going on. When Wurtzel saw the conditions that the company was working under and the quality of the film that had been shot, he thought that John might be doing his best work. From Wadsworth he went directly to New York and urged Fox to stick with the picture.

John, meanwhile, not sure if the studio was about to pull the rug out from under him, kept shooting. He was under pressure to ship exposed film, almost any exposed film, to Hollywood. Time and time again he made adversity work to his advantage. At one point, while shooting an exterior along the railbed, a huge flock of sheep approached the setup and stopped on the tracks. Instead of halting the camera until the flock passed, John kept it rolling and photographed the herd. He eventually used this sequence, which was beautifully backlit with natural light, for the opening title shot.

Despite the pressures, John was determined to make *The Iron Horse* as authentic as possible. He used the two genuine Central Pacific and Union Pacific locomotives, "Juniper" and "116," to re-enact the wedding of the the rails and Promontory Point. He also devised a number of original shots, including the technique of placing the camera in a pit and stampeding a herd of cattle overhead. This shot has become commonplace today, but in 1924 it was a remarkable and stunning thing to see.

John celebrated his twenty-ninth birthday during the filming of *The Iron Horse*. Mary came to Wadsworth with a birthday cake, which was placed on a coupling between two cars and shared by the entire company. "He had the maturity and leadership of a much older man," says George O'Brien. At twenty-nine, he was already being called Pappy by some of his co-workers.

But John wasn't such an authority figure that he was above playing practical jokes on his actors. While filming an Indian attack, John had Pardner Jones shoot a clay pipe out of actor Justin McCluskey's mouth. He got a great take, but McCluskey was reduced to a trembling wreck. Eddie O'Fearna took McCluskey's side, and the two brothers actually got into a fistfight—not the only battle they had on *The Iron Horse*. O'Brien remembers Eddie throwing a clock at John in the recreation room one day. "J. Farrell McDonald was living in there and stepping on clock springs for days," he recalls.

The Iron Horse troupe returned to Hollywood in mid-March 1924 and John went to work pulling together the miles of footage he had shot. *The Iron Horse* is the work of a mature John Ford, containing scenes that eventually became his trademarks: Indians on a ridge line, riders disappearing into the sunset, slapstick juxtaposed with action, humor with violence. Although it is often compared to *The Covered Wagon*, *The Iron Horse* is a much more sophisticated film, its action shot with more angles, cutaways, and closeups, its editing far more complex.

The Iron Horse represented an enormous investment to William Fox, and to ensure that the picture earned back its costs, a massive promotion campaign was devised. To attract female viewers, the film was billed as a "battle of woman against woman in a romance of East and West, blazing a trail of love and civilization." Another pitch centered on George O'Brien: "He's not a sheik or a caveman or a lounge lizard, he's a man's man and the idol of women."

The Iron Horse opened in Los Angeles on August 24, 1924, at Sid Grauman's new Egyptian Theater, the first picture to play there. Fox brought three hundred Piute Indians and the Central Pacific's "Juniper" down from Sacramento and paraded them up and down Hollywood Boulevard. Lefty Hough was to attend the premiere with Eddie O'Fearna but, he says, "Eddie never made it. When I went over to pick him up, he said he wasn't going because he'd seen the goddamn thing." The New York premiere was held in Manhattan's Rialto Theater. John and Mary went East as guests of William Fox. John brought his parents down from Maine and they spent a week together in New York.

The Iron Horse was my grandfather's first major box-office success and established him as a premier Hollywood director. He always looked back on this picture with a special fondness. In 1972 he recalled taking his parents to the New York premiere:

"This was my parents' first trip to New York and, as I remember, they were both a bit overwhelmed by it all. We were staying at the Waldorf and every day Winnie Sheehan took them out shopping in his Rolls-Royce town car. They sat in the back seat, ramrod straight, while Sheehan was in front spitting tobacco juice out of the window. My mother had never learned how to read or write English, but she could read numbers, so that week she ordered all her meals from the price column. If something was $7.00 and something else was $5.00, she'd order the $7.00 item.

"William Fox had us out to his home on Long Island for the weekend. It was a gorgeous estate right on the sound with rolling lawns and a yacht moored in front of the house. He was a grand man and a great gentleman who knew this was a big outing for both Nana and Grampy, and he did everything to make them feel at home. During dinner, a butler came over to Grampy with a bottle of Jamison's Irish Whiskey, and he lit up like the bulb on a

Christmas tree when he saw it. He took his water glass, dumped the water into a potted plant, held it up for the butler, and didn't let him stop pouring until the glass was filled right up to the brim. Then he gulped the whole glass down in a shot. He didn't bat an eye. I remember Mr. Fox staring at him in disbelief.

"The next day was the premiere and Mary and I, Nana and Grampy, and Mr. and Mrs. Fox arrived in a limousine. We walked down a red carpet between bleachers filled with applauding fans and big searchlights sweeping the sky. Inside the lobby were big photographs of everybody connected with the picture, William Fox, Sol Wurtzel, George O'Brien, and myself. Nana walked up to each one of the pictures and stared at each one for a moment, then, just as straight as Queen Victoria, she walked over to William Fox and said, 'Mr. Fox, there's something I don't understand.' 'What's that?' he asked. 'Where's Eddie's picture?'"

The Iron Horse went on to become a great critical and commercial success. Today, it is remembered as one of the classics of the silent screen, and it's a great favorite among critics and John Ford buffs.

Although John had taken liberties with the actual events of the building of the transcontinental railroad, *The Iron Horse* was a historical picture that conveyed a strong sense of national pride. It was a celebration of heroic enterprise, of hope, of the country stretching gloriously to its full length. In the picture's final scene, George O'Brien and Madge Bellamy walk along the tracks toward each other while a photographer is preparing to take the historic picture of the driving of the Golden Spike. John Ford had found his great theme as a chronicler of the American experience: personal happiness is tied to national progress.

His vision was never more optimistic.

Despite the success of *The Iron Horse*, John fell back into a routine of grinding out studio potboilers and program fillers in the years immediately afterward. In 1925 he made six consecutive pictures— *Hearts of Oak*, *Lightnin'*, *Kentucky Pride*, *The Fighting Heart*, *Thank You*, and *The Shamrock Handicap*—which had in common only their lack of distinction. They were commercial pictures, mass entertainment, made to make money. Yet with each of them John continued to develop his technique, to nurture his style. Though they were mediocre pictures, he gave each of them something extra, enough so that the reviewers of all six films repeatedly called attention to the skill of their direction.

The fourth of these films, *The Fighting Heart*, was the story of a town outcast, a perennial loser, who in desperation enters the ring, becomes successful, and finally gets a title shot. It featured three actors who would have a long association with John. One was George O'Brien, whom *The Iron Horse* had launched as an action star and resulted in a long-term contract at Fox. Another was John's brother Francis, who had failed to keep pace with the new developments that by 1926 were making silent films so sophisticated and was now working as a character actor. Then there was an actor whom John would one day direct in his greatest performance: Victor McLaglen.

A big, colorful man with the kind of grace and expressive features ideal for silent films, Victor McLaglen had one of the most unusual backgrounds in Hollywood. Born in 1885 in South Africa, where his father had been an Anglican bishop, McLaglen ran away from home at sixteen and became a journeyman prizefighter, boxing his way across the United States and Canada.

In 1905 he went to England, addressed himself seriously to the art of boxing, and eventually became the heavyweight champion of the British Empire. When the First World War broke out he joined the British Army, became an officer, and was posted to Mesopotamia, where he became the Deputy Provost Marshal for the City of Baghdad. After the war he drifted into acting and made twenty films in England before Vitagraph brought him to Hollywood in 1924.

McLaglen was blustery and outspoken, with a rich sense of humor. He was, however, a vain man, preoccupied with himself and insensitive to what went on around him. As such, he left himself open to the incisive, sometimes cruel, manipulations of John Ford.

The Fighting Heart's climactic scene where O'Brien and McLaglen slug it out for the title was McLaglen's first scene with John Ford and his introduction to the director. Before he rolled the camera, John tried to bait his two actors into fighting for real.

They began to spar and dance around the ring, according to a prearranged routine. After they had run through it, though, John yelled through his megaphone, "Cut, Cut, Cut. What the hell do you think this is, a dance? Give me some goddamn *ACTION*."

They went at it more vigorously, but still not enough to please John. "CUT CUT CUT," he bellowed. "Come on, Vic, what the hell's the matter with you? You afraid of him? I told him not to hurt you."

"It's funny how he was able to get to us," says O'Brien today. "Vic and I suddenly began feeling each other out. We clinched and I don't know exactly what happened, but we came out of it and Vic hit me with a left hook on the ear and knocked me down. I got up and hit him in the eye with a succession of quick jabs, then landed a right cross. We really got into it, and the crowd of extras was roaring. After a couple of rounds, Vic's eye was bleeding pretty badly and started to close. Jack rang the bell and stopped the fight in the middle of the fourth round. Vic's eye was swollen shut and blood was running out his nose."

The Fighting Heart was released in October 1925. While Victor McLaglen took most of the punishment, its director seems to have taken most of the critical acclaim. The review in *Motion Picture News* was typical: "Director Ford ... has managed to put over double audience appeal ... scrap stuff and human interest."

Though he was grinding out picture after picture in the years after *The Iron Horse*, John made only two more really exceptional silent films; an epic-scale western called *3 Bad Men*, and *Four Sons*, a pacifist drama set in Germany in World War I. The two films, made in two distinctly different styles, represent the different ways in which John's directorial technique was evolving.

3 Bad Men, adapted from a Herman Whitaker novel called *Over the Border* and set against the Dakota land rush of 1877, was the story of three good-bad outlaws who give up their lives to protect a young couple from a corrupt sheriff and his gang. It was conceived as a sequel to *The Iron Horse*, and Fox lavished an enormous (for the time) $650,000 budget on it. The studio planned to use its three leading western stars—Tom Mix, Buck Jones, and George O'Brien—as the three heroes, but John convinced Sol Wurtzel that unless the "bad men" were presented as working cowboys, earthy, crusty, and real, who were both good and bad at the same time, the story simply wouldn't make any sense. In the end he prevailed, and three character actors—Tom Sanschi, Frank Campeau, and John's

36

pal J. Farrell McDonald—were cast. George O'Brien was added as a romantic lead.

In March 1926 *3 Bad Men* began shooting in Jackson's Hole, Wyoming. Snow was still on the Teton Mountains, which served as a magnificent backdrop. The company lived in tents, ate off chuck wagons, and bathed in a nearby river that was still choked with ice. Despite the hardships, this was John's favorite kind of location. Remote and inaccessible, he was far from the nitpicking interference of studio brass and was surrounded by a familiar group of actors and technicians over whom he reigned supreme.

Some scenes in *3 Bad Men* were as rugged as the location. One, which was to be done with doubles, called for the three outlaws to swim their horses across the icy waters of Jenny Lake. Pardner Jones, J. Farrell McDonald's double, couldn't swim, and was dreading the scene. But he was even more afraid of John Ford than he was of the water, so rather than admit his fears he went to George O'Brien and asked the actor to keep an eye on him. O'Brien recalls the scene:

"When Jack took his seat beside the camera, he noticed me standing by. 'What the hell are you doing here?' he asked. 'I'm your lifeguard,' I said. 'Lifeguard, my ass. I don't need a goddamn lifeguard.'

"When the camera was ready, Jack hollered 'Action' and the three riders started across the lake. Almost immediately Pardner's horse began to struggle, kicking and splashing and falling behind the others. Then he went under and Pardner panicked and started crying for help. I started to run into the water, but Jack grabbed me. 'I told you I don't need a lifeguard.' He hung on to my arm, and a grin broke out over his face. Then the horse went under again, but when he surfaced Pardner wasn't in the saddle. Jack let go of me and said, 'Go get him.' I swam across the lake, reached Pardner, and pulled him ashore. He had been kicked in the head by the drowning horse and was unconscious, but he was all right.

" 'See if you can get the horse,' Jack told me. Eddie O'Fearna and I got a boat and a large coil of line. The water was clear and moving with a good current and I could see the horse upside down in the water. The current was rolling him along the bottom. I dove in and got down to him. I pulled the mouth open, ran the line in behind the bit and pulled it through. Then I swam to the surface, and Eddie and I pulled the horse up and rowed ashore. The wranglers tried jumping on him, but it was too late. The horse was dead. The reins had become wrapped around his forelegs.

"I was stunned and exhausted by the whole thing. I was too young and dumb to know what to do so I went over to a tree and I just broke down and had a good cry. I cried for Pardner, I cried for the horse, I cried for everybody. I started thinking about all the wild chances we took, all the crazy things we did, the *esprit de corps* among us. Jack came over to me and said, 'You all right, kid?' He put his arms around me. 'You want to go in?' 'No, I'm OK,' I said, 'just let me catch my breath.' We would have done the same for Jack Ford as we would have for Knute Rockne."

The climactic scene in *3 Bad Men* was the land rush, in which a cannon goes off and hundreds of wagons dash into the new territory. This scene was shot on a dry lake bed in Victorville, California, just outside Los Angeles. It was the last scene actually filmed.

There is a shot in this scene in which the rushing wagons race toward a baby accidentally abandoned on the dry lake bed; creating action within action, it multiplies the suspense tenfold and is perhaps the most famous single shot in a John Ford silent film. The stunt was an old idea of Harry Carey's and John had been waiting for a chance to try it for years. In this period before process or trick photography it had to be done for real: An actual baby had to be set down in front of the onrushing riders. John knew that no mother in her right mind would volunteer her own child and that he'd have to resort to trickery. By coincidence, a woman with a baby girl visited the location the day before the scene was shot, and John knew this was his chance.

"I'd like to use your child as an extra," John told the woman. "She'll ride on one of the wagons, and I'll personally guarantee her security." The woman agreed, and a moment later Eddie O'Fearna drove up and hustled her off the set. "We never let parents stay around while we're working with child actors," he explained. "But don't worry. Jack Ford just loves children."

They set the child down on the dry lake bed and started the land rush. The riders were bearing down on her, and just as she was about to be trampled an arm reached into the frame and picked her up. The arm belonged to Lefty Hough, who remembers how the stunt was done. "It was set up for a left-handed man. The camera was shooting out of a pit and I was on the running board of an automobile standing off to the side with the motor idling. As soon as I had a grip on her, the car raced off just ahead of those galloping horses. If I'd missed, I would have fallen on the kid."

3 Bad Men finished shooting in May and was edited during the summer of 1926. In August, Fox previewed it in Los Angeles. The reaction was not good, and the picture was recut and shortened considerably.

On September 10, Winnie Sheehan and Sol Wurtzel took the recut version to Modesto, where they previewed it again, this time successfully. Very much relieved, they wired Ford, "Congratulations. Long may the Irish survive..."

Like *The Iron Horse, 3 Bad Men* is readily available today and is often shown at retrospectives. The film has the same feel, the same "aura," indeed many of the same shots, as John Ford's later sound westerns. *3 Bad Men* was one of the most violent films made up until that time. There are innumerable fight scenes, all with the most graphic kind of kicking and gouging. At one point the corrupt sheriff burns down a church and brutally beats a preacher. Offsetting the violence, the three heroes—J. Farrell McDonald, Tom Sanschi, and Frank Campeau—move through the film projecting an irresistible charm and camaraderie.

3 Bad Men was released in October 1926 to outstanding reviews, but despite its success with the critics, its glossy production values, splendid scenery, and rough-and-tumble action, *3 Bad Men* took years to recoup its costs. Why it wasn't more popular is hard to say. Public tastes are always fickle. *3 Bad Men* was released just before Charles Lindbergh's flight across the Atlantic, and the aviator, not the cowboy, was soon to become the hero of the day. Also, the industry converted to sound a few years after its release, and silent pictures, even epic silent pictures, were a drug on the market. Nevertheless, *3 Bad Men* stands as one of John Ford's better films, and quite possibly his best silent film.

Although he was upset by the commercial failure of *3 Bad Men*, John took refuge in the fact that he was a working director with other projects to pursue. As he had done after *The Iron Horse*, he followed *3 Bad Men* with a string of studio program fillers, the first of which, ground out even before *3 Bad Men* was released, was a navy adventure film with George O'Brien and Janet Gaynor called *The Blue Eagle*.

After *The Blue Eagle* came *Upstream*, a comedy about life in a

London boardinghouse for actors. This in turn was followed by *Mother Machree*, the story of an Irish housekeeper who sacrifices everything so her son may have a better life. *Mother Machree* marks the beginning of John's great friendship with John Wayne and therefore stands as a milestone in his life.

Wayne, whose real name is Marion Michael Morrison, was then a sophomore at the University of Southern California, working his way through school on a football scholarship. In the summer of 1928 his football coach, Howard Jones, arranged for Morrison—who even then was known as Duke—to get a summer job at the Fox studios, where he worked as a swing-gang laborer, striking sets and moving furniture from one set to another. One day Morrison was told to report to the set of *Mother Machree*, where Lefty Hough put him to work herding geese that were being used in the film's background. That afternoon John went up to him and said, "You one of Howard Jones's boys?"

"Yeah," said Morrison.

"What position do you play?"

"Guard."

"Guard, huh?"

"Yeah."

"I used to be a fullback. You think you could take me out?"

Morrison looked at the director. "Yeah, I know I could."

John and Duke Morrison crouched down, knuckles on the stage floor, and started slamming into each other. But "Bull Feeney," at thirty-three hadn't broken a tackle since 1914, and Morrison, at 6'4" and 200 pounds, was in prime physical condition. John couldn't budge the U.S.C. guard. Going back to a corner of the stage John said, "See if you can stop me." He started running at Morrison and slammed into him, then tried to break free. But Morrison had him, not cleanly, but he had him. Then, just as John was breaking free, Morrison kicked the director squarely in the chest and sent him sprawling.

There was dead silence on the set. All eyes were on Morrison, whose brief career in pictures was surely at an end. But John simply got up, dusted himself off, and said, "Come on, let's get back to work. That's enough of this bullshit."

In 1928, Marion Morrison looked very different from the John Wayne of later years: tall, thin, and with distinctly Irish features, he looked like his son Pat does today. Wayne once recalled for me his first impressions of John Ford, the man who was to become the most important influence on his professional life:

"I was going to U.S.C. studying to be a lawyer, and had no particular interest in the motion picture business—working at Fox was just something to pay the bills at school. I wasn't thinking about a future in the studios, and that helped Jack and me develop a nice relationship. Jack was interested in football, and we were just starting to have good teams on the West Coast, just beginning to get some national recognition. Jack appreciated the fact that I was more than just another propman, that I was trying to get an education.

"I watched how he handled people, how he got his actors to communicate without the spoken word. I saw him as a very sensitive, very learned man, and I began to appreciate what a great artist he really was.

"When I went back to school in the fall I started thinking about my future. The other kids who were going to law school all had connections—fathers or uncles who had law firms. I had none and began to realize that if I went into law, I was going to spend ten years in a back room writing briefs before I could get started. This really started playing on me, and the more I thought about the picture business, the more attractive it became. I had no thoughts about becoming an actor—I wanted to be a director like Jack Ford. He was my mentor, my ideal, and I made up my mind: I wanted to be like him."

By the late 1920s silent films were becoming increasingly sophisticated, moving away from the clean, simple compositions of D. W. Griffith to increasingly ornate and elaborate designs. Toward the end of the silent era, Hollywood was greatly influenced by the German cinema, which, led by directors Ernst Lubitsch, G. W. Pabst, Fritz Lang, and F. W. Murnau (most of whom would eventually be lured to Hollywood), had the second largest and possibly the most creative film industry of the period. Steeped in the tradition of German romanticism, the films of these directors were surreal, fogbound, and highly stylized, shot on elaborate indoor sets and meticulously blocked out, frame by frame, before a foot of film was shot. Every setup, every camera angle, was planned in sketches made by artists—or designers, as they were called—who had come to motion pictures from painting. Herman Warm,

41

Walther Rohig, Albin Grau, and Erno Metzner were among the most famous, and they brought the concepts of expressionism, cubism, and constructivism into film.

The German cinema had a direct and profound influence on John. In April 1927 he went to Germany to shoot background scenes in the Bavarian countryside for his next picture, *Four Sons*. While he was there, John got a firsthand education in the techniques of the German film makers.

Docking in Hamburg after a stormy Atlantic crossing, John and Mary, who was accompanying him, traveled to Berlin to meet F. W. Murnau, whom Fox had recently signed to come to Hollywood. Welcoming them warmly, Murnau allowed John to examine artists' renderings and design sketches, and explained in depth the preproduction techniques of German expressionistic cinema. Fascinated, John screened the films of the German Golden Age: Lubitsch's *The Cabinet of Doctor Caligari*, Lang's *Destiny* and *Metropolis*, Murnau's own *Nosferatu* and *The Last Laugh*—films that used design and lighting techniques of the greatest sophistication to translate their stories to the screen in purely visual terms. John studied them scene by scene, making mental notes on their techniques, their slow deliberate rhythms. Many of the lessons he learned in Berlin would become a vital part of his own visual style.

After a month in Berlin, John assembled a German camera crew and, leaving Mary behind, traveled to Munich to shoot his background footage. From Munich he went to Vienna, where Mary rejoined him.

Four Sons, based on a short story by I.A.R. Wylie called "Grandma Bernle Learns Her Letters," was made in the summer of 1927. Back in Hollywood, John went way beyond cutting in the background footage he had shot in Bavaria. At every opportunity he put the lessons he had learned from Murnau to work, deliberately seeking to create an expressionistic classic. When the film is viewed today one cannot help but be aware of the self-conscious artistry with which it was made. Although an essentially sentimental story celebrating mother love, stylistically *Four Sons* was John's most sophisticated silent film. Its dissimilarity from the Hollywood norm helped to create a critical storm when released in 1928.

4

The
Sound
Revolution

Al Jolson's famous line "You ain't heard nothin' yet" in *The Jazz Singer* (1927) marked the beginning of a sound revolution that changed the entire film industry. Within eighteen months the cinema was ripped by its roots out of the silent era and transplanted into richer if unfamiliar new soil. Silent films, which in 1928 were so fluid, so astonishingly beautiful, and so adept at telling a story visually, were suddenly dated. Sound was everything, and King Mike ruled motion pictures. Volumes could be (and have been) written on how the coming of sound changed Hollywood. Careers were ruined and fortunes were made as the industry changed overnight. When films moved indoors, veteran movie men like John Ford were told that stylized films and rugged outdoor pictures had gone the way of the clipper ship, the stagecoach, and the pony express.

In the early days of sound there were a number of competing systems. Fox used one called "Movietone" that had been developed for use in the company's newsreels, Fox Movietone News, then the largest newsreel organization in the world. The studio's first talkies, made with newsreel equipment, were called Movietone Shorts.

John's first talking picture, *Napoleon's Barber*, had a simplistic plot typical of primitive talkies. The making of it was an exercise in chaos. The whole atmosphere of picture making changed with the introduction of sound. No one in silents was used to working quietly. These films had been shot with carpenters hammering and sawing, directors shouting, atmosphere musicians playing, and, if a scene were funny, crews laughing. Now, with sound, everyone but the actors had to be deathly quiet, to whisper and to tiptoe about with newfound restraint and unaccustomed grace.

Early motion picture cameras were as noisy as Model A Fords. To accommodate sound they, too, had to be silenced, which was accomplished by stuffing them into thick padded booths, wrapping them in horse blankets and asbestos, and locking them in ugly pillboxes.

Lighting was another problem. Silent film ran through cameras and projectors at a speed of sixteen frames a second, sound film at twenty-four—fully 50 percent faster. (Old silent films are usually projected today at twenty-four frames a second, which is why they look so hurried and jerky.) Speeding up the film meant cutting down the exposure time, so twice as much light was required, which in turn meant more heat on the actors. Already apprehensive about speaking lines, actors sweated off their thick makeup under the hot lights.

There was a new man on the set of *Napoleon's Barber*, that wizard of Western Electric, the sound man. He shackled and bound film making to the needs of his infant technology and in the process set it back twenty-five years. Only with time did film makers like John regain control of their art and subordinate sound to the larger problems of film making.

Much later, sound became a magnificent tool of the film maker. In addition to dialogue there was background music and sound effects—gravel crunching underfoot, bacon frying in a pan, horses clomping on concrete—that added a dimension of realism unknown in silent pictures. Technology eventually solved some of the problems that sound had created: Eastman Kodak developed film with faster emulsions which needed less light; the Mitchell Camera Company developed a noiseless sound camera; a single-directional microphone working on an overhead boom replaced the many cumbersome mikes hidden in vases and flowerpots.

But the biggest change that sound brought to motion pictures wasn't in technology or working conditions, but rather in personnel. Hollywood needed actors who could handle dialogue, and to get them the studios turned to the theater. Talent scouts swarmed over Broadway, signing every actor who could get a table at Lindy's or the Lamb's Club. They brought west the likes of Irene Dunne, Barbara Stanwyck, Bette Davis, Claudette Colbert, James Cagney, and Edward G. Robinson. They brought out carloads of dialogue directors and drama coaches to teach silent actors like George O'Brien, Victor McLaglen, and J. Farrell McDonald how to enunciate, to project, and to elongate their vowels.

Before the introduction of sound, writers had played a relatively minor role in film making. Now, that suddenly changed, and the studios scrambled to sign the best writing talent in the land. Ben Hecht, Charles MacArthur, Sidney Howard, and S. N. Behrman were among those who were enticed to Hollywood. At one time, MGM had Anita Loos, F. Scott Fitzgerald, Ring Lardner, Aldous Huxley, and P. G. Wodehouse under contract. Although many writers looked down on motion pictures and complained, as Dorothy Parker did, that Hollywood was a "warm

Siberia," there is no doubt that they changed the industry and gave picture making some of the respectability that the theater had enjoyed.

In 1928 a writer named James Kevin McGuinness came to Fox. A dapper, charming Irishman with a sharp wit, he had been a publicist and contact man for the Catholic Church and was well connected in Catholic and Irish circles. Partly because of their Irish connection, and partly because McGuinness was a congenial companion who liked to drink, McGuinness, whom John called Seamus, and John, whom McGuinness called Sean, hit it off immediately. They first collaborated on a railroad yarn starring Victor McLaglen, called *Strong Boy*, followed by an adaptation of the Talbot Mundy novel of love and intrigue in British India, *King of the Khyber Rifles*. The film version, called *The Black Watch*, and starring Victor McLaglen and Myrna Loy, was shot as a silent in January and February of 1929. Working with a generous $400,000 budget, an excellent supporting cast, and a small army of extras, John took his time and went after expressionistic lighting and effects, including some beautiful tracking shots. He also pulled a fine performance out of Victor McLaglen, who had recently achieved a degree of stardom with *What Price Glory?* and was emerging as one of Fox's principal romantic leads. Nevertheless, despite his success, McLaglen remained an actor with a limited emotional range, and John had to browbeat a performance out of him.

The Black Watch also marked the beginning of John's professional relationship with Mary's brother, Wingate Smith, who went to work for John on this picture as an assistant director. An engaging fellow with dark hair, a small mustache, and a quick wit, Smith was a much-decorated veteran of the First World War who had been seriously wounded at the Battle of Chateau-Thierry and had spent five years recovering in V.A. hospitals.

As John was putting the finishing touches on *The Black Watch*, Fox released *In Old Arizona*, an all-talking western that Raoul Walsh had made with Movietone equipment. It was enormously successful and prompted Sol Wurtzel and Winnie Sheehan to decree that henceforth all the studios' pictures, including any silents still in production, were to be talkies. When John finished *The Black Watch*, it was turned over to a British stage director named Lumsden Hare for the addition of dialogue scenes.

Having no concept of film, Hare added a number of long,

static dialogue scenes, mostly between McLaglen and Loy, which upset the symmetry of the picture and turned what had been a beautifully made action-adventure film into a disjointed and inconsistent semitalking picture. To make matters worse, the dialogue was poorly written, as when Myrna Loy's character says at one point to McLaglen's, "They will torture thee; they will put out your eyes."

When *The Black Watch* was released in May 1929, reviewers unanimously called attention to the contrast between the dull dialogue and the masterfully staged and photographed action scenes. Unfortunately, though he had nothing to do with it, most critics blamed John for the picture's unevenness.

For John, 1929 was shaping up as a very precarious year, and for a while, at least, it was questionable whether he was going to be able to survive the transition into sound. Three of his pictures in a row had been box-office failures; he needed a hit and he needed it badly.

It was at this point that Jim McGuinness, demonstrating just how clever he really was, came up with an absolute nugget of an idea. Taking a cue from Raoul Walsh, who had made *In Old Arizona* as far away from the studio as he could get, McGuinness concocted a story set 3,000 miles from Hollywood at the United States Naval Academy in Annapolis, Maryland. The story, called *Salute*, was about two brothers, one a West Point cadet and the other an Annapolis midshipman, who are bitter rivals. Both are the stars on their respective football teams, both are in love with the same girl. Their rivalry comes to a head at the Army-Navy game. In April 1929, John sold the front office on the idea, and with Jim McGuinness, cinematographer Joe August, and George O'Brien, who was to play the lead, they went east to work on the script and scout locations.

John, who wanted a lot of football action in *Salute*, needed twenty-five football players to use as extras. The best players available in those preprofessional days were those on Duke Morrison's old team, the U.S.C. Trojans, which had been the number-one team in the nation the previous fall and had won the Rose Bowl.

When he got back to Los Angeles, John approached the university and asked if he could use its players. But *Salute* had a starting date for the beginning of May and the university wouldn't let the students out early. Playing his trump card, John turned to

Morrison, whom he hoped might be able to pull some strings. Going directly to U.S.C. President Rufus E. von Kleinschmidt, Morrison gave every reason he could think of why the players should be let out of school early. There was the travel, the opportunity to see Annapolis and Washington, D.C., to learn something of the country's military and political traditions—and to make some money too. Morrison's arguments were forceful and convincing, and finally von Kleinschmidt agreed. After taking their final exams early, the players could go.

Sol Wurtzel had authorized Morrison to offer the football players seventy-five dollars a week, but Duke, anxious to make a name for himself at the studio, offered them fifty dollars instead. When they accepted, Wurtzel complimented Morrison on his shrewdness. Then he told him how stupid he was. "I forgot to mention to you, Duke, that you're doing double duty on this picture. You're propping it and playing football too. Congratulations! You just screwed yourself out of twenty-five bucks a week."

A chance to get out of school early and to be in the movies was an attractive proposition. Morrison had more volunteers than he had jobs, and in recruiting players he naturally favored the men of his own Sigma Chi fraternity. The morning the *Salute* company was to pull out of Los Angeles' Sante Fe depot, however, an extra player showed up who was not one of Morrison's fraternity brothers. He was a 220-pound tackle with thick lips and big ears, whose only baggage was a bottle of bootleg gin. His name was Ward Bond.

Morrison knew him and didn't like him. "You're not getting on this train, Bond," he said. "You're too ugly to be in the movies."

"Screw you, Duke," said Bond, as he shoved his way aboard the train. "Not everybody on this gravy train is going to be a sweetheart of Sigma Chi."

Salute marked the beginning of John Wayne's real friendship with John Ford. "Jack was a distant figure before that," he says today, "and I suppose I had been more loyal than close. But on *Salute*, Jack and I learned to share all the secrets of friendship." In the course of his work on *Salute*, Wayne even learned to like Ward Bond, who also became a lifelong friend. "You couldn't help but notice Ward in a crowd," Wayne observes. "He was always getting himself into trouble by opening his mouth before he knew what he was going to say. But he was really fun, and right away Jack kinda' took to him."

At the Naval Academy John borrowed a Marine Corps drill instructor, a tough old topkick on his last tour of duty, to teach the U.S.C. football players how to drill and act like midshipmen. Soon after they arrived at the Academy John had the D.I. hold a formation on a grassy knoll so he could look over the players and select a few to play bits.

"All right, you ragtag scruffy college boys, I'm going to teach you to act like gentlemen and midshipmen," said the drill instructor. "You there, Mr. O'Brien, you've been in this man's outfit before. Post yourself up here."

O'Brien did as he was told.

"You gentlemen will notice how Mr. O'Brien assumes the position of attention. You will notice that his heels are together, that his fingers are extended and joined with the thumb touching the first ring of the forefinger. His stomach is in, his chest is out, and he looks straight ahead. This, gentlemen, is the proper position of attention. ASSUME IT!"

"What is this bullshit, anyway?" came a voice from the back of the crowd. It was Bond's.

"Who's that great big ugly guy?" John asked Morrison.

"Which one?"

"The one with the liver lips and the big mouth."

"His name is Bond, Wardell Bond. He's just a big loudmouth who *thinks* he can play football. Now, over here are some real football players. There's Don Williams and Ernie Pinckert and Russ Saunders, and—"

"What did you say his name was?"

"Bond, Wardell Bond. We call him 'the Judge' because he spends so much time on the bench."

"He sure is ugly."

"He's a rotten football player, too. We also call him 'Wrong Way Bond,' because last year during the Stanford game he spent the entire sixty minutes sitting on the bench—with his back to the field. Now, over here are some real football players—"

"I'm going to use the ugly one," said John.

"Ward had an unshakable ego and all the gall in the world," says Wayne today. "He was just unbelievable. One night we wanted to go out drinking, but we were broke. Ward said, 'Come on, I'll get

49

some money from Jack Ford.' He didn't know Jack nearly as well as I did, but he just marched up to Jack's door and banged on it and said, 'Hey, it's me, Ward, open the goddamn door and let me in.' Jack was sitting in the bathtub shaving, as was his wont. We went in and on top of the dresser was about fifteen dollars in cash. Ward reached up and said, 'Jack, I'm taking fifteen bucks,' and before he could say anything, we were out the door! That's something I would never have had the nerve to pull."

Jim McGuinness had been very cagy in developing the *Salute* script. Not only was the Annapolis location a long way from an interfering front office, but the script was written in such a way that sound couldn't ruin its cinematic qualities. The picture had a lot of football action that John was able to shoot without recording the sound. Later he would dub in voices and sound effects. The dialogue scenes were brief, to the point, and were used only to convey essential exposition.

Aside from teaching him how to subordinate sound to the larger problems of film making, *Salute* provided John with his first real introduction to the navy. He found that he relished the Academy's atmosphere: the neat white buildings, the well-clipped lawns, the midshipmen marching by counting cadence. He liked the simple, manly principles and the traditional atmosphere that he found there. Moreover, while making *Salute*, John met a number of officers who would become vital contacts in the years to come, the most important of whom was a Catholic chaplain, Father Joseph Brady, who had influence into the highest ranks of the navy.

Salute is remembered as a very special picture by all those connected with it, largely because of the strong sense of comradeship that developed among the company. George O'Brien can't remember having had more fun on a picture, and even Ward Bond was caught up in the prevailing spirit. Only Eddie O'Fearna was unhappy; he resented this young upstart, Duke Morrison, who was beginning to act as though he knew something about making pictures. Their relationship took a decided turn for the worse on the train ride home when Ward Bond ate a twenty-dollar breakfast, an incident Eddie used to limit everyone's meal allowance to ten dollars a day. Morrison went to John and complained that football players needed to eat big meals. "Jack and George O'Brien went in and ate a forty-dollar breakfast and signed Eddie's name," Wayne recalls. "Eddie got sore as hell and blamed it on me. I don't think he ever forgave me for that."

Salute finished shooting in July 1929 and was released the following October. A simple, inexpensive picture with lots of action and comedy, it was moderately popular with the critics but, more important, extremely popular at the box office, and became Fox's biggest grosser in 1929. *Salute* was the hit that John had been looking for, and it helped secure his position as a director of talkies.

After *Salute*, Jim McGuinness developed a story about a disabled submarine trapped on the ocean floor, whose crew finally escape by shooting themselves out of the torpedo tubes—all, that is, but one man who must remain behind. When McGuinness completed his draft, John turned it over to a new writer on the Fox lot, a navy veteran named Dudley Nichols, who was familiar with military detail. He was a very different man from Jim McGuinness. One of many journalists then coming into motion pictures, Nichols had been a reporter on the New York *World* and had gained national recognition for his coverage of the Sacco-Vanzetti trial. Tall and thin, with soft brown hair and watery blue eyes, Nichols habitually dressed in tweeds and corduroy.

John and Nichols hit it off immediately and made an ideal team. Dudley Nichols was the butterfly, John the bull. John was bursting with enthusiasm and energy while Nichols was subtler, more controlled. His were the Athenian qualities of logic and grace, while John's were the Spartan ones of ruggedness and perseverance. In the years ahead, Dudley Nichols would have a great influence on John, implanting in him the seeds of social consciousness and coloring the director's cinematic style.

Nichols went to work on *Men Without Women*, adding salty speeches and characterization. At a time when films were full of self-conscious talk, he kept the dialogue terse and to the point. Then John, who was not a writer himself but could direct the writing of others, went over the drafts of Nichols and McGuinness and selected the best of both. These he wove into a finished script.

John shot *Men Without Women* in the fall of 1929 on the Fox lot and on locations at Catalina Island. Almost all the action takes place inside the stricken submarine, and John had to use every conceivable device, tracking shots and fast-paced cutting, to keep the film from becoming static.

Men Without Women was photographed by Joe August, whose skill at intricate composition beautifully captured the claustrophobic feeling of life aboard a submarine. At one point, in a brilliant cinematic stroke, he mounted a camera in a waterproof glass case on the deck and ran it by remote control as the ship submerged. In the years since then this shot has become commonplace, but in 1930 it was nothing less than sensational.

Men Without Women was an important turning point for another man who worked on it: Duke Morrison. Writing the propman a small role as a navy lieutenant, and giving him a close-up and a few lines, John gave Morrison his first part that was more than a walk-on, his first with any flair.

A few months later Raoul Walsh was casting a big-budget western called *The Big Trail* and needed a big, rugged, good-looking kid who wouldn't cost too much. Did John, he asked, know of anybody? John suggested Morrison, and showed him the clip from *Men Without Women*. Walsh was impressed. He tested Morrison and showed the results to Winnie Sheehan.

"What's this guy's name?" asked Sheehan.

"Marion Morrison," said Walsh.

"Jesus, that's a terrible name," Sheehan said. "I'd like to use the kid, but tell him he'll have to change his name."

When Morrison heard that he had got the part, he went to John with the good news.

"They want me to change my name," he said. "I don't know what to call myself."

"Why don't you take the name of somebody in American history that you admire?" John suggested.

"I've always liked the Revolutionary War general Mad Anthony Wayne."

"Anthony Wayne, hmm." They mulled it over.

"How about Tony Wayne?"

"Nah, sounds too Italian. How about John Wayne?" said Ford.

The Big Trail was made in the winter and spring of 1930 on locations throughout the west. An epic film, made in a 70-mm process called "Fox Grandeur," it was, in terms of sheer size and action, one of the most impressive westerns ever made. Yet the film was a box office disaster.

The Big Trail launched John Wayne as an actor, but hardly as a successful one. He next appeared in a musical called *Girls Demand Excitement*, then in a comedy called *Three Girls Lost*. Both were box-office failures and Fox didn't pick up his contract. He would have to bide his time and pay his dues for nearly a decade before the vehicle came along that would propel him into stardom.

In the spring of 1930 the inmates in New York's Auburn Prison rose up, disarmed their guards, and took the warden hostage. The Attica of its day, it caused New York's governor, Franklin Roosevelt, to remark, "This is a hell of a way to begin a depression." Thanks to the Auburn riots, prisons suddenly became topical, and *The Last Mile*—a prison play starring two unknowns, Spencer Tracy and Humphrey Bogart—became the surprise hit of the season.

Seeking to cash in on the sudden interest in prisons, MGM prepared a picture called *The Big House*, and at Fox a writer named Maurice Watkins began developing a prison script called *Up the River*. Winnie Sheehan assigned the picture to John and sent him to New York to find a leading man. On his first night in New York John saw *The Last Mile* and got his first look at young Spencer Tracy. Noting the strong resonant voice, the energy, the warmth, and the deep intelligence Tracy brought to his role, John knew he was looking at a superior actor. After the play he went backstage and introduced himself. Similar types—gruff, companionable, and without pretense—the two men liked each other right away. The next day John reported his find to Winnie Sheehan, only to learn that Fox had already tested Tracy and decided that he was terrible. Undaunted, John dug up the tests, screened them, and discovered that Tracy, made up with a scarred face and a beard, had been tested as a character actor instead of a leading man. John persuaded Sheehan to let him test Tracy again, this time with no makeup at all. The test was so successful that Fox signed not only Tracy but, on John's advice, Humphrey Bogart as well.

Up the River was dealt a temporary setback when MGM got *The Big House* into release in the summer of 1930 and Sheehan decided to cancel the Fox picture. But John saved it by selling the front office on the idea that the picture could be played for comedy and, as such, wouldn't compete with *The Big House*. In a ten-day writing marathon, John and gag-man William Collier completely overhauled the script, focusing not on the prison riot, but on a comical prison baseball game so important to the cons that escapees actually break *into* prison to play in it.

Shot in the summer of 1930, *Up the River* had the same relaxed improbability as *Salute*, and when released in October it was enormously popular with audiences and critics. Though Spencer Tracy and Humphrey Bogart were superb in the film, Fox foolishly allowed both their contracts to expire soon afterward. Like John Wayne, they had to go elsewhere to make their marks.

5

Tits
and
Temples

U*p the River* was followed by *The Seas Beneath*, a navy adventure film shot in November of 1930 off Catalina Island. Written by Dudley Nichols and starring George O'Brien, it was the story of a disguised raider, a "Q ship," trying to lure an elusive German submarine into a fight; the navy had lent Fox two submarines, the V-4 and S-47, and a minesweeper for the film. The movie company and ships' crews lived and worked together on that sunny island near Los Angeles on the California coast. They played baseball, held swim meets, and, as often happened in John's films, a strong comradeship grew among all involved. At times it was hard to tell where Hollywood ended and the navy began.

John and George O'Brien, to a lesser extent, had been spending so much time around the navy with pictures like *Salute*, *Men Without Women*, and *The Seas Beneath* that they were beginning to feel like navy men themselves. They didn't sleep with the movie company in their bungalows ashore, but rather aboard the V-4, anchored in the Isthmus harbor. They ate with the officers in the wardroom, where they participated in the shop talk and read the "flimsies" from the radio room that were passed around the table.

In the mornings, the three-thousand-horsepower engines hammered alive, the anchor chain rattled up through the hawse, and the submarine got under way. Water rippled under the bow and she headed out into deep water as John, a pair of binoculars hanging from his neck, stood in the conning tower beside the captain. A woolen watchcoat kept off the morning chill. The smell of the sea, of fresh painted steel, and diesel fumes filled his nostrils.

John liked this clean and orderly world; he was comfortable in it. He liked the discipline, the crisp salutes, the "Yes sir" and "No sir," the purposeful coming and going of the men. It was all very different from Hollywood. These men had a nobility, a quiet dignity, a sense of service that the greedy hucksters of the motion picture business could never even comprehend.

Another factor drawing John to the military during these years was Mary, whose family connections in the service were numerous. She and John often drove down the coast to San Diego to make social calls and to attend luncheons and parties at the navy officers clubs at Coronado and North Island. There, on verandas that overlooked the wide blue bay, they would dance to brass bands and mix with the officers and their wives. Mary was also active in the Navy League, and when high-ranking officers and their wives came to Los Angeles, she entertained them and saw to it that they got studio passes to visit John on the set.

But there was a darker side to the John–Mary–Navy triangle. Despite John's success in motion pictures, Mary was unimpressed by his accomplishments. She regarded his movie career as flashy and "low Irish" and let him know that she felt it lacked substance. What he needed, she told him, was something "more substantial," something that "Hollywood could never take away." John had an underlying self-doubt and felt a need to vindicate himself in Mary's eyes, to prove his worth to her. Thus he looked to the Establishment world of the military for much of his social life.

In the fall of 1929, a decade of unprecedented boom and prosperity came crashing to an end. On October 23, at the New York Stock Exchange, there was a spectacular drop in the last hour of trading. The next day, October 24, the bottom fell out, and stocks plunged to new lows. Almost overnight the mood of the times shifted from frivolity and hope to dark despair. So ended the decade of the 1920s. Historian A.R.M. Lower said it most eloquently: "The revelry on the warm sandy beaches of the 1920s was followed by the freezing rain of the 1930s."

For most people the years 1930, 1931, and 1932 were lean and bitter ones. In an age before unemployment insurance, welfare, or social security, 12 million people, fully 33 percent of the labor force, were unemployed. Yet, as the Depression settled in over the land, Hollywood remained largely unscathed. During the early 1930s, motion pictures were one of the most solvent industries in America as films offered visions of hope and escape at prices most could still afford.

But what was true for the industry as a whole was not true for all the studios. In 1931, at the William Fox Film Company, everything seemed to go wrong at once. For one thing, Fox's Movietone sound system had been modeled on a German system, and after a protracted legal battle William Fox was ordered to pay enormous royalties. For another, the Fox Film Corporation owned the largest chain of movie theaters in the country, but the cost of converting its 800 outlets to sound had been enormous. To make matters worse, in 1925 William Fox had committed his company to 70-mm and had begun to convert his theaters, a project that had required tremendous additional outlays. In good times Fox might have been able to pull it off, but in 1931 it all came tumbling down. That year Fox declared itself bankrupt and was put into receivership. *The Seas Beneath* was the last picture made on Fox's Western Avenue lot.

John Ford, as a valuable corporate asset, was kept under contract and continued to receive his regular salary, but with only a few "B" pictures scheduled for production, there was simply nothing for him to do. For the first time in his life John was forced to be idle.

At first he enjoyed the break from his usual hectic race, lolling around the house, eating, reading, and sleeping. But after six weeks of enforced idleness he was restless and tense, itching for something to do. Unused to having John around the house for more than a day or two at a time, Mary also felt the strain, and their relationship began to suffer from overexposure.

With no end to this paid unemployment in sight, John decided that he might as well take a sabbatical, an extended vacation, and he began planning a cruise to the Far East with Mary and the children. But a few days before their ship was to sail, John and Mary quarreled over some trivial matter, and John decided not to make the trip with Mary and his family. Eschewing the stiff formalities of a cruise ship, he and George O'Brien, who also had been idled by the production slowdown, booked passage on the Norwegian tramp steamer *M.S. Tai Yang*, leaving Mary to take the children on vacation to Honolulu.

There were many tensions working inside of John besides those caused by his disagreement with Mary, and he had probably wanted this kind of trip in the first place. George O'Brien says that John was resisting success at this point in his life. "He was fighting it off. He wanted to go out and work in the barn and be one of the boys for a while." He was more interested in being a man among men than a man of power whom others sought out. John also had a romantic notion of himself as a man of action, a Lord Byron who experiences his material firsthand. He wanted to share the lives and adventures of other men, and to give his life some of the vigor, color, and adventure that his films had.

After going aboard the beat-up, rusty hulk in which they were to cross the Pacific, O'Brien began to have second thoughts about the trip. After settling into a tiny cabin off the bridge, he and John met their skipper, Captain Earling Crapp, who recognized O'Brien right away.

"I am happy to meet you, Mr. O'Brien. *The Iron Horse* is one of my favorite pictures." He turned to John. "And you, Mr.—"

"Ford," said John.

"Yes, Mr. Ford. Tell me, what do you do?"

"For Chrissake," John replied, "this dumb son of a bitch wouldn't know when to turn around if I didn't tell him."

The two passengers were standing on the bridge and the ship was just pulling away from the dock when John's car drove up and Mary, Pat, and Barbara stepped out. O'Brien, seeing tears welling up in Mary's eyes, was very touched.

"Gee, isn't that sweet," he said. "They've come to see you off." John said nothing but continued to lean against the rail puffing away at his pipe. Then, as the last line was cast off, he tapped the ashes out and said,

"You'd cry too, if you were her."

"Why?" asked O'Brien.

"Because you've got her ticket."

The only other passenger aboard the *Tai Yang* was a Department of Agriculture expert on tropical insects named William Clauson. He gave the all-but-baggageless O'Brien some clothes to wear, and the three passengers settled into a shipboard routine of playing cards, sitting in the sun, and drinking beer. As the ship plowed west and south across the Pacific, the days became increasingly hot and humid, relieved only by occasional squalls.

The monotony of the passage ended abruptly nine days out when the ship was hit by a raging typhoon, with rain so hard that it seemed to have been shot from a fire hose, enormous seas, and winds so fierce that every protrusion on the little ship, even the rivet heads, sang or howled or hummed according to its shape. The ship pitched and rolled crazily, and the passengers huddled on the bridge with Captain Crapp as he attempted to maneuver the little ship through the storm.

While the fore and aft motion was uncomfortable, it was the ship's roll that worried Captain Crapp. A degree too much to either side and the *Tai Yang* would keel over on its back like a top-heavy turtle. All empty fuel tanks had been filled with salt water for ballast—but the ship was rolling between 35 and 40 degrees, and all eyes on the bridge were fixed on the ship's inclinator, the instrument that measured its roll. After some hours there was a lull in the storm; the waves continued, but the rain stopped and the air was calm. Captain Crapp opened the hatch on the windward side and peered out.

"It's calming down," he said.

Just then a gust of wind hit the ship and slammed the hatch shut, hurling Crapp across the bridge. The gust caught the ship on a roll and everyone knew they were in trouble. The inclinator swung to 40, 45, 50, then an incredible 54 degrees, and the ship hung there, suspended on its side. There was nothing to do but hang on. Finally the wind let go, and the ship swung 50 degrees in the opposite direction with an awful compensating lurch. From below came the sound of dishes slamming, machinery breaking loose, men screaming. But the ship swung back, righted itself, and plowed on through the storm.

The *M.S. Tai Yang* was in the storm the better part of ten days. John kept a diary of the trip in the form of a letter to Mary which he mailed when he arrived in Manila. It tells the story of the typhoon, his need for a rest and reveals a twinge of guilt at having left Mary behind. Some excerpts:

"*M.S. Tai Yang*. At Sea, 20 days. Well gang, Greetings, etc. Just a few notes to let you know how the old man is getting along. We've had ten days of typhoons, hurricanes, gales, etc. The weather has been terrible. The ship was under water all the time. Mountainous waves broke over the bridge. This is the first time its been steady enough to even write a letter. We'll probably be 10 days late. In spite of that I've had a good time. Slept twelve hours a day, ate four meals, and five days out I've read all the books I brought. In between times we've kidded the Captain who got sea sick. George and I laughed at Mama's suggestion at laying on the deck and getting tanned. If you laid on the deck you'd only get water logged.

"Now the weather is lovely and we're making up time. It's getting warmer and we can take long walks on deck. . . .

"O'Brien's behavior has been exemplary. I am proud of him. Never once had he been disorderly or uncouth and at all times he is a credit to the industry. Well, Ma, I hope you are having a nice vacation in Waikiki, enjoying the sun and the brown boys. If you swim by the time you get home, it's grounds for divorce.

"Well, this trip has done me a lot of good. I've never felt better and certainly never looked better in my life. Even O'Brien looks at me admiringly. (However it will do him no good.) I look and feel twelve years younger. . . ."

After a twenty-seven-day crossing, ten days longer than scheduled, the battered *Tai Yang* pulled into Manila Bay. John, O'Brien, and William Clauson gathered on the bridge and studied their first landfall in nearly a month. The ship tied up at the quay and a navy officer named Cap Cleland, who was a friend of George O'Brien's, was there to greet them along with a delegation of Filipino newspapermen. John was upset when he saw the reporters.

"What the hell is this?" he said.

"We gave it to the press that you were coming," said Cleland. "George O'Brien and his director, John Ford."

"Yeah, well if these jerks are going to bug us," John said, "they'd better get the billing right. It's John Ford and his actor, George O'Brien."

With that straightened out, John and O'Brien talked to the reporters.

After saying good-bye to Clauson, Crapp, and the *Tai Yang*, John and O'Brien set out to savor the good life on the far shores of the Pacific Empire. They bought white linen suits and formal mess jackets, *de rigueur* attire for gentlemen in the tropics, and stayed in a government B.O.Q. as guests of General Hines, the commandant of the Manila garrison.

One of the first people they met in Manila was the Philippine distributor of Fox Films, Larry Deprita, who had been ordered by Sol Wurtzel to look after the two Fox VIPs. Charming, handsome, and sociable, Deprita sang and played the guitar, was fluent in English, Spanish, and several Tagalog dialects, and became their unofficial guide. They also met Father John McGuire, the navy chaplain would later become famous for saying, during the Japanese attack on Pearl Harbor, "Praise the Lord and pass the ammunition." He gave a luncheon for the two Hollywood dignitaries at the Army-Navy Club. Motion picture celebrities were oddities in Manila, and "John Ford and his actor, George O'Brien" were very much in demand.

Wanting to see more of Manila than the American Colony, they got Larry Deprita to take them one night to a tough waterfront hangout, a smoky, sweltering dive called The Spanish Casino. Inside was a long ornate bar and on three sides louvered windows that looked out on wharves lined with small interisland steamers and trading schooners. As they were leaning against the bar, trying to blend in and look inconspicuous, a short bull of a man with a shaved head and sailor's bell bottoms recognized O'Brien, whose photograph had appeared in the local papers.

"So it's George O'Brien, the great American movie star. Out slumming, huh?"

"Those are your words, not mine," said O'Brien.

"You probably think you're as tough as those guys you play in your pictures. You think you could take me in a wrestling match?"

Within seconds a crowd gathered, eager to see a fight between the sailor, a Filipino Moor named Hassen Bagues, and the American movie star. Although neither John nor O'Brien wanted trouble, there was apparently no way to avoid it.

"What do you think?" John whispered. "Can you beat him?"

"Yeah, I'm pretty sure I can," said O'Brien, surveying the hostile crowd. "But this doesn't seem to be the place to do it."

"No, let's not wear out our welcome," John said, as O'Brien handed him his shirt. "Let him take you."

Squatting, with their arms extended, the two men circled, then clinched, then went at it on the sawdust floor. Bagues got O'Brien in a hammerlock, but with a great deal of effort the actor was able to break out of it. He got back on his feet and the two men circled again. O'Brien was sweating and breathing hard, his face flushed. John sensed that his temper was getting the best of him, that he was about to mop up the floor with the belligerent sailor.

"Remember, let's not wear out our welcome," he whispered.

O'Brien nodded and relaxed a bit. The two men clinched again. O'Brien used his stunt-work expertise and put a touch of showmanship in the match, kicking over tables and spilling pitchers of beer. Then he let Bagues beat him, but just barely. The crowd was delirious with excitement. Hassen Bagues was the man of the hour.

Flushed with his victory over the great George O'Brien, Bagues did a complete about-face and became a friendly, expansive, and congenial host. He was, he explained, the second mate on a small interisland steamer that was leaving Manila that night for the islands of the southern archipelago, and he invited John, O'Brien, and Larry Deprita to come with him on the three-week trip. Hungry for adventure, they agreed, and a few hours later they moved aboard Bagues's ship.

The little steamer made the *Tai Yang* look like a modern luxury liner. Tar and oil were spilled everywhere, the paint was blistered and peeling, and the decks were stacked haphazardly with crated cargo. The crew's quarters, below the amidships wheelhouse, were crowded and poorly ventilated, and reeked of smoke, cooking oil, and sweat.

The three passengers found a corner of the deck and made bunks out of unused tarpaulins. A few hours after coming aboard they were steaming out of Manila harbor, past the Bataan Peninsula, past the silent guns of Corregidor. As they sailed south, John, O'Brien, and Deprita passed the days sitting in the shade playing cards; at night they lay on the deck gazing at the millions of bright southern stars overhead. They ate with Bagues and the crew, sharing their rice, curry, and warm tea. Despite the primitive conditions, John loved life aboard the little ship. He relished the clean sea air, the spray, and the tropical sunlight that sparkled on the water.

The steamer's regular rounds included stops on the islands of Cebu, Illoweila, Dumagita, Jolo, Zamboanga, and Mindanao. John delighted in exploring the little tropical ports along the way, savoring their waterfronts where the sea and the jungle met, feeling the heavy wet breezes coming out of the mountain valleys carrying the land smells of burning copra and rubber being processed.

On Zamboanga, where they were to stay for several days, Hassen Bagues arranged a special treat for his guests, a luncheon in their honor given by the local sultan, who was also his uncle. Then they sailed on for Mindanao, where, because of sporadic fighting between government soldiers and Moslem separatists, they stayed each night at an outpost of the local constabulary. After its three-week run the little steamer returned to Manila.

John, O'Brien, and Larry Deprita had left for the southern islands in such haste that they hadn't told anyone where they were going, and neither General Hines nor the people at the Fox Film exchange had been able to answer the many queries from California concerning them. A few days after their return, the three men were

63

guests of General Hines at the Manila Polo Club. They were seated at a large round table when the General pulled out a telegram.

"I have a telegram from your father," he said to O'Brien. "I'll read it to you. 'Dear General Hines: I am requesting your assistance in locating my son, George O'Brien. I know he is all right, but I am looking for the man who sailed with him, Mr. John Ford, motion picture director and friend. His wife is quite concerned about him. She has not heard from him since he first arrived. Regards. Daniel J. O'Brien, Chief of Police, City of San Francisco.'"

John didn't miss a beat. "George, I'm ashamed of you. You should have sent Mary a card and told her where we were."

At the end of March, after more than two months in the Philippines, John and O'Brien piled their souvenirs aboard the S.S. *President Cleveland* and followed the route of the old Dollar Line to Hong Kong and then Shanghai, which O'Brien remembers as "boiling over in those days." There they disembarked and stayed at Sir Victor Sassoon's Cathay Hotel. John found China cold and filthy but fascinating, and vowed to return. From Shanghai, the *President Cleveland* sailed to Yokohama, then eastward across the Pacific. After a week-long sojourn in Honolulu, they boarded a Matson freighter bound for San Francisco.

By coincidence, George O'Brien had been a deckhand aboard the ship as a young man, and the same Captain Anderson he had worked for then was still in command. O'Brien had been just another kid off the beach in those days, but now he was a movie star traveling with a distinguished director, and the first night at sea Captain Anderson invited the two celebrities to eat at his table. John, who knew how to pick a fight in an empty room, didn't waste a minute with idle chatter.

"How long have you been aboard, Captain?" he asked.

"Oh, quite a few years now, Mr. Ford. Sixteen years."

"Well, then, you must have been aboard when Mr. O'Brien here was a member of your deck crew?"

"What? Mr. O'Brien, you were?"

"Yes, Captain, in 1919."

"Well, then I welcome you back on board. Have you gone forward?"

But John wasn't about to let it end there.

"Tell me something, Captain," he said. "How is it that you never invited Mr. O'Brien to eat at your table *then*?"

Next day Anderson got his revenge when John asked him for some gunnysacks to put his souvenirs in. When John returned to his room it reeked with a sickeningly sweet odor: Anderson had it stacked full of gunnysacks which had recently contained raw sugar. John pulled the sacks out, but the nauseating smell persisted in the cabin all the way to San Francisco. "It's a good thing you got off this ship ten years ago," John told O'Brien. "That son of a bitch has no sense of humor."

The freighter docked in San Francisco on April 11, 1931, and leaving O'Brien behind to visit his family, John took the night train down the coast. He was home the next day.

George O'Brien had traveled half way around the world with John. They had been in every kind of situation, from the typhoon aboard the *Tai Yang* to the social whirl in Manila, from seedy waterfront bars to remote Malay villages. Yet O'Brien says that John remained an enigma to him. "I had known him, first as a cameraman and then as an actor, for nearly ten years. Yet after four months in which I was with him every second of every day, I think I knew less about him than ever before. He was the most private man I ever met, and even though I loved him I guess the truth is that I never really understood him."

Arriving back in Los Angeles, John found his professional life showing signs of his neglect. Things were in turmoil at Fox as the company was undergoing radical reorganization. William Fox was out. Most of the top management, with the exception of Sol Wurtzel and Winnie Sheehan, had been fired, and John didn't know if he would be too.

Up until this point in his career, John had never felt the need of an agent. As a contract director he had been continuously employed for fifteen years. But now, with Fox in upheaval, he put out feelers to a number of agents including Edward Small, Myron Selznick, and Harry Wurtzel. A short, fat, cherubic man who chain-smoked cigars, Harry was Sol Wurtzel's brother, and was in a position to do a lot for John. He became John's agent.

Wurtzel soon proved his value to John when he got his brother to revoke the exclusive clause in John's contract and let him work at other studios. John would remain under contract to Fox and would continue to receive his regular salary. But as long as the production slowdown remained in effect, as long as there was no work at Fox for him, he was free to work elsewhere. Wurtzel promptly found work for his new client: the direction of the Sam Goldwyn version of Sinclair Lewis' Nobel Prize-winning novel, *Arrowsmith*.

Released in December 1931, *Arrowsmith* was a very successful film that helped John out of his professional doldrums.

John was having less luck in reversing the ominous drift of his marriage. Mary refused to forgive him for going off to Manila with George O'Brien and was into what John referred to as her "martyr act." John was determined to save his marriage but seemed unable to placate his wife. In September 1931, after a summer of continued tension, John decided to go for broke. Because the crux of the problem was Mary's resentment over the Manila trip, he decided to go to the Philippines again, but this time he would take Mary along.

They sailed October 31, 1931, on the Matson liner S.S. *Wilhelmina*. Traveling with them was John's niece, Cecile McClain, a Max Factor representative on her way to Singapore. When they reached Hawaii, John and Mary disembarked and checked into the Royal Hawaiian Hotel, and Cecile went on to the Far East.

John and Mary made a number of friends on this trip, including Kim Wai and his wife, Rosina. Kim, an executive with Honolulu's Bishop Bank, was both a proper businessman and one of the hardest-drinking men John ever met. Then there was Francis Brown, a wealthy Bostonian who had left the frigid climate of New England to make his home in the warm paradise of Hawaii. Brown invited John and Mary to his seaside cattle ranch in Kona on Hawaii, and there, amid swaying palm trees and the bright tropical moon, the Fords' marriage showed signs of mending.

Despite his good intentions, however, John's good behavior was short-lived. When he drank he became petty and sarcastic, and hardly a day went by that didn't find him saying something cutting about the trunkloads of clothes Mary had brought or the fact that they needed an entourage of porters and servants everywhere they went. In John's mind, everything that he had run away from last year he had brought with him this time.

John's drinking began to get out of hand in Kona, and when he and Mary returned to Honolulu he pulled out the stops altogether and began drinking with abandon. The Irish morbidity always latent in his nature now came to the surface, and for five days he sat in a darkened room at the Royal Hawaiian, sobbing and slobbering. After he had been drunk for the better part of two weeks, Mary had him taken to Queen's Hospital. He was suffering from alcoholic dehydration.

While John was hospitalized, Mary sent for the children in the hope that their presence would keep him from going on any further binges. They arrived in early December with their nurse, Maude Stevenson, and on December 20, the party of five boarded the Canadian Pacific liner *Empress of Asia* and sailed for Manila. They arrived nine days later, after having spent Christmas at sea.

In Manila they were met at the dock by Larry Deprita, who helped them check into the Manila Hotel. A beautiful high-rise tower overlooking Manila Bay, the Manila Hotel, with its liveried servants and high-ceilinged rooms, had hosted maharajahs, presidents, and kings, and was considered one of the best hotels in the Far East. John took Mary on the social rounds of the year before: the Army-Navy Club, the Manila Polo Club, luncheons and dances at the various officers clubs, all of which Mary thoroughly enjoyed. But John had done it all before and was easily bored. Predictably, his restlessness won out over his consideration for his wife. After a few days in Manila he and Larry Deprita began planning a side trip to the Dutch East Indies. They would go beyond the islands they had seen last year and visit Bali, Java, and Sumatra. It would be a "man's trip"—Mary and the children would stay at the Manila.

Late in January, John and Deprita boarded a Java-China-Japan liner, an old coal-burning derelict called the *Tjbadak*, and steamed south through the Philippine Archipelago. On board the *Tjbadak* was the sculptress Malvina Hoffman, on her way to Bali to sketch and eventually sculpt that island's famed dancers. John's passport was in his real name, John A. Feeney, and to avoid confusion he usually traveled under that name. As they sailed south through the Philippines, Malvina Hoffman got to know this bright, energetic "Feeney," and her curiosity was aroused.

"Just who in the hell are you, anyway? What do you do?" she finally asked him.

"I'm a movie director. People know me as John Ford," he said.

In Bali, John and Larry Deprita hired a car and driver and toured the island with Miss Hoffman, joining her in studying the Balinese dancers. John thought they were the most beautiful women he had ever seen. Their dancing, graceful and highly controlled, seemed strongly sensual. But John was never one to take such things too seriously. From Bali he wired George O'Brien: "Miss you. Nothing here but TNT—Tits and Temples."

Leaving Miss Hoffman in Bali, John and Deprita returned to the *Tjbadak* and sailed for Surabaya on Java, where they left the ship once again and traveled across the island in a rickety jungle train. They stopped to visit the water castles and the native temple of Borobudur, then went over the Poetjak Pass and into the old Dutch capital of Batavia, where they reboarded their little ship. From Batavia they sailed on to Singapore, where they were met by Cecile McClain. After a few days, John returned to Manila, but Larry Deprita, having discovered the charms of Cecile, stayed in Singapore with her. Six months later they were married.

Mary, meanwhile, had stayed at the Manila Hotel occupying her time with her children, her clubs, and her lunches with navy wives. On this trip, intended to achieve marital harmony, she had been taxed to the limit. John's bachelor side trip made her more aware than ever that life with John would be a life alone. She resigned herself to it.

On February 24, John, Mary, their children, and Maude Stevenson boarded the S.S. *President Cleveland* and made their way back home.

Money
and Politics:
The
Two-Sided
Man

John returned from the Far East to find the situation at Fox still chaotic, and his own financial situation uncomfortably precarious. His salary had been cut off, and he had less than $5,000 in savings. When he went back to work it was with one purpose in mind: to make as much money as he could in as short a time as possible.

The first picture he made was for Universal, an aviation adventure film called *Air Mail*, for which he received a flat fee of $36,000. *Air Mail* had been written by one of the most remarkable men that ever came into John Ford's life: Lieutenant Commander Frank "Spig" Wead. Tall and angular, with the graceful good looks of an "Arrow Collar Man," to recall a popular advertisement of the 1930s, Wead had attended Annapolis and had been a pioneer naval aviator. He had led a team of navy fliers to victory in an around-the-world race, and had later set an altitude record for seaplanes. A celebrity in the world of aviation, Wead had been considered one of the brightest young men in the navy until an accident in his home ended his military career: he fell down a flight of stairs, broke his neck, and was completely paralyzed.

Retired from the navy, Wead took a small beach house in Santa Monica and began a new career as a writer, first of pulp fiction and eventually of motion picture scripts. Wead's military background, his skill as a raconteur, and his courage won John over immediately, and in the course of their work on *Air Mail* the two men became quite close.

John was at work on his next picture, an MGM wrestling potboiler called *Flesh*, even before *Air Mail* was released in November 1932. Then, in January 1933, production began to pick up at Fox, and John returned to his old studio to work on an adaptation of an I.A.R. Wylie short story called "Pilgrimage."

John had made three pictures between June 1932 and June 1933. While none of them would be remembered as being among his best work, he had accomplished what he set out to do: he had made a lot of money. The combined fees for *Air Mail*, *Flesh*, and *Pilgrimage* came to over $86,000. While this was a long way from the $145,000 that John had made in 1930, he was clearly climbing out of the financial trough his trips to the Far East had put him in. Perhaps even more important, John's confidence in his money-making ability was revived. He bragged openly to Sol Wurtzel, Fred Totman, and others that he was a "money director," a man who could be counted on to bring in "a good commercial picture" on time and within its budget. He told Harry Wurtzel that he was "a journeyman director, a traffic cop in front of the camera, but the best traffic cop in Hollywood."

The Fox Film Corporation, too, was making a comeback. In 1929 they had signed cowboy-philosopher Will Rogers to an exclusive contract. Rogers was already a big star with the Ziegfeld Follies and America's most popular newspaper columnist, and his pictures were also proving to be enormously popular. That year he was number two in *Motion Picture Herald*'s chart of box-office stars. More important, he was the financial mainstay of the Fox Film Company. In May 1933, after John completed *Pilgrimage*, Sol Wurtzel told him that he wanted him to become "Will Rogers' director."

In the spring of 1933, John was so optimistic about his financial prospects that he bought Mary a $20,000 Rolls-Royce limousine. It was an enormous car with huge spoked wheels and running boards wide as decks. John hoped that it would placate Mary, that she would forgive him for some of his failures as a husband.

Things may have been going well for John, but in 1933 the country was in the grips of the Great Depression and he was very much aware of how difficult things were for others. Many of his friends had turned to the Left during those years, and they were continually trying to enlist John's support for their various causes. It struck them as reprehensible that a film maker of John's stature should occupy himself with military melodramas when he should join them in the great task of saving the world.

John's deepest instincts may have been liberal, but his growing income, Mary's Southern-conservative roots, and his own desire for social acceptance all tended to pull him to the Right. A man of intuition, not ideology, he vacillated on the issues of the day. He was liberal on some issues, conservative on others. If there was one common denominator in his political thinking, it was that he had never taken a public stand.

Dudley Nichols was one friend who argued with John often about politics. After their story sessions the two men would adjourn to the Hollywood Athletic Club for a steam bath and a rubdown, and Nichols would lecture John on his political and intellectual responsibilities.

In the early 1930s, another writer who would play an important role in shaping John's political thinking came into his life: Liam O'Flaherty, a voice in the Irish Renaissance known for compassionate and compelling novels including *The Neighbor's Wife*, *The Black Soul*, *Mr. Gilhooley*, *The Assassin*, *The House of God*, *Sketerrt*, and *The Informer*. A rugged-looking but shy man with sandy-colored hair and blue eyes, O'Flaherty was a dreamer with a high-strung temperament, an idealist with Marxist sympathies, who had trouble fitting the world of his imagination into the world of reality. O'Flaherty, like so many people in the world of John Ford, had a weakness for the bottle. In 1932, O'Flaherty came to Hollywood to find work at the studios, and John met him soon after he arrived. Similar types, the two men soon became friends.

Although all of Liam O'Flaherty's novels stirred John, the one that most moved him was *The Informer*, the story of Gypo Nolan, a Communist IRA man who, during the Sinn Fein revolt, betrays and thus dooms his friend, Frankie McPhillip. *The Informer* had already been filmed in England by the German director Arthur Robeson, but the film had not been distributed in the United States.

John was deeply moved by the uniquely Irish flavor of *The Informer*, by the way it caught the essential mysticism in the Irish soul, the simultaneous brilliance and stupidity of the Irish people, and he was intrigued by the novel's possibilities as a stylized expressionistic film. In the winter of 1933, John took an option on the property. O'Flaherty was of course delighted. He had never made much money on his writing, and Marxist or not, he liked the idea of selling his material to Hollywood. But John was frank with the writer about the chance of selling it. "It's going to be very hard to find a studio that will back this picture," he warned. "It's very different from the usual fare. Don't get your hopes up too high."

To Liam O'Flaherty, *The Informer* was much more than the story of Gypo Nolan: it was an allegory of both the British rape of Ireland and the exploitation of labor by capital. In marathon discussions with John, lubricated by generous amounts of Guinness Stout, O'Flaherty hammered his ideas home, and in time they began to sink in. Influenced first by Dudley Nichols and reinforced

72

by O'Flaherty, John's political thinking swung, like a heavily weighted pendulum, to the Left.

The first fruit of his emergent liberalism was his active support of Franklin D. Roosevelt in the presidential campaign of 1932. With his growing liberal awareness, John was almost as enthusiastic about Roosevelt's promise to reshuffle the economic cards, his "New Deal," as he was about the candidate's promise to repeal the Volstead Act.

But John soon had reason to question the wisdom of that support. In March 1933, the bank holiday declared by the newly inaugurated President brought the full weight of the Depression to Hollywood. Studio executives, long believing that actors, writers, and directors were grossly overpaid, used the bank holiday as an excuse to make pay cuts and to lay off thousands of employees. Some studios notified employees that they would receive no salaries at all until the banks reopened. Others suspended all contracts.

The studio employees appealed to the only organization in Hollywood that cut across studio lines: the young Academy of Motion Picture Arts and Sciences. But the Academy, an organization then controlled by the studios, appointed an emergency committee which recommended that the studios be allowed to make pay cuts of up to 50 percent. In the resulting furor, writers, actors, and directors resigned from the Academy *en masse* and joined the professional craft guilds, which had been in existence for some time but were still struggling for recognition. The major studios did everything they could to stop them, short of calling out the troops, and the battle left scars that would last for years.

John had long been active in the Screen Directors Guild and its predecessor, the Motion Picture Directors Association. In March 1933, when the Guild called a general meeting to discuss the Academy's action, he was its treasurer and was scheduled to give a financial report to the assembled members. But instead of dwelling on the Guild's financial condition, John used the occasion to give a fire-and-brimstone trumpet call for a united stand against the studios, Wall Street, and the forces of monopoly capitalism. His speech marked the end of his long silence on political issues:

"Gentlemen," he began, his Yankee voice nasal and intense as it rang out over the smoke-filled hall. "I am going to give you a few dry and gloomy facts. Possibly a little dull, but facts we all should know. In the past few weeks, despite the most profitable year that the motion picture industry has ever known, there have been more studio people fired than at any other time. Hundreds have been let go at the studios, directors and assistants, writers and stock players, craftsmen and office workers of every classification. Now, after this eminently successful year, why is this going on? Why are so many people being let out? The usual answer is, of course, business depression. Stock market going down, business is bad. Well, I don't believe it! Your Board of Governors doesn't believe it. The President of the United States doesn't believe it! The Attorney General's office in Washington doesn't believe it! In fact, he boldly states that the banking industry is going on a sit-down strike. Why? To bring about a financial crisis so that wages and organized unions can be pushed down and beaten. So that wages and wage earners can be pushed back to where they were in 1910..."

John's speech established him as one of the real firebrands of the Guild, a central figure in what was developing into a full-fledged labor war.

One near-casualty of the five-year struggle for Guild recognition was the young Motion Picture Academy, which was caught in a withering crossfire from the two sides. In an effort to deny management the promotional value of the Academy Awards, the various guilds urged their members to boycott both voting and ceremonies, and more than a few Oscars were turned down during those years. Conversely, many producers withheld their financial support from the Academy. The split between the guilds and the Academy lasted until the guilds were recognized in 1938.

Financially, 1933 was a good year for John, but 1934 was even better. His income from Fox came to just under $100,000, a comedy he made for Columbia called *The Whole Town's Talking* earned him another $50,000, and his total income that year was over $165,000.

In June 1934, John bought a 110-foot gaff-headed ketch called the *Faith*. Designed by John Hanna and built in Essex, Massachusetts, in 1926, she had a high bow, good lines of sheer, and a wide transom. Below decks she had quarters for six crewmen, a large galley and pantry area, and a mammoth six-cylinder Atlas and Imperial diesel engine. Aft, in the "owner's area," was a large main saloon paneled in polished mahogany, with cabins on either side and a large master suite. Aft of the suite were a navigator's station and two small cabins to either side. The *Faith* had been owned by a Pasadena financier who had fallen on hard times. She had seen little use and had not been well maintained; nevertheless, the $30,000 John paid for her was a great bargain.

John rechristened her the *Araner*—after the Aran Islands off the Galway coast from which his mother's people had come—put her in the Fellows and Steward Yard in San Pedro, and spared no expense in refitting her. He had the engine and generator over-hauled, replaced the main shaft and screw, put in a new mast, had the bow and stern sections completely rebuilt, and added a luxurious teakwood deckhouse. He also had the bottom recop-pered, built a walk-in freezer, and replaced sails, batteries, awnings, stanchions, and standing rigging. Mary picked out new rugs and furnishings, and bought linen, silverware, and dishes. Finally, John bought two small boats, an 18-foot lapstrake tender and a 21-foot Chris-Craft speedboat with a varnished hull. To run the *Araner* John hired a licensed master, a grizzled veteran of the sea named George Goldrainer.

When work on the *Araner* was finished, she was one of the most beautiful yachts on the West Coast, an impressive symbol of the wealth and power of her owner. John was enormously proud of her and spent the month of August and part of September aboard her at Catalina Island's Isthmus Harbor.

More important than the *Araner*'s value as a status symbol was the fact that she was a place where John could relax in complete privacy and enjoy the company of people he really liked. John Wayne, Ward Bond, Wingate Smith, Dudley Nichols, Preston Foster, and Grant Withers were all frequent guests aboard the *Araner*, and spent many hours with John fishing, carousing, drinking, and playing cards. In April 1935, Bond and Doris Sellers, his girl friend of many years, were married aboard the ship.

John Wayne remembers that after he became an actor, there was a long period when he didn't see much of his former mentor. It was the *Araner*, he says, that brought them back together:

"I hadn't seen much of him for two years. I don't know if he was mad at me or what. Then the first summer he had the *Araner* I was sitting in Christian's Hut, the bar at the Isthmus, and Barbara, who was about ten years old, came in and said, 'Duke, Daddy's out on the boat and he wants to see you.' I said, 'All right, tell him I'll be right out.' So out I went and Jack was in the main saloon holding court with a lot of people around him. In the middle of a sentence he said, 'Hi, Duke, sit down,' and went right on talking. After about an hour he said to everybody, 'The shore boat will take you all in now. Duke, can you stay for dinner?'

"After that I found myself spending a lot of time on the *Araner*. Sunday afternoons we'd drive down to San Pedro just to have a cup of tea on board. I'd usually sneak a shot of tequilla to get rid of my hangover. We'd go over to Catalina for two or three weeks at a time. Jack would bring in a cord of books, and I'd read one while he read three. We'd say hello at breakfast and again at lunch and after dinner we'd play some cards. We had a nice comfortable relationship that didn't depend on continuous or continual conversation, and we never had to explain each other. On most of those trips Jack never drank. The *Araner* was one place where he felt completely relaxed without belting the brew."

On September 12, 1934, John was appointed a Lieutenant Commander in the naval reserve. The swearing-in was conducted by Captain Herbert Jones at a ceremony in San Diego.

Why did John, with his lucrative and satisfying career, and his busy schedule, take the time to seek out a commission in the navy? As a product of Hollywood, John had a romantic, idealized notion of what the navy was all about—it was like being in a yacht club, with fancy white uniforms and Sunday brunches on the officers' club lawn. But it also meant respectability, for in those years before the technocrats took over the military, a commission, and particularly a naval one, gave a man status as a gentleman.

Determined to make his career in the naval reserve as successful as his career in motion pictures, John attacked his new job with enthusiasm. He bought every uniform the navy had: summer khaki, winter wools, dress whites and blues, watchcoats, and greatcoats. Perfectly tailored and carefully kept, his uniforms stood in marked contrast to the casual work clothes he normally wore. John didn't miss a chance to win favor or influence. He presented an expensive oil painting of the U.S.S. *Constitution* to the Officers' Mess at the U.S. Naval and Marine Corps Armory in Los Angeles. He cultivated his commanding officer, Captain Claude Mayo, taking him to Catalina on the *Araner* and showering him with theater tickets and studio passes. In 1935 he gave Mayo a set of dishes with scenes of life at Annapolis.

John also became friendly with Commander Ellis M. Zacharias, head of Intelligence in the 11th Naval District. During the mid-1930s, Japanese fishing trawlers were active in Mexican waters and Zacharias believed they were making hydrographic surveys for the Imperial Navy—possibly also stockpiling fuel, supplies, and spare parts for submarines in the remote regions of Baja California. When Zacharias learned that John was planning to take the *Araner* into Mexican waters in the winter of 1936, he asked him to be on the lookout for any signs of Japanese activity on Baja's western coast. John was only too pleased to accept the job.

In March 1936, with the *Araner* anchored outside Baja's Scammon's Lagoon, John, George Goldrainer, and several *Araner* crewmen took the yacht's two launches and motored into the wide shallow bay. For the next two days they carefully combed the waters and the surrounding sand dunes. John photographed the area, made a detailed chart, and prepared a written report in which he noted that although he had seen no signs of the Japanese, Scammon's Lagoon was remote and inaccessible by land, offered good shelter, and was "close enough to shipping lanes to serve as an ideal place to either stockpile supplies or to serve as a rendezvous point for submarines and sub tenders." When he returned to Los Angeles, John turned the photographs and the report over to Naval Intelligence. His willingness to undertake such "intelligence missions" at his own expense did not go unnoticed.

In the summer of 1936, after years of growing unrest, a bloody civil war erupted in Spain. On one side were the Loyalists, a duly elected popular-front coalition of Republicans, Socialists, and Communists. On the other side was Francisco Franco's Falange España, which had the support of the Catholic church, the army, and major Spanish industrialists. The Loyalists were supported by liberals in the U.S. and Europe, and by Soviet Russia. Franco was supported by the Italians and Germans, who hoped to create a Fascist state in Spain. Although it was far more complex, the Spanish Civil War looked to many like a showdown between communism and fascism, and in 1936 it was impossible for anyone to be indifferent to it. The Spanish Civil War became the focal point of the growing cleavage of opinion in the U.S. between Right and Left.

In July 1937, the Spanish Civil War was made immediate to John when, along with a number of other Hollywood notables, he was invited to the home of Fredric and Florence March to meet Ernest Hemingway. The writer had just returned from Spain, where he had helped make a propaganda film called *The Spanish Earth*, and was using it to raise money for the Loyalists. Hemingway screened his film and gave a talk in which he said that every $1,000 donated would send another ambulance to Spain. His stance as a fighting liberal, his obvious sincerity, and the film itself made a deep impression on John and the others present, who dug deep into their pockets and contributed thousands of dollars. During these years there was an élan, a very special glory, about the Loyalist cause that both the bully-boy Irishman and the liberal man of letters in John were drawn to. After this encounter with Hemingway, John became a fervent and active supporter of the Loyalists. Shortly thereafter he joined the pro-Loyalist Motion Picture Artists Committee.

That summer John also joined a group called the Motion Picture Democratic Committee. It was a liberal, internationalist, pro-Roosevelt organization that believed fascism to be a more serious threat to world peace than communism. John was sympathetic enough to its views to allow his name to appear on the masthead as vice-chairman, along with writer Philip Dunne and actor Melvyn Douglas.

John also got a vicarious involvement in the Spanish Civil War through his brother Francis' son Bob, who fought with the International Brigade in Spain. When Bob Ford heard that his famous uncle had come out on the side of the Loyalists, he wrote:

"I just received a letter from my Grandmother in which she told me that you had given an ambulance to the Spanish government. I didn't know you were interested in our cause, or I would have written before now. It is good to know that we are supported by liberals in the states...

"The reports reaching America all give the impression that the Loyalist army is Red. This is out and out Fascist propaganda. Outside of the 5th Regiment, which was organized by the Communist Party and then turned over to the government, the Spanish army is the same as the government. That is, made up of everything from Revolutionary workers to Republicans. In fact, they're almost as few Communists in Spain as there are in the States. As for the

International Brigade, the papers have it that we are all Stalinist shock troops. The I.B. is anti-Fascist and while there are a number of Reds in it they are not the whole Brigade...."

John answered his nephew's letter immediately:

"It was swell of you to write me. I treasure the letter. Here, owing to the very hide-bound and conservative papers, we get little or no information as to what is happening in Spain. Your letter is *very illuminating*. I got some idea of it from Hemingway—have you met him?

"I am glad you got some of the good part of the Feeney blood—some of it is God damn awful—we are liars, weaklings and selfish drunkards. But there has always been a stout rebel quality in the family and a peculiar passion for justice. I am glad you inherited the good strain.

"*Politically*—I am a definite Socialistic Democrat—always left. I have watched the Russian experiment with great interest. Like the French Commune, I am afraid it might lead to another Bonaparte. Mussolini was in early manhood an anarchist—Hitler—almost."

As to whether John felt running in his own veins the good or bad strains of the Feeney blood, the letter is tantalizingly silent.

7

The
Informer

When John had warned Liam O'Flaherty that *The Informer* was going to be a tough picture to place, he wasn't kidding. Sol Wurtzel had given him such an emphatic no, that his refusal became a point of real tension between the two men. But Fox wasn't the only studio that turned *The Informer* down; so did Warner Brothers, Columbia, Paramount, and MGM. Everywhere he went, John heard the same things: "This is not commercial material"; it was "too political"; it had "no love interest and no hero." Determined to make the film, John pressed on, and after trying almost every studio in Hollywood he finally presented his case to RKO Radio.

Located in a run-down neighborhood of lean-to shacks and old wooden buildings, RKO was one of the smallest studios in Hollywood. It was also one of the most fought-over: no company in the history of motion pictures ever had more dissident stockholders, proxy fights, and manipulations by Wall Street financiers. At various times in its history, controlling interest was held by such financial luminaries as Joseph P. Kennedy and Howard Hughes. In 1933, management had just been reshuffled again. David O. Selznick was now in charge, and the studio was looking for properties—even, perhaps, offbeat properties by Irish Marxists.

Selznick's number-two man at RKO was Merian C. Cooper, a congenial Southerner with one of the most fascinating backgrounds in motion pictures. John made his pitch to Cooper, and, although neither man realized it at the time, this was the beginning of a long and important friendship.

If he was nothing else, Merian Cooper was a man obsessed by dreams of military glory. He had attended the naval academy at Annapolis but was expelled in his senior year. He joined the army and became an aviator, and when the United States entered World War I, he was among the first Americans sent to France. Six weeks before the armistice, Cooper was shot down over Mannheim, Germany. Severely wounded, he spent the waning weeks of the war in a German hospital.

In 1919 Cooper was offered a commission in the Polish Air Force and flew with great distinction in the Russo-Polish War. After this he teamed up with a cameraman named Ernest B. Schoedsack and in the next three years they traveled all over the world making documentary films, classics of their kind: there was *Grass*, filmed in the mountains of Persia; *Chang*, filmed in the jungles of Siam; and *Four Feathers*, an African adventure story. These films, comparable to the works of Robert Flaherty, opened all the right doors for Cooper and launched him on his career in motion pictures.

When John met him in 1933, Cooper had just produced one of the most original and profitable films that had ever been made. On the strength of his documentaries with Schoedsack, Cooper had become a prominent member of the New York Explorers Club. There he had met a man named W. Douglas Burden, who had given him a fantastic idea. Burden had explored the islands of Komodo and Wetar in the Dutch East Indies, where he had found a large lizard of a type thought to have been extinct for millions of years. A major zoological event, it had created much interest in the scientific community. Intrigued with Burden's find. Cooper had soon begun to think about the possibilities of a motion picture about it.

Back in Hollywood, Cooper concocted the story of a motion-picture company that goes to an uncharted island and finds an enormous gorilla-god called Kong. First called *The Beast*, then *The Eighth Wonder*, and finally *King Kong*, the film was released in the summer of 1933. Although panned by most critics, *King Kong* was a tremendous box-office success and stood as Hollywood's top-grossing film until surpassed by Selznick's *Gone With the Wind*.

John was very impressed by Merian Cooper's worldliness, his military background, his achievements as aviator, adventurer, and film maker. Cooper, in turn, was impressed by John's achievements and by the obvious depth of his commitment to *The Informer*. Although the film seemed to have limited commercial prospects, it looked to Cooper like a serious picture, a critic's picture, and after the lambasting he had taken for *King Kong*, the idea of making such a picture was not without appeal.

In October 1934, Merian Cooper gave John the go-ahead to make *The Informer*. But RKO was less than enthusiastic about the project. The studio assigned the picture a budget of $243,000, a figure that precluded production values, location work, or the use of big-name stars. John told Merian Cooper that the money didn't make any difference, he was "going to build all the production values into the camera." If he had to, he asserted, he "could make the picture for half that amount."

John envisioned *The Informer* as a deliberately stylized film, as mystical and fogbound as *Four Sons* had been. Before the script was written, long meetings were held with art director Van Nest Polglase, set director Julia Heron, cinematographer Joe August, and RKO's master musician, Max Steiner, who, like Merian Cooper, had made a name for himself with *King Kong*. Before one word was put on paper, John's approach to the picture was made clear to all concerned: *The Informer* was to be an aesthetic experiment, with bold photography, venturesome effects, dramatic lighting, low angles, and double exposures. Like James Joyce's fiction, *The Informer* would be soaked in Dublin's atmosphere and topography; expressionistic mists of fog would serve as a visual metaphor both for the city and for the psychological fog inside Gypo Nolan's head. John didn't hesitate to remind everyone that he believed so strongly in the story that he was "making it for free," and that he was going to demand the best from himself and from everyone connected with it.

Dudley Nichols was first to bear the brunt of John's enthusiasm for *The Informer*. They worked on the script in the living room of John's Odin Street house, where John, dressed only in a bathrobe and chomping on endless cigars, dictated the script scene by scene. Nichols often found himself standing up and shouting to make himself heard. John's typical response if they didn't agree was that Nichols didn't "understand the Irish temperament" or that he had no "firsthand experience with the Irish people." When that didn't work, John exploded in a tirade of personal insults, calling the writer a "supercilious egghead" who wanted to write "a doctoral dissertation on the origins of the Irish proletariat." When they finally did agree on a scene, Nichols would write it down and John would go over it, making brutal cuts in Nichols' dialogue.

When the first draft was completed, Nichols typed it up and the whole process began again. Only after countless rewrites and the most intense effort did John consider the script ready. By then, Nichols was so exhausted from the work and from John's bullying that he vowed never to work for him again.

Nichols' feelings aside, the effort that went into *The Informer* paid off. The writing was extremely cohesive, and the dialogue almost unbelievably sparse. In an era of wordy talkies, there was so little dialogue in *The Informer* that the picture could have been shot as a silent film.

After completion of the script, the other elements of the production were painstakingly worked out. Artist's renderings were prepared for every camera angle, every setup; effects of light and contrast were carefully designed to heighten and accentuate the inner drama of Gypo's treachery.

In casting *The Informer*, John knew of only one man who had the brutish looks and the physical explosiveness to play Gypo Nolan: Victor McLaglen. But there was a problem in using him, and it was a big one. McLaglen was an actor with a limited emotional range. Long ago McLaglen had found his niche playing soldiers and heavies. He had a generous contract at Fox and spent most of his time on his San Joaquin Valley ranch. When he did do a picture, McLaglen, a favorite among Hollywood's swizzle-stick set, was more interested in getting out and socializing than in concentrating on his work. John took a calculated risk that he could pull a performance out of him.

After McLaglen's services had been engaged, the other parts were quickly cast. Wallace Ford was cast as Frankie McPhillip; Preston Foster, a drinking and card-playing crony of John's, as rebel leader Dan Gallagher; and Margot Grahame as Gypo's sweetheart, Katie Madden.

The RKO front office assigned John an ancient sound stage located across the street from the main lot. Filthy, drafty, and unheated, it had long been used as a storage shed for props. Shooting began there on St. Valentine's Day, 1934.

Once shooting actually began, *The Informer* was one of the easiest films John ever made. A small picture with a small cast, it had been meticulously prepared. The front office had little faith in it and gave John complete freedom to shape it as he wished.

Dudley Nichols' script was superb, and Joe August's photography the same. But perhaps *The Informer*'s most enduring strength was Victor McLaglen's performance. His Gypo Nolan was a lumbering animal, a hapless victim of his own lust and greed, who somehow conveys the higher instincts of faith, love, and loyalty. To bring these qualities out, John did everything he could to keep McLaglen off balance and thus inadvertently in character. He juggled the schedule without telling his leading man, so that McLaglen, a slow study under the best of circumstances, would have to learn new lines when he arrived in the morning. As the day progressed, John hurried McLaglen on and off the set at dizzying speed, showering him with abuse if he dared to slow down. In the afternoons, under the pretext of a rehearsal, John ran McLaglen

85

through his "next day's" scenes, while the camera rolled away. McLaglen's tentative efforts with the unfamiliar dialogue resulted in some of his best takes.

The key scene in *The Informer* takes place at the rebel court of inquiry where Gypo, full of guilt and anguish, breaks down and confesses his betrayal of Frankie McPhillip. A difficult scene for the best of actors, it was a particularly rough one for Victor McLaglen, and John had to reach deep into his bag of tricks to pull it out of him. The night before the scene was to be shot, he took his leading man aside.

"Vic," he said, "I've changed the schedule. This is a critical scene. I don't want to shoot it until you've got a better grasp on your character. You're not working tomorrow. Take the night off."

McLaglen's mouth watered.

"Go out tonight and relax."

John's Hawaiian friends Kim and Rosina Wai happened to be in town, and John had them take the actor to a party where the wine freely flowed. By midnight, as John intended, McLaglen had drunk himself unconscious and passed out on the piano. Early the next morning a painfully hung-over McLaglen was summoned to the studio. John went right to work on the court-of-inquiry scene, and McLaglen's thick-tongued, confused, anguished performance owed much to his very real hangover.

John pulled the performance of a lifetime out of Victor McLaglen, but he also reduced the actor to a trembling wreck. He shook, lost weight, and couldn't sleep at night. At least a dozen times during the making of the picture, McLaglen swore that he was going to quit acting—just after he killed John Ford.

John's handling of McLaglen raises the question of whether he did it for the picture or for his own pleasure. Wingate Smith, who was there, isn't sure. "You had to wonder where the line was in Jack's mind. Sure, he was getting great stuff from Vic, but I also think he enjoyed seeing him suffer. He was like a mean little kid playing with a bug."

So far the RKO management had paid little attention to *The Informer*; not even Merian Cooper knew what John had been up to in the old sound stage across the street. But when John screened it for the front office, they could scarcely believe what they were looking at. Most of them had never seen such eye-opening photography, such visual effects, such stylized direction. Some liked it, some didn't, but to a man they were no longer indifferent. The question was, what would audiences think?

RKO first previewed *The Informer* in Los Angeles in April 1935. Taking a chance, John invited Richard Watts, the distinguished film critic from the New York *Herald Tribune*, to the screening. The preview was a failure. The audience wasn't prepared for this very unusual picture, and after it was over, John, so depressed that he was physically sick, sneaked past a cluster of grim-faced RKO executives. He went out to his car, sat down on the running board, and vomited. Then Richard Watts came over and told John not to worry about the preview audience's reaction. He said that the picture was over their heads, but that he thought it was a great film.

Buoyed by Watts's encouragement, John talked Merian Cooper into previewing *The Informer* again, this time billing it as a "special production" of a "literary classic." The second preview attracted a highbrow audience that gave the picture such an enthusiastic reception that RKO decided to get behind *The Informer* 100 percent, mount a major publicity campaign, and book it into some first-class theaters. John was euphoric. The dream project of a lifetime was shaping up like a winner.

The Informer opened at New York's Radio City Music Hall on May 9, 1935. Its reception was excellent. *The New York Times* wrote, "*The Informer* is an absolute masterpiece fashioned by a man with a sensitive feel for his material, an unerring eye for visual detail, and a sharp objective style. He tells his story with a camera instead of relying on dialogue; he employs double exposures, expressive angle shots, a moving camera and other ingenious devices. Many masterful directorial touches live in the memory ... *The Informer* is certain to take its place as both a model for future film artisans and among the classic films of all time."

Jim McGuinness, now an important executive at MGM, summed up the industry's attitude toward the picture when he wrote John:

"I saw *The Informer* last night and when I got home I stayed awake for several hours thinking about it. To me it takes place among the very few memorable things I have seen in my lifetime, either on the stage or screen. You know how sparing and gun shy I am about motion picture superlatives, but if ever I could honestly apply the word great to anything this is the time.

"In the direction, you surpassed even yourself—and that's as far as I can go in the way of compliments. Vic was superb, I don't know how you did it, but he was really magnificent. Dudley's screenplay caught brilliantly the spirit of the novel. There wasn't a single person in the cast, or a single scene that didn't rouse my highest admiration. This letter may seem too fulsome, but believe me, it is an honest and reverent genuflection before mastery."

The picture's initial run at Radio City Music Hall was, however, a disappointment. It opened poorly and did not draw an audience. In an effort to cash in on the film's excellent reviews, RKO put it into general release. Then, in the "provinces," the miracle happened. People who had expected the film to be another tough-talking Victor McLaglen vehicle soon realized that they were watching a masterpiece of direction. The word quickly spread, audiences increased, and by year's end *The Informer* was RKO's top-grossing picture. In the summer of 1935, three months after its first opening there, *The Informer* even made a triumphant return to Radio City.

Before *The Informer*, John's name carried little weight with the critical establishment. He had been looked upon as a workmanlike "money director," known for action films. But *The Informer* changed that, elevating him into the ranks of Hollywood's premier directors. In January 1936, *The Informer* was unanimously named the best film of the year by the New York Film Critics, and John was selected the best director.

The big pictures in the 1935 Academy Awards balloting were *Dangerous, Alice Adams, The Life of Louis Pasteur, Captain Blood*, and MGM's *Mutiny on the Bounty*. But on the evening of March 6, 1936, RKO's low-budget masterpiece, *The Informer*, surprised everyone by capturing more gold hardware than any other film. John won for his direction, Victor McLaglen for his acting, Dudley Nichols for his adaptation, and Max Steiner for his score. (Other awards that year went to *Mutiny on the Bounty*, as best picture, and to Bette Davis for her role in *Dangerous*.)

But for John, the Academy Award was marred by the continuing strife between the Academy and the craft unions. The

Writers', Directors', and Actors' Guilds had declared a boycott of the Academy Award proceedings and were pressuring their members not to accept Oscars. Victor McLaglen accepted his, but Dudley Nichols, who was active in the Writers' Guild, declined his. So, initially, did John. But a few months later he changed his mind and quietly accepted his Academy Award. He was widely criticized by some of the more militant members of the Directors' Guild, was voted out of office, and was never again active in Guild affairs.

8

Studio
Director

Though *The Informer* is remembered as John's first great success, his real bread and butter were the Will Rogers program fillers that he was making at Fox during the same period. Between 1933 and 1935 John made three films with Rogers: *Dr. Bull*, *Judge Priest*, and *Steamboat Round the Bend*, Rogers' last film before his tragic death.

First signed by Fox in 1929, Rogers worked according to a rigid formula. He played a thinly disguised caricature of himself, a seedy, simple common man, an underdog speaking out against the special-interest groups and the politicians they owned. He was philosophical and kind, moving through a world that was gentle and predictable. His pictures were an affirmation of American values. If they were not the kind of films John wanted to make, they were the kind of films that people wanted their children to see.

In the summer of 1935, Darryl F. Zanuck came to Fox. A five-foot, two-inch human dynamo, Zanuck hummed with energy. Like Zukor, Goldwyn, Mayer, and Cohn, he was a film "mogul," a Hollywood potentate in every sense of the word. But unlike them, his ancestors had never escaped from a Czarist pogrom, and he had never pushed a cart on the Lower East Side. He was a middle-class, Midwestern Protestant from Wahoo, Nebraska.

Zanuck began in motion pictures as a writer at Warner Brothers. A remarkably fast and facile worker, he wrote nineteen feature films in 1925, half of Warner Brothers' entire output. There is a famous anecdote about Zanuck's productivity. At the annual sales meeting in 1926, an angry distributor complained that because so many of the studio's pictures were being written by the same man, the company looked cheap. He demanded that they hire more writers. But Jack Warner was never one to throw money away. Instead he had Zanuck start using three aliases: "Gregory Rogers" when he wrote comedies; "Mark Canfield" when he wrote melodramas; and "Melville Crossman" when he wrote "A" pictures. Warner was soon calling Zanuck "three charming fellows."

In 1927, Zanuck became head of production at Warner Brothers and was soon making his mark on Hollywood. He gave directors Ernst Lubitsch, William Dieterle, Michael Curtiz, and William Wellman their starts. While others followed trends, Zanuck started them. His *Little Caesar* ushered in a cycle of gangster films; *Disraeli*, a cycle of biographical ones. When everybody was saying that musicals were passé, Zanuck made *Forty-Second Street* and brought them back. He also looked to the issues of the day: *I Am a Fugitive From a Chain Gang* was a landmark film that championed prison reform.

In 1933, Zanuck and Joe Schenck formed a company called Twentieth Century Productions. They made eighteen pictures in eighteen months. Seventeen of them made money. Two years later, Zanuck and Schenck merged their tiny but prosperous company with the huge and ailing Fox—a marriage of Fox's facilities and distribution system with Zanuck's and Schenck's ability to make the product. At the time of the merger, the net worth of Fox was $36 million while the net worth of Twentieth was only $4 million. But the earning power of the two companies tells the real story: Fox earned $1.8 million in 1934 while Twentieth earned $1.7 million. Joe Schenck became president, Darryl Zanuck, vice-president in charge of production. They insisted on—and got—top billing in the merger. Thus the company became Twentieth Century-Fox.

When Zanuck took command he surveyed his domain like a field marshal and swept the studio clean, firing producers, directors, and guards off the gate. Winnie Sheehan's contract was bought out for $360,000, and he was let go. Sol Wurtzel was the only major executive to survive the purge.

Zanuck set out to turn Fox, which had been wallowing along since its 1931 bankruptcy, into a truly modern studio. Believing that motion pictures were a collaborative medium, shaped not by one man but by the efforts of many, he set out to create a modified version of MGM's "Producer System," in which he would personally supervise the preparation of all "A" scripts. When they were ready, he would turn them over to a producer, who would oversee the preproduction. The director would not be called in until the picture was ready to go before the camera. This system would free his best directors from tedious and time-consuming detail; they would thus be available to shoot four, five, and even six pictures a year. But it also took decisions about the basic content of the films out of their hands.

Zanuck also had definite ideas about what the studio's product should look like. In long, detailed memoranda he decreed that stylized "directorial touches" such as extreme closeups, long shots, and the use of a mobile camera were to be eliminated. So as not to

93

detract from the actors, lighting was to be clear, bright, and even. Scenes were lit for stars, to make pretty people prettier, rather than for dramatic atmosphere. From the day he assumed command, Zanuck let it be known in no uncertain terms that he was going to have a hand in every picture made at Fox; that directors, including John Ford, were no longer independent warlords ruling over their own fiefdoms.

John was initially delighted when Zanuck took over the reins of the company. The new studio chief had a reputation as a mover and shaker, and John was sure that he was just the man to breathe life into Fox's tired operation. But John's delight was destined to be short-lived.

Zanuck insisted on making the final cut of all "A" pictures himself. He also liked pictures with hard-hitting themes and fast-paced story lines, and disliked slapstick humor and bits of business not essential to the plot. Everyone that I talked to who was close to Darryl Zanuck said that if he and my grandfather had a conflict, it was over the issue of pacing. In Nunnally Johnson's words, "John liked his films to meander, to stop and focus on something inconsequential and make a comment of some sort. Darryl liked them to *move*."

Soon after taking command, Zanuck canceled twelve pictures in various stages of preparation and another six already in production. Then he took a good hard look at those about to be released, including *Steamboat Round the Bend*. He took the Ford-Rogers comedy and recut it, picking up the pace and cutting out some of the broader sight gags. John, who was used to almost complete autonomy under the old Wurtzel-Sheehan regime, was appalled. He complained openly that Zanuck had "ruined my picture," that he was "showing off," and was more interested in letting everyone know who was in charge than in getting out a good picture. John's attitude did not improve when *Steamboat Round the Bend*, as edited by Zanuck, opened to rave reviews.

The first new film John made under the Zanuck regime was *The Prisoner of Shark Island*. Written by Nunnally Johnson, it was based on the life of Dr. Samuel Mudd, the physician who treated John Wilkes Booth's broken leg the night he assassinated President Lincoln. Mudd was tried as an accomplice and sentenced to life imprisonment at Shark Island, a fetid, malaria-ridden prison off the coast of Florida.

In the years to come, Nunnally Johnson would become one of John Ford's most important collaborators. A fine wit and raconteur with a dewy Southern charm, he recalled for me his introduction to John:

"I met him at a party given at the home of some friends. He had a reputation as having a fierce Irish temper. I had heard that there were two producers at RKO, Cliff Reid and Joe Haight, who were so terrified of him that they'd flip a coin to see who would go and look at the rushes. Naturally, I approached him with some trepidation.

"We had a discussion about 'director's touches.' I said that they were so much nonsense, made up by the critics who had no way of knowing if something was made up by the director on the spot or if the writer had included it in the script. They just automatically gave the director credit for any odd bit of business. I told him I didn't think it was fair. I remember that John said, 'You're quite right. Why, just this afternoon I read a script which was offered to me to direct. It had a scene where a wagon pulls out and runs over a bouquet of roses. That's exactly the sort of thing some critics would call a director's touch.' I was staring at him with my mouth open. He was talking about a scene from *The Prisoner of Shark Island*. Then he smiled and we both started to laugh."

Perhaps it was inevitable that John and Zanuck would clash before *The Prisoner of Shark Island* finished shooting, and clash they did. Their first confrontation came when Zanuck learned that John seldom bothered to look at his rushes but relied on the judgment of his editor and assistant director instead. (John was able to do this because he shot very little film and rarely printed more than one take. Without a lot of takes to choose from, the only reason to look at the rushes at all was to check them for technical mishaps—negative scratches, poor sound recording, and the like.) Zanuck, the editor supreme, thought it inconceivable that a director, and particularly a director of John Ford's caliber, could make a picture without many long hours bent over a movieola. It seemed careless and irresponsible, and he sent John a memo to that effect.

Zanuck's memo made John furious. He resented the studio chief's meddling in his affairs. Zanuck had already taken the preproduction and the postproduction out of his directors' hands, and now he seemed bent on moving onto the set and taking over the actual filming as well. How far was he going to go? When was it going to end?

John decided that the best way to deal with Zanuck's memo was to obey the letter of it while flagrantly disobeying the spirit. The next day, John had his editor bring the rushes onto the set; he settled back into his chair, picked up the exposed strip of film, and began studying it—not in the projection room, but through a magnifying glass.

When word of John's stunt got back to Zanuck it was his turn to be furious. He had no intention of being intimidated by a director. It was clear to all that a showdown was coming. The only question was when.

In preparing *The Prisoner of Shark Island*, it had been decided that Warner Baxter would play Dr. Mudd with a Southern accent. But a week into the picture it became apparent that the actor couldn't do the accent convincingly, and Zanuck told John to have him play his part with no accent at all. But Baxter refused to go along with Zanuck's decision, claiming that the accent was essential to the character. He was so adamant that John decided not to make an issue of it. If it meant that much to Zanuck, then he could deal with the actor personally. Baxter kept the accent. John kept shooting.

A few days later, when Zanuck saw that Baxter was still using the accent, he went down to the set and called John aside. "What the hell's going on here?" he demanded. "I told you to have Baxter drop that accent. Aren't you the director of this picture? Can't you control him?"

"See here, Darryl," John replied, "if you don't like the way I'm directing this goddamn picture, then take me off of it." He turned to walk away.

But Zanuck, not about to be intimidated, jumped on John like a terrier. "Don't you ever threaten me again. If I didn't want you on this picture, you wouldn't be on it. Let's get one thing straight right now. I'm in charge of this studio and when I say do something, you sure as hell better do it."

In a rare capitulation, John went back to shooting the picture and Warner Baxter dropped the accent.

The Prisoner of Shark Island was personally edited and prepared for release by Zanuck, who gave it all the verve and pacing that was his trademark. *The Prisoner of Shark Island* was perhaps the first picture in which John managed to combine the sophisticated visual style which had so distinguished *The Informer* with the realism of his American subjects. Released in February 1936, it was very well received by the press and public. But John's problems with Zanuck had left him with a bitter taste in his mouth. His misgivings about the studio boss, first aroused by his recutting of *Steamboat Round the Bend*, were reconfirmed by the Warner Baxter incident. John saw the diminutive Zanuck as a "hyperactive manipulator" with a "Napoleon complex," and behind his back began calling him "Darryl F. Panic." Shortly after the release of *The Prisoner of Shark Island*, John gave a rare interview to a writer from *New Theater* magazine. Sounding very different from the man who just a few years before was calling himself "the best traffic cop in Hollywood," he articulated his feelings about the studio system and the right of directors to control their films: "They've got to turn the picture making over to the hands that know it. Combination of author and director running the works, that's the idea. Like Dudley Nichols and me or Riskin and Capra ... As it is now, the director arrives at nine in the morning. He has not only never been consulted about the script to see whether he liked it or feels fit to handle it, but he may not even know what the full story is about. They hand him two pages of straight dialogue or finely calculated action. Within an hour or less he is expected to go to work and complete the assignment the same day, all the participants and equipment being prepared for him without any say or choice on his part. When he leaves at night, he has literally no idea what the next day's work will be...."

If John wasn't free to control his films or deal with meaningful subjects at Fox, he at least had something very few of his contemporaries in Hollywood had: the freedom to go elsewhere. His contract at his home studio was still nonexclusive.

While Zanuck was cutting *The Prisoner of Shark Island*, RKO asked John to film the Maxwell Anderson play *Mary of Scotland*, which David O. Selznick had purchased as a vehicle for Katharine Hepburn. Besides Hepburn there were Fredric March as Mary's lover, Bothwell; Florence Eldridge as Queen Elizabeth; and John Carradine and Donald Crisp in supporting roles. Shooting began just after New Year's Day, 1936.

Working with Katharine Hepburn was an entirely new experience for John. A leggy, toothy New England blueblood from a patrician WASP family, an intellectual, a snob, and an heiress, she made it clear, in her broad Bryn Mawr vowels, that she had nothing but contempt for Hollywood. Headstrong and opinionated, flashy and feminine, Kate Hepburn caused a stir wherever she went and had been pursued by some of the most eligible men in motion pictures. Katharine Hepburn and John Ford were as opposite as positive and negative. He was a man's director, she was a woman's woman. They fought, bickered, and fussed all the way through *Mary of Scotland*.

On the first day of shooting, John walked onto the set and found Kate seated in his chair, mimicking him by wearing a hat pulled down over her eyes and smoking an Irish clay pipe. But John wasn't about to let Kate have her gag.

"How can you smoke those goddamn things?" he asked. "They make me sick."

Kate even dared to criticize the mighty Ford's direction. Once, while shooting a scene with Mary and Bothwell, John said, "This is a lousy scene. I don't know why I'm bothering with the goddamn thing."

"I beg your pardon," said Kate. "I happen to think that this is the best scene in the script."

"Well, if you like it so much, then you direct it." John walked off the set. Kate directed the scene.

At one point John offered his leading lady some advice.

"You're a hell of a fine girl. If you'd just learn to shut up and knuckle under, you'd probably make somebody a nice wife."

John Ford and Kate Hepburn had the rollicking, bickering, cockeyed attraction of opposites. And attracted they were. During the filming of *Mary of Scotland* they fell in love. They met at Kate's Laurel Canyon home, and stole away together for weekends aboard the *Araner*. This was one of the happiest interludes in John's life. He was obsessed by Kate and found with her a degree of happiness and a peace of mind that he had never known before. She was not only beautiful and graceful, but had charm, nerve, and humor, topped off by a fierce competitive spirit.

After *Mary of Scotland* finished shooting in the spring of 1936, they went East together and spent a month at Fenwick, Kate's family home at Saybrook Point, Connecticut, where they sailed on Long Island Sound and played absurdly competitive golf matches at a nearby country club. Then they went to New York and caught the latest Broadway plays and visited Kate's friends from her days in the theater.

As much as John and Kate may have felt for each other, there were limitations on their relationship. Whatever the shortcomings of his marriage, and they were many, John's ties to Mary were strong. A relationship was one thing; divorce was something else. As for Kate, she was a steadfastly independent woman whose primary devotion was to her career. Even if John had considered leaving Mary to marry Kate, he must have sensed that Kate would never "knuckle under" and marry him.

In the summer of 1936, John returned to Hollywood. Kate, meanwhile, perhaps as a way to cool off the relationship, went on an extended national tour with the play *Jane Eyre* that kept her on the road until February 1937. The long separation took its toll.

John and Kate, opposite in so many ways, were in fact very much alike. Both were volatile, creative, strong, and self-centered. Both were opinionated, pigheaded, and difficult to live with. John's masculine ego would never tolerate Kate's independence, and Kate instinctively knew that John Ford's house had to be a cold and lonely place for a woman. John was better off married to someone who had a stabilizing effect on him, a woman who could tolerate his energies and absences and could make him a home. Deep down, he knew he was better off with Mary, and he let the relationship end.

By 1937, Hollywood had completely recovered from its 1933 slump and the motion-picture business was booming. That year 80 million people, fully 65 percent of the entire population of the United States, went to the movies *every week*. To meet the demand for films, the studios had been made over into modern efficient factories, with specialization and division of labor the pillars of the system. Films, like automobiles, moved down the assembly line from story idea to final cut.

The late 1930s are remembered as Hollywood's golden age. Feeding on a cycle of production, distribution, and exhibition, the studios enjoyed a phenomenal prosperity. Yet the studio system, so often praised for its vitality today, certainly had its drawbacks. Most films were made according to formula. Plots were standard and generally superficial. The studio chiefs exercised the power of feudal barons, while directors were handed detailed scenarios they could not alter and studio crews they had not chosen. It was more important that they be able to weld together the ideas of others than to be original themselves. Stylistic differences tended to be erased, and Hollywood films took on a slick, impersonal sheen.

As much as he decried the loss of his freedom, perhaps more than any other director, John Ford thrived under the studio system. It steered him toward the kind of films he was really good at: commercial, less pretentious ones, most of which had American settings. With his powerful personality and reputation for irascibility, he was able to browbeat even the strongest producers and more often than not make the system work for him.

Perhaps the strongest producer in Hollywood was Sam Goldwyn, an independent in the age of the big studio, he operated out of his own lot at 1041 Formosa Avenue in Hollywood, and released his pictures through United Artists.

Sam Goldwyn was famed for being a shrewd negotiator. Indeed, he operated with a great advantage: he had his own language. Goldwyn had a way of coming up with a phrase that somehow conveyed the feeling of the moment, but didn't make any sense logically. Such verbal oddities were called Goldwynisms in Hollywood.

Goldwyn exercised dictatorial control over his pictures. He was the dominant force on every one he ever made. He had a hand in every decision, from casting and budget to the details of wardrobe and makeup. A great admirer of writing talent, Goldwyn had some of the best writers in America working for him: Robert Sherwood, Francis Marion, S. N. Behrman, Lillian Hellman, and Ben Hecht, to name but a few. But because he insisted on being the dominant force on his pictures, Sam Goldwyn traditionally didn't get along with directors.

In May 1937, Sam Goldwyn asked John to make a film version of the Charles Nordhoff–James Norman Hall novel, *Hurricane*. Set on a peaceful South Sea island, it was the story of a well-intentioned but doctrinaire European governor who sends a native boy to prison. Unable to stand the confinement, the boy breaks out again and again, but each time he is caught and his sentence is extended. Finally, a terrible storm, as though sent by the gods, devastates the island.

Hurricane was a big picture, a full-blown disaster epic, and Sam Goldwyn was convinced that John Ford was the man to direct it. He thought enough of John's ability to pay him an astronomical fee of $100,000 and 12 percent of net profits, escalating to 15 percent when and if *Hurricane*'s profits exceeded $1 million. Goldwyn further sweetened the deal by chartering the *Araner* for use in the picture, and by giving John contractual control over the film's production, script, and editing.

Goldwyn had assembled a first-rate cast for *Hurricane*. Terangi, the native, was to be played by Jon Hall, the tall and muscular nephew of the book's co-author. As his bride Goldwyn had cast sarong girl Dorothy Lamour; some of the best actors in Hollywood were in supporting roles: Raymond Massey as the governor, John Carradine as the sadistic guard, Thomas Mitchell as a kindly but drunken doctor. Shooting began in the summer of 1937 on the Goldwyn lot and at the Isthmus Harbor on Catalina Island. There the crew lived ashore in tents while John stayed aboard the *Araner*, anchored in the bay.

Always sensitive to his company's morale while on location, John traditionally made it a point to provide some sort of entertainment that would keep the crew from becoming bored off-hours and keep them in line. On *Hurricane*, he put Tommy Mitchell in charge of an entertainment committee, and Mitchell had the entire company, actors and technicians alike, participate in sketches. One night, however, John slipped ashore to see what Mitchell's entertainment committee was up to. He entered the camp unnoticed and made his way to the tent where the sketches were in progress. Pulling the flap open, John looked inside and saw an electrician with a pipe clenched in his mouth and a fedora pulled down over his eyes, barking orders in a thin New England accent. He was doing an impersonation of John Ford. John slipped back to the *Araner* unnoticed. The next day the electrician was fired.

Despite his personal and contractual assurances that he would not interfere with its filming, Sam Goldwyn was too strong a producer not to get involved in the making of *Hurricane*. He sent one of his most trusted lieutenants, an associate producer named Merritt Hulburd, to the Catalina location to supervise the picture and to look over John's shoulder. Resenting the intrusion, John picked on Hulburd unmercifully, belittling him at every opportunity and even refusing to let him come aboard the *Araner* to attend the nightly production meetings.

Despite his differences with Hulburd, John had only one relatively minor clash with Sam Goldwyn on *Hurricane*. It happened after the company had moved back to Hollywood and the producer decided that John wasn't shooting enough close-ups of Dorothy Lamour. He went down to the sound stage to tell his director to shoot more.

"You bothered me about *that*?" John exploded.

"Yes," said Goldwyn. "It's not personal enough."

"Well, let me tell you something," roared John, shaking his fist at Goldwyn. "I'll determine when to shoot the close-ups on this picture."

The producer looked apprehensively at John, then turned and walked away muttering, "Well, anyway, I put the idea in his head."

And in fact he had: the more John thought about it, the more he agreed that Goldwyn had a point. Before the picture was over, he shot a number of close-ups of Lamour and cut them into the film.

Released November 9, 1938, *Hurricane* opened to mixed reviews, but was very well received by audiences. A romantic action picture praised for its special effects, it was a big money-maker for both Sam Goldwyn and John.

After *Hurricane*, John returned to Fox to make two quickie program pictures—*Four Men and a Prayer* and *Submarine Patrol*—both straight adventure films, studio potboilers made on the assembly line. *Four Men and a Prayer* was the story of four brothers who try to avenge their father's death at the hands of Indian gunrunners. *Submarine Patrol*, an excellent film of its type, was very well received, with *The New York Times* going so far as to praise it as John's best film in years.

In the two years between November 1936 and November 1938, John had made four program fillers: *Wee Willie Winkie*, *Hurricane*, *Four Men and a Prayer*, and *Submarine Patrol*. While only *Hurricane* is remembered today, all four films were popular with audiences and were big money-makers, their financial success reflected in John's earnings: over $131,000 in 1937, and in 1938, thanks largely to the success of *Hurricane*, over $215,000. Perhaps even more important than the money they brought in, these four films reestablished John as a commercial director.

In a very real sense the period between 1935 and 1938 was John's golden age. His reputation as a commercial director was well established, and barring any disastrous illness, injury, or indiscretion, he was assured of a secure, lucrative position in the Hollywood community for the rest of his life. He had grown up with an infant industry, matured and prospered with it, and now, in the late 1930s, as Hollywood was entering its own golden age, he was in a position to reap the spoils of his success.

This was a particularly happy time in John's personal life as well. His marriage had survived the tempest of the Hepburn period, and his relationship with Mary had moved onto a new plateau, as they reached deeper levels of understanding and learned how to give and take and tolerate each other. This was no small feat on Mary's part. Living with John was not easy. In her years with him, Mary had acquired considerable diplomatic skill. As John grew older, his temper grew shorter and his disposition became more and more volatile. Mary, on the other hand, became smoother and more diplomatic. She not only learned how to live with John, but she also learned how to walk behind him and repair some of the fences he crashed through.

As in all marriages—and particularly long marriages—John and Mary lived together with certain matters understood. The Hepburn relationship had changed things. It had blown the lid off any pretense of monogamy, and after it was over, Mary seemed to have given John a free rein to indulge in extramarital affairs—her only stipulations being, first, that she wasn't to know about them, and second, that they were not to become public knowledge. Over the years John had several minor affairs, but they didn't really amount to much. He was not an excessively promiscuous man; his real vice was alcohol, not women.

Despite John's financial success, he and Mary lived modestly by Hollywood's imperial standards. With the notable exception of the *Araner*, they kept a fairly low profile and didn't try to compete with their peers. Rather than moving out to the plush new suburbs of Beverly Hills and West Los Angeles they kept adding on to their comfortable Odin Street house, and by 1937 it went up the hill in three different directions.

Neither John nor Mary particularly liked to entertain, at least in traditional Hollywood ways. They gave few dinner parties, avoided premieres, and seldom screened films. Although John generally shunned publicity, the nature of the Hollywood system demanded that he occasionally step into the limelight to help promote his movies. The Fox publicity department, for instance, used his name extensively in promoting *Submarine Patrol*. Among other things, he was the subject of an Associated Press feature that appeared in 114 newspapers across the country. Prepared by a reporter named Robin Coons, the piece featured eighteen photographs of John aboard the *Araner* and at home, and a brief, somewhat idealized account of his life-style:

"John Ford, at 43, is a $100,000 per film Hollywood director and motion picture Academy Award winner, but you'd never suspect it from the way he lives. His idea of a swell time isn't a night club party, but a quiet evening at home with baked beans for dinner, a good book and a pipe. His home has nine rooms and a modest garden, but no swimming pool. His favorite pastime is a game of hearts with Mrs. Ford and some friends, and he prefers to spend most of his free time aboard his yacht to escape from Hollywood's bright lights between jobs.

"He is an omnivorous reader who wears glasses and smokes a pipe most of the time. Both his parents spoke Gaelic, and he collects books on Irish subjects by Irish writers. Frequently he revises scripts for his pictures and he tries to colloquialize his lines whenever he can ... Once a picture is finished, Ford tries to forget all about it. He never attends previews or gala premieres; 'I'm no judge of my own work,' he explains modestly."

Though John and Mary led an essentially conservative existence, it was by no means austere. They were both very much a part of Hollywood's golden era, and judged by any standard they lived well. Mary, in particular, enjoyed her wealth. With her Rolls-Royce and her charge accounts in every Beverly Hills store, she was very much the Hollywood matron. She appreciated John's success and enjoyed the good life it earned her. Yet she was not a "flashy" woman. She had impeccable taste, a great sense of style, and she looked down on garish displays of wealth. While she liked nice things, she liked the idea of financial security even better.

John, on the other hand, was less interested in spending money and hated all forms of conspicuous consumption. His wardrobe was ludicrous, considering his income. His collars were always frayed, the seat of his pants was always shiny, and his socks rarely matched. As often as not, he showed up at work with an old necktie wrapped around his waist for a belt. The older he got, the more contemptuous of his dress he became. On one occasion in 1938, Louis B. Mayer invited him to MGM to discuss a picture, and John showed up at the Culver City studio dressed like a skid row wino. He hadn't shaved or changed his clothes in about three days, and the guard wouldn't let him in the gate. "But I'm John Ford the director," he protested. "I've got an appointment with Mr. Mayer."

"You don't look like a director to me," said the guard. He never did let John on the lot.

John had little interest in material possessions (with the notable exception of the *Araner*), and the larger and more important the item, the more he tended to neglect it. His car, a Ford roadster in the mid- and late 1930s, was always filthy. The seats were littered with script pages, and he always seemed to leave it parked under eucalyptus trees. The contrast between John's beat-up roadster and Mary's immaculate Rolls caught the attention of many Hollywood wags.

Just as John and Mary had very different ideas about money, they also had very different ideas about raising children. Mary tended to be indulgent and overly protective, particularly with Barbara, while John tended to be a stern disciplinarian, particularly with Pat. Most of the actual child rearing was left to the children's nurse, Maude Stevenson, who remained with the family until Pat and Barbara were well into their teens. "Mama Steve" was a surrogate mother, and there was considerable distance between John, Mary, and their children.

As was the fashion in upper-class Hollywood, both Pat and Barbara went to the best private schools, Barbara to Marymount and later to Westlake, and Pat to the Black-Foxe Military Academy, a popular private school among Hollywood's elite. Since there was no bus service to the latter, Cadet Ford was driven to school every morning in his mother's Rolls-Royce.

After the Lindbergh kidnapping in 1932, John and Mary became concerned about the children's safety. Reasoning that they would be safer and more insulated from their father's fame away from Hollywood, Pat and Barbara were sent to the Punahoe school in Honolulu, where they thrived. At Punahoe they became friends with the children of Kim and Rosina Wai, and spent most of their holidays with them. Pat developed into an outstanding athlete in the Islands, winning football letters all through high school and developing into an outstanding swimmer and surfer.

The differences between Pat and Barbara were apparent from a very early age. Barbara, who had Mary's beauty and John's wit and energy, was clearly her father's favorite. Pat, on the other hand, wasn't so indulged. Robust and masculine, he was a good if not great student, who readily accepted life on its own terms. He thrived in the rough—but not too rough—boarding schools he was sent to. John went to great lengths to "stiffen Pat up," to offset some of the advantages that his son enjoyed. He encouraged him to play football and had him work aboard the *Araner* during the summer, sleeping in the forecastle with the paid hands. One summer Pat set up in his own business at Catalina Island: John let him use one of the *Araner*'s launches to go around the Isthmus harbor and collect garbage from the yachts moored there. Although Pat collected a fee for this service, he was determined to milk the operation for all it was worth. At the end of the day, Pat took the garbage to the other side of the island and fed it to a half dozen pigs he was raising. At the end of the summer, Pat sold the pigs to an island restaurant, and on Labor Day they were slaughtered and cooked in the ground, Hawaiian style.

Despite John's interest in his children and his genuine affection for them, on balance he was not a particularly good parent. He was too busy, too absorbed in his work, and his children were constantly being told that their father was "away on location" or "in production and could not be disturbed." They grew up having to compete with an endless parade of writers, actors, and producers who were always passing through John's life, and in the end they always had first call on his attention.

The demands of the movie factory always came first.

John's family life and his professional life cannot be cleanly and evenly divided; there was a good deal of overlap. Two of the people closest to him were his brother and assistant, Eddie O'Fearna, and his brother-in-law and second assistant, Wingate Smith. Eddie and

Wingate were two very different people with two very different approaches to their work. Eddie had come to Hollywood in 1917 and had been working as John's assistant since 1920. He had a quiet, low-key approach, and a relaxed, almost diffident manner. If his electricians were taking too long to light a scene, Eddie would say, "Gentlemen, I'm afraid that this just won't do. Try and hurry it up a little, will you?" If the set was too noisy, Eddie would quietly admonish everyone, "Now, now, children, let's have some quiet, please."

Wingate, on the other hand, was a graduate of a much rougher school—the army. While Eddie was refined and diffident, Wingate was loud and rough. Everywhere he went there was noise and commotion, and his booming voice could be heard from every corner of the set. He was always bawling, "If you jokers think you're going to break my heart whining like a bunch of old whores on Sunday, then you've got a lot to learn. NOW GET CRACKING!"

Despite Wingate's rough approach and badgering tactics, there was something about his fierce gusto that made him popular with crews. They would do anything for him. His words and tone may have been unpleasant, but he was so enthusiastic, so efficient, so obviously ready to jump in and do the job himself that the men loved him.

Despite the differences between them, Eddie and Wingate liked each other and got along well, but as the years wore on, rivalry began to get the upper hand over friendship. There was a lot of verbal sparring between them, and by 1937 it became apparent that one of them would have to go: that year Eddie went to work for William Wellman and Wingate became John's first assistant. In time, Wingate became a fixture on every John Ford film, the "First Sergeant" of the John Ford stock company. He ran the day-to-day operations, hiring the crews, selecting the locations, casting the smaller parts, and making up the budgets and the payrolls. He became a liaison between John and the Fox front office, and made it easier for John to concentrate on the pictures, on the actual "product" that was their life's blood. In time Wingate lost some of his rough edge. Because he was Pat and Barbara's uncle he was dubbed "Unc," and he carried that nickname for the rest of his life.

Wingate and John spent a lot of time together off the set, too. Wingate also liked his bottle, and the two men went on more than an occasional toot together. They played golf and Wingate was almost always aboard the *Araner* in her weekend trips to Catalina.

There was another fixture on the set of every John Ford picture: his script supervisor, Meta Stern. A short, frumpy woman with red hair, Meta's trademark was a hat with an enormous wide brim. She had started with John at RKO and for some strange reason got along with him. Like Mary, Meta had highly developed diplomatic skills and she was able to help in the day-to-day dealings. When they were not shooting, Meta acted as John's secretary, and there her diplomatic talents really got a workout. One morning when John was preparing *Hurricane* with Dudley Nichols, he told Meta that he was afraid he might be browbeating the writer too much. "If you hear me screaming at Dudley, write me a note and tell me that I'm supposed to take it easy," he told her.

Later that morning the story session began, and Meta could hear the muffled tones of ordinary conversation coming from John's office. Suddenly she heard her boss unleash a fusillade of the foulest language she'd ever heard. She wrote out a note and ran into the office. John was pacing the floor, glowering at Nichols with such intensity that sparks seemed to be flying off him. When Meta handed him the note, he crumpled it up and threw it in the wastebasket. "Goddammit, Meta," he shouted, "mind your own business. How do you expect me to get anything out of this idiot if you're always barging in here?"

Perhaps it was fortunate that John surrounded himself with relatives and long-term associates, for by the late 1930s his reputation as a bellicose Irishman was so well established that not everyone in Hollywood wanted to work for him.

By 1937 John's working routine was so deeply ingrained that all his pictures flowed together in a blur of continual activity. There was no letup, no break between pictures. Only the sets, the wardrobes, and the actors varied. Over the years John had developed a reputation for being an extremely fast director. Part of his secret was momentum. Mornings, he liked to get right into it, and as often as not his first setup was a scene that he had blocked out the afternoon before but had saved to establish his momentum the next day. But the real secret of his speed was the fact that he shot so little film; he got what he was after with a minimum number of takes and camera setups. Wingate Smith once recalled how he worked:

"He never shot a lot of film. A lot of directors will make sixteen or seventeen takes, but Jack always tried to do it in one. On an important scene he shot two. The second one was a protection which he seldom printed. He avoided close-ups, didn't shoot a master shot, then a series of close-ups, the way a lot of directors do. Jack didn't like to break up the rhythm of a scene. This is the biggest single reason why he was able to work so fast. He didn't shoot the same thing from a lot of different angles.

"He picked up some quirky habits over the years. Jack never looked at his rushes. After he broke for the day, the editor would screen them and unless there was something terribly wrong—a negative scratch or something—that was it. Late in the afternoon we always broke for tea. During the tea break he never talked about the picture. I would rather have gone in and faced a lion than have gone up to him and asked something about the picture. The break lasted about fifteen minutes. Guys would sit down, play a few hands of cards, and drink their tea.

"About five o'clock he would call the gaffer over and say, 'Bring your flashlight.' He would point it to his watch and say, 'Goddamn, it's getting late.' The cameraman would pick it up and say, 'Yeah, the light's starting to go.' He'd take a couple more shots, then we'd go home. We never seemed to work very hard, and we always broke early, but we always got a lot done. After work we'd drive out to the California Country Club and play a few rounds of golf or go down to the Hollywood Athletic Club and take a steam and get a rub. Then he went home to Odin Street and ate dinner. Afterwards he would curl up in his den with a book on his lap and read the night away."

Other than sailing on the *Araner*, John's favorite sport during these years was golf. He was a member of the California Country Club and the Lakeside Country Club, that venerable Hollywood institution in Toluca Lake. Though John was a good golfer, the pace of the game didn't suit his temperament. He was too high-strung and hot-tempered for it. He was famous for cheating, for subtracting points from his score and adding them to an opponent's. If his ball went into the rough, he was not above "finding" it in his golf bag.

But John was even more volatile when he was playing cards. Although he liked hearts, poker, and pitch, his favorite game was bridge, and stories about his conduct at the bridge table are legend. One time John was playing two-handed "honeymoon bridge" with John Wayne in the *Araner*'s main saloon when Barbara bounded down the gangway and asked what they were playing.

"Honeymoon bridge," said Wayne.

"Why do you call it that?" Barbara asked.

"Because we're trying to screw each other," said John.

Although John was a superb bridge player, he was so bellicose, so profane, and so hated losing that he often had trouble finding partners. Not many people could take the abuse he handed out, and finding a fourth was often a problem. John Wayne remembers one rainy day when he was aboard the *Araner* in San Pedro with Ward Bond. "Jack decided that it would be a nice day to play bridge. We called just about everybody we knew looking for a fourth, but we couldn't find anybody that would come down and play. Finally Jack sent George Goldrainer ashore and had him scour through the waterfront bars to find a fourth. He came back with some guy who had been drunk for about five days. He was so drunk he couldn't even sit up at the table. But that's not the half of it. The worst part of it was that Jack made me take this guy for a partner."

John may have been difficult, but he wasn't stupid.

9

John Ford's
Yacht Club

In the 1930s the Hollywood Athletic Club, located on Wilcox Street between Sunset and Hollywood boulevards, was a gathering spot for some of the most prominent men in motion pictures. The club had a weight room, a swimming pool, several masseurs, a barbershop, and a steam bath that was run by an affable, charismatic black man named John "Buck" Buchanan. In addition, the club offered other services to its members. There were, for example, half a dozen rooms upstairs that were an ideal place to retreat to after a fight with one's wife or to sleep off a bad drunk.

Throughout the 1930s, John was a regular at the Hollywood Athletic Club. After a long day of shooting he liked to stop off and relax from the tensions of the day with a steam bath and a rubdown. Indeed, many writers discovered that the best place to pitch John on a story idea was in the club steam room. Not only could they corner him there and be free from interruptions and ringing telephones, but they would invariably find the great man in a relaxed and open frame of mind.

Over the years, John and a group of friends that included Emmett Flynn, Tay Garnett, Wingate Smith, Liam O'Flaherty, Dudley Nichols, Harry Wurtzel, Fox producer Gene Markey, Merian Cooper, Johnny Weissmuller, Preston Foster, Frank Morgan, John Wayne, and Ward Bond became such regulars that the management discreetly set up a bar in one of the rooms upstairs for their use. Big drinkers all, the group was soon spending more time in the bar than in the steam room, and in time the Hollywood Athletic Club transcended its function as a health spa and became their meeting place, their social club.

Since everybody involved in the group was in show business and, as such, was barred from the better country clubs in Los Angeles, they took great delight in mocking clubs that required their members to be from the social register. They began calling themselves the "Young Men's Purity Total Abstinence and Snooker Pool Association." The only requirement for membership was an affinity for steam baths and alcohol, and not necessarily in that order. They adapted "Jews but no dues" as their slogan and elected the steam room attendant, Buck Buchanan ("The distinguished Afro-American") as their president. In their "charter" they stated that the club's purpose was to "promulgate the cause of alcoholism," and they jokingly required any applicant to be a "career-oriented" or at least a "gutter-oriented" drunkard.

One of the running gags of this mock club was Dudley Nichols' application for membership, which was repeatedly denied because his liberal politics were deemed "socially reprehensible." Although Nichols liked to claim that he was a big drinker, and loudly boasted of his alcoholic exploits, he really drank very little, at least when compared with the likes of Messrs. Wayne, Bond, and Ford.

In the summer of 1937, when it was discovered that many of the members shared an interest in boating, the "Young Men's Purity Total Abstinence and Snooker Pool Association" changed its name to the "Young Men's Purity Total Abstinence and Yachting Association." Over the years John kept gag minutes of the group's "meetings." In addition to Dudley Nichols' politics and his unpardonable temperance, another issue of great concern was the outrageous alcoholic behavior of Brother Ward Bond. If Dudley Nichols was only marginally qualified for membership, Brother Bond was overqualified. Some excerpts from the club's minutes:

"At the last meeting of the Young Men's Purity Total Abstinence and Yachting Association, Mr. Ward Bond was summarily dropped from our rolls for conduct and behavior which is unpleasant to put in print. Mr. Dudley Nichols, the well-known Irish-American screen writer, was elected in his place.

"Mr. Nichols' first action on becoming a member was to put forward a motion changing the name of the Association from the YOUNG MEN'S PURITY TOTAL ABSTINENCE AND YACHTING ASSOCIATION to THE YOUNG WORKERS OF THE WORLD'S ANTI-CHAUVINISTIC, TOTAL ABSTINENCE LEAGUE FOR THE PROMULGATION OF PROPAGANDA CONTRA FASCISM. This motion was defeated. Then Brother Nichols arose and presented each member with an autographed copy of his brochure thesis on the 'Origin, Development and Consolidation of the Evolutionary Idea of the Proletariat,' which he has recently sold to Sam Briskin to do as a musical with the Ritz Brothers. The copies of the pamphlet were refused by the members.

"The following is a statement from Brother Commodore John A. Buchanan (colored) who was recently elected Commodore of the Yachting Division: 'On Saturday night, February 27th, while fulfilling my duties as towel-boy and locker room attendant of the Hollywood Athletic Club, I was amazed by seeing Brother Bond taking a bath. This, I noted at the time, was most unusual. Later I saw him in the barber shop having a manicure. When I reported this unusual procedure to Brother President Ford, he at once doubted my veracity, intimating that I was prevaricating. Upon my insistence, Brother President Ford, Brother Gene Fowler and Brother Corresponding Secretary Smith proceeded to the barber shop. There we found Brother Bond in a state of total intoxication, drinking Irish whiskey with gin chasers, attempting to kiss the manicurist on the back of the neck with a lighted cigar in his mouth, cutting his own hair and whispering to the barber confidentially to put two bucks on the nose of Napoleon Bonaparte in the Battle of Waterloo. Upon being reprimanded by Brother President Ford, Brother Bond's excuse was very lame, his alibi for drinking being that Troy had been last in the Tri-State league. Brother Bond then proceeded to drink the cigar and bite off the end of the glass. This I swear on my honor as a gentleman or a Harvard graduate or both, to be the truth, the whole truth and nothing but the truth, so help me God."

In the summer of 1938, "The Young Men's Purity Total Abstinence and Yachting Association" became the Emerald Bay Yacht Club, named after a cove located near Isthmus harbor on Catalina Island, and because it had an Irish ring to it. The Emerald Bay Yacht Club was no more a yacht club than its predecessor had been. It was not recognized by any national or regional yachting associations, there was no clubhouse, and there were no dues. "Meetings" were held, as they had always been, either in the steam room of the Hollywood Athletic Club or in the bar upstairs. The Emerald Bay Yacht Club was a spoof, a sham; it was a drinking society, whose purpose, like that of its predecessors, was to mock the high-hat snobbery of Establishment yacht clubs. The club motto remained "Jews but no dues" and "The yacht club for people who don't like yacht clubs." To carry out this sham, the members developed an elaborate table of organization. John was Commodore, Fox producer Gene Markey the Vice Commodore, and there was a Port Captain, a Fleet Captain, a Regatta Chairman, and a Fleet Chaplain. Everyone bought the most elaborate uniforms imaginable, caps and blazers covered over with insignia, and burgees that were correct in every detail.

The Emerald Bay Yacht Club was, above all else, an Irish Yacht Club, and the major social event on its calendar was a Saint

Patrick's Day dinner. The first one was held at the Coconut Grove at the Ambassador Hotel, but because it was so boisterous and loud and ended up in a food fight, the management asked them not to return. John wrote the Coconut Grove, "I neither understand nor condone your allegations regarding our behavior at a recent *fête galante*, but unfortunately, I am not in a position to remember it."

The following year, the dinner was held at the House of Murphy restaurant in Hollywood, whose management proved to be far more tolerant. The members gathered in full regalia. As Commodore, John sat at the head of the table; as Vice Commodore, Gene Markey, resplendent in his cap, muttonchop whiskers, and gold braid, sat at the opposite end. Also at the table were members emeritus Harry Wurtzel, Frank Morgan, Liam O'Flaherty, Dudley Nichols, Preston Foster, Philip Dunne, Johnny Weissmuller, Frank Borzage, Buck Buchanan, Owen Churchill, Wingate Smith, Tay Garnett, Emmett Flynn, John Wayne, and Ward Bond.

In the best tradition of Saint Patrick's Day, everyone proceeded to get speechlessly drunk.

While John Ford never went to nightclubs and was seldom seen on the "Bel Air circuit," his social and recreational life was by no means confined to the steam room at the Hollywood Athletic Club. Throughout these years his principal avocation was the *Araner*, far and away his most beloved personal possession. In John's mind she was more than an inanimate object, more than wood, canvas, and a maze of complicated machinery. In his mind she seemed to be alive.

John's love for the *Araner* was reflected in the immaculate way in which she was kept. Her white paint was always fresh; her varnish always glistened; below decks her mahogany paneling was always polished and the deco chrome trim always shined. The big oak table in the main saloon was regularly holystoned with sand and sea water and left to bleach white in the sun. Her engine was kept in top condition. A powerful block of pure logic, it was kept spotlessly clean, the moving surfaces shining and damp with oil, the green paint fresh and new on the housings. The engine-room floor was clean and all the tools polished and hung in their places. One look into that room inspired real confidence in the *Araner*'s owner and master.

Throughout the mid- and late 1930s, John spent as much time as he could aboard the *Araner*. Summers he kept her moored at Catalina Island. John would leave Mary, Pat, and Barbara aboard her and zip back and forth in one of her launches. But it was during the winter that he got the most use out of her. For four consecutive winters between 1936 and 1939, John took her to Mexico and spent several months cruising the West Coast and the waters of the Gulf of California. Although the guests varied with each trip, they almost invariably included a collection of congenial pals, the same people who made up the Emerald Bay Yacht Club: Wingate Smith, Dudley Nichols, Preston Foster, John Wayne, and Ward Bond, among others.

Despite John's frequent boasting of his seamanship and his navigational skills, he showed little interest in the actual mechanics of running the *Araner* on these extended voyages. That was left to George Goldrainer and a crew that included an engineer, a cook, a steward, and a half a dozen deckhands. John was much more interested in drinking, fishing, and playing the paternal host.

Although the itinerary varied with each trip, the *Araner* always stopped in San Diego to top off her fuel tanks and take aboard last-minute provisions. Then she sailed south along the mountainous coast of Baja California, around the peninsula's southern tip over to La Paz, then north through the Sea of Cortez and into the tranquil solitude of the Gulf of California. After cruising the gulf, the *Araner* turned south and sailed down the west coast of Mexico, as far south as Acapulco.

A good part of each trip was devoted to some serious sport fishing. There were the bonitos, which struck hard on the line and made the reels sing; when they were landed, they beat the deck with their tails and their colors pulsed and faded as they went through their death throes. There were the dorados, which sounded deep after they hit and were good for at least one or two good runs before they could be landed. These were filleted on the spot and the tender white steaks put in the freezer below. But most sought after was the king of all sport fish, the marlin, and a good part of each trip was dedicated to searching for them. John's admiration for these great fish was boundless. He liked to claim that they were "strong as bucks," "incredibly fast," and had "mouths of steel." They jumped higher and more often, and fought harder, than any fish he had ever seen.

In Mexican waters they weighed upwards of 1,200 pounds. Twice in 1937 and three times in 1938 the *Araner* got involved in virtual "boils" of marlin. At one point in 1937, John Wayne caught seven of the fish in three days, John himself caught three, and Smith, Foster, and Nichols caught several each. Ward Bond didn't catch any, but somehow managed to get his picture taken beside the biggest ones. At one point on the 1938 trip, John Wayne hooked one that he remembers as "the biggest damn thing I've ever seen." Sweating mightily, he played it for over two hours, only to have it throw its hook just before coming to the gaff. He was so disappointed that he sat panting and cursing for half an hour until a sudden rain squall came and cooled him off.

There were other kinds of fishing too. In March 1937, at Puerto Escondido, on the east coast of the Baja Peninsula, Dudley Nichols took one of the *Araner's* skiffs and rowed in close to shore. He got in the water with a face mask, a snorkel, and a long-handled spear and was trying to stab some fish when an enormous manta ray, with wing tips more than ten feet apart, appeared and headed toward him. From the *Araner* John shouted for him to swim for the skiff, while Wayne dashed below and came up with a rifle. By the time he got a bead on the giant fish, it was passing under Nichols, who was already in the skiff. They shouted for him to spear the ray, but Nichols just sat there trembling. For some time afterward he remained motionless, contemplating his close call. One hit from the great fish's wing could easily have flicked him and the skiff high into the air. For hours afterward, all he could say was, "Jesus, did you see the size of that goddamn thing."

The fishing was always accompanied by some serious drinking. John Wayne remembers a classic incident when John and Ward Bond went fishing together:

"One day Ward and Jack got a couple of cases of beer, took one of the *Araner's* launches, and went out fishing. When they got out to sea, Jack told Ward to hand him a beer. Bond reached into the cooler and got the beer, then realized he had committed the unpardonable sin: he had forgotten the opener. Ward rummaged through the tackle box looking for something to use, and all the while Jack was all over him calling him a 'liver-lipped baboon' and telling him, 'I've met eggplants with higher IQs.' Finally Ward said, 'Dammit, Jack, I'll open it.' He raised the beer up to his mouth and opened it with his teeth. That day Jack made Ward open a whole case of beer with his teeth. By the way, the beer wasn't in bottles. It was in cans."

Few cantinas in the towns and villages along the Mexican coast were not visited at least once by the *Araner's* well-oiled travelers, but their favorite stopping-off place, their favorite "liberty port" on all these Mexican trips, was Mazatlán. It was near the really good marlin grounds at the mouth of the Gulf of California, and, as John Wayne remembers, "there was an ambiance about it." At night John and his band, barefoot, unshaven, and dressed in khaki work clothes splattered with fish blood, came ashore to comb the bars on the beach. George Goldrainer usually tagged along behind, picking up the checks and seeing that nobody got in trouble. Always a lover of mariachi music, John usually hired any local musicians to tag along, strumming their guitars and singing their sad, sentimental songs.

John's favorite bar in Mazatlán was in the Belmar Hotel which was located on the beach. The long low bar looked out over the water and had big heavy wooden chairs from which one could watch the sunsets. The owner of the bar had a pet boa constrictor that had the run of the place. One night Ward Bond passed out early, as was his custom, and John picked up the snake and set it on his lap. When Bond came to, he looked down, saw the snake, and popped up like a coiled spring, throwing the snake at John.

After a night (or day) of drinking, they would return to the *Araner* and bring the mariachis with them. Then they would settle back in the deckhouse, swill tequila, and have the Mexican musicians play.

Although these trips aboard the *Araner* were great fun and John enjoyed himself to the hilt, there was another, less attractive side to them. John did not surround himself with his creative peers, but rather with sycophants who were willing to serve him and obey his every whim. There was Ward Bond, the "class clown," and Dudley Nichols, "the class coward," both willing to go to any length to please John. There was Wingate Smith, whom John sometimes called "the ideal subaltern." John Wayne, who would later grow in professional stature and become a giant in his own right, was during these years still a struggling young actor all too willing to be a humble servant before a paternalistic Ford.

Then, too, there was the drinking, which was getting worse all the time. John Wayne says today: "Drinking was the one way

Jack could really relax and shut off his mind. Unfortunately, as he got older he found that he was less able to handle it. He always kept it in control and saved those real benders for times when he was around people he felt comfortable with, and who he felt he could trust. You'd think he was tight all the time, the way people talked about him. Maybe once a year he would really pin one on, but I'll tell you, they were long ones when he did it. The strangest thing about Jack's drinking was that he remembered everything right down to the drop of a pin when he sobered up. He never had the lapses of memory, as a lot of people who disparaged him when he was drinking found out."

On every trip the drinking got more and more out of hand. John drank for the effect, for oblivion. He would go for days, sometimes whole weeks, without eating and without sobering up. He would lose weight until he looked frail and dangerously thin. His eyes would become clouded and curiously distant. The drinking brought out the blackness, the Irish morbidity, and he became tearfully sentimental.

He was well on his way to becoming an alcoholic.

10

Stagecoach

T hroughout the 1930s westerns were out of favor with the Hollywood Establishment. When sound moved film making indoors, it brought with it tough-talking gangsters, musical extravaganzas, and sophisticated comedies, but it had relegated westerns, which had been enormously popular in the 1920s, to "B" picture status. By 1938 the major studios shunned westerns, which were now made almost exclusively by poverty-row producers and aimed at juvenile and rural audiences.

But not everybody shared the majority's belief that "A" westerns were a thing of the past. John, who had not made a western since *3 Bad Men*, believed that the genre had long been overlooked, that the public was ready for an "A" western with a first-rate cast. In the summer of 1937 he bought a short story, "Stage to Lordsburg" by Ernest Haycox, that had appeared in *Collier's* magazine the previous spring. It was a tightly constructed story about a collection of characters who make their way by stagecoach across the New Mexico Territory in the midst of an Apache uprising, and are rescued just in time by the U.S. Cavalry. There was a gambler, a drunken doctor, a whiskey drummer, and a prostitute; the key character was a lonely gunfighter known as "Malpais Bill." John bought the film rights for $2,500.

In August 1937 John and Dudley Nichols worked up a script, broadening the characters and developing the relationships between them, along the way making "Malpais Bill" the more heroic-sounding "Ringo Kid." Taking a lesson from *Hurricane*, they constructed the story, now called *Stagecoach*, so that events moved with increasing speed and tension toward the final chase scene.

But selling *Stagecoach* proved to be much more difficult than writing the script. Darryl Zanuck refused even to read it. John tried *Stagecoach* at MGM, Warner Brothers, Paramount, and Columbia, without positive result. Everywhere he went, he heard the same thing: "Nobody goes to westerns anymore," "You're ten years too late," or simply, "This isn't commercial material."

With his options very nearly exhausted, John finally approached independent producer Walter Wanger, who, he had heard on the Hollywood grapevine, was committed to make a picture for United Artists and was looking for a property. A tall, handsome Ivy Leaguer, Wanger was famous for his classy drawing-room films and his reputation for fairness.

After reading the Ford-Nichols script, Wanger decided to go ahead with the project. Contracts were signed in October 1937.

But there was another problem that had to be dealt with before *Stagecoach* could be made. United Artists was skeptical about making a western, and to get them to go along with it, Wanger had to limit the budget to $392,000. Since *Stagecoach* had a lot of action and required location work, its actual production cost—the "below the line"—would be high. To keep the film within its budget, the fees paid to the writer, the actors, and the director—the "above the line"—would have to be kept small. John may have found a taker for his western, but he was going to have to do it for a small fee. In the end, he agreed to make it for a flat $50,000. Although a respectable amount of money in 1938, it was still considerably less than the $75,000 per picture he was getting at Fox—and much less than the $100,000 plus 12 percent he had gotten for *Hurricane*.

The $392,000 budget left John with only $65,000 to spend on the cast, but he was able to get some of the best character people in Hollywood for the money. As the female lead, the prostitute called Dallas, he cast Claire Trevor; John Carradine was cast as the gambler, Hatfield; and Thomas Mitchell as the drunken doctor (a role he played in *Hurricane* the year before). Donald Meek played the whiskey drummer, and Andy Devine, the rotund, rasping cowboy from Kingman, Arizona, was set as the stage driver. George Bancroft, Louise Platt, and Tim Holt, plus Ford regulars Francis Ford, Jack Pennick, and Harry Tenbrook, rounded out the cast—except for the part of the Ringo Kid. Wanger had originally hoped to cast Gary Cooper in that role, but the tight budget precluded the use of such a high-priced star. Besides, John had other ideas about who should play the Ringo Kid. From the very outset he had seen it as an ideal part for his prodigal-son, his drinking, fishing, and card-playing crony John Wayne.

The Ford-Wayne friendship was unique in all of Hollywood. Wayne had admired and emulated John since his days as a propman at Fox. He was drawn to him as a mentor, an older brother, a man to whom he could look for advice and guidance. John, in turn, was drawn to Wayne's gregariousness, his natural good humor, and his shared affinity for booze and boating. But John also saw other qualities in Wayne. For some years he had believed that once Wayne shed his youthful callowness, once he put on some age, weight, and character, he could become a first-rate actor. Even with his six-foot, four-inch frame, John noticed that Wayne "moved like a dancer." He sensed in him a charm, a charisma, a vulnerability with which he thought audiences would identify. John also knew that Wayne had the phenomenal, almost pathological drive that it took to survive in Hollywood. He was hungry. Several times, says Wayne, John had told him that he had the kind of personality that was "successful in any business," and that "if he stuck to it he would eventually make it in pictures."

Over the years John had watched Wayne grow as an actor. He had seen him pay his dues and learn the basics of his trade: how to play to the camera and say the straight lines convincingly and without affectation.

In 1938 Wayne was under contract to Republic Pictures, grinding out a "B" western every eight days. He was well established in Hollywood, but only in the realm of children's pictures. Every agent and casting director knew who he was, but they all had the same mental notation beside his name: "John Wayne. Ex-jock. Western leading man. Mascot, Monogram, Republic. Looks good, moves and rides great. Can't act." Wayne had no money to speak of, no prestige, no importance in the eyes of his peers. He was frustrated at being a second-rate actor and bored by trite, cliché-ridden shoot-em-ups.

If Wayne's career was going nowhere, neither was his ten-year-old marriage to the former Josephine Saenz. The daughter of a prominent doctor and part-time diplomat, Josie, as she was called, was aristocratic and sociable, a prominent member of Los Angeles society, who regularly entertained well-heeled friends in her elegant home on North Highland Avenue. But Wayne was uncomfortable around those friends, who seemed to regard him as just another uncouth actor who didn't know which fork to use. After a fourteen-hour day of getting shot out of the saddle, the last thing Wayne wanted was to dress up, stay sober, and be nice to boring, bloodless, supercilious sons of the rich with whom he had nothing in common. By 1938 his marriage to Josie was all but over, a façade maintained for the sake of their four children. More and more, Wayne had been retreating from his marriage and spending his free time with John aboard the *Araner*.

In the summer of 1938 John invited Wayne to spend a weekend at Catalina. As the *Araner* powered past the San Pedro breakwater, John handed the actor a copy of the *Stagecoach* script and told him to read it. That night the two men sat up late playing cards. Finally John said,

"I've got Claire Trevor, George Bancroft, John Carradine, and Tommy Mitchell, but I need your help on something. You know a lot of these young actors. Do you know anybody who could play the Ringo Kid?"

Wayne grimaced. He knew he was being set up.

"Why don't you get Lloyd Nolan?" he answered.

John didn't acknowledge Wayne's sarcastic reply.

"Jesus Christ," he said, "I just wish to hell I could find some young actor in this town who can ride a horse *and* act. Goddammit, Duke, you must know somebody. But then you've been out at Republic. You're not likely to see a hell of a lot of talent out there."

The next day, as they sailed back across the channel, John continued his roundabout recruiting, fully intending to offer Wayne the part but wanting to see him squirm a bit first. The hand of the giver always did have a vicious backhand. Finally, on Sunday evening, as the *Araner* was docking in San Pedro, John broke the "news."

"Duke, I want you to play the Ringo Kid."

"Yeah, coach," answered Wayne, "I know."

Stagecoach began shooting in late October 1938 in Monument Valley, a spectacular region of desert plateaus and majestic rock formations located on the huge Navajo Indian reservation in southern Utah. John had first heard about Monument Valley from Harry Carey, who had stumbled into it while exploring the Navajo country in the 1920s. No other film company had ever worked there, and John had been waiting for years for a chance to do so. But in 1938 Monument Valley was an exceptionally difficult place to work. One of the least accessible points in the United States, it was a 200-mile drive over washboard dirt roads from Flagstaff, Arizona. There were no telephones, no telegraphs, and no bridges over the countless streambeds that cut across the single road. At an elevation of almost 5,000 feet, it was bitterly cold in winter and unbearably hot in summer. Nevertheless, Monument Valley offered a backdrop of matchless beauty, and John felt it would be well worth the extra effort.

Monument Valley was populated by Navajo Indians who, as they had for thousands of years, worked as sheepherders and subsistence farmers. Their homes, called hogans, were low rounded structures made from mud and thatch. Plumbing, sanitary, and medical facilities were unheard of. Malnutrition, disease, unemployment, and alcoholism were the four horsemen of the Navajo's apocalypse. In 1938, Monument Valley had been hit by a series of bitter winters, and the Navajo economy was in worse shape than ever.

Feeling distressed by the plight of these proud and noble people, John decided that they should receive some of the residual benefits from the film he was making in their midst. He hired hundreds as extras, bit players, and laborers, forming relationships with local people, Navajos and whites, that would continue throughout all the future pictures he made there. There were the Brady Brothers, Navajos who acted as translators and John's liaisons to the Navajo tribal council. There was a Navajo medicine man named "Old Fat," whom John put on retainer; his job was to predict weather and invoke big medicine to arrange scenic cloud formations. These men John hired would gladly have accepted the smallest pittance, but he insisted that they get full Hollywood scale. He cast Navajos like Fred Big Tree and Chief White Horse, among others, in small bits. John's favorite bit player was not a Navajo but an Apache, who had a classic Indian face and lived in a remote canyon far from Monument Valley that was accessible only on horseback. His name was Many Mules and he played Geronimo, the Indian the camera pans to at the start of the chase in *Stagecoach*.

John enjoyed the remoteness of Monument Valley almost as much as its scenery. Here there were no "front office spies" sneaking onto the set; here he could lord it over his troupe like an Old Testament patriarch. Each morning he arrived on the set in the station wagon of Harry Goulding, the proprietor of the local lodge and trading post. John's favorite atmosphere musician, Danny Borzage, heralded his entrance by playing traditional songs like "Bringing in the Sheaves," "Red River Valley," or "Wild Colonial Boy" on his accordion. A propman handed John a mug of steaming coffee, and he sat in the front seat, sipping from the mug and staring through his thick glasses out across the valley. As the crew hunkered around small fires and chatted among themselves, John decided how to shoot the first setup. Then he would bolt from the car.

"Set the camera up over here. We'll be shooting across the valley."

He would walk up to a wrangler.

"Can the horses cross the river there?"

"Well, where I went in the water—"

"Don't tell me the goddamn story of your life," John would cut in, throwing his cigar on the ground. "Just answer the question."

The company was headquartered at Goulding's lodge, and in the evenings a big western-style dinner of steak or barbequed ribs was served. After dinner there would be a game of pitch in John's room. It was played with silver dollars because John liked the sound the heavy coins made as they were tossed into the pot.

The isolation of Monument Valley freed John of rigid studio schedules and allowed him to work "off the cuff." He could juggle his schedule and, if the opportunity presented itself, he was free to take advantage of dramatic backlighting, a beautiful cloud formation, or a desert squall. Midway through the location scenes, a snowstorm hit the valley and left a blanket of snow over the area. Most directors would have shut down until the snow melted, because the footage of Monument Valley draped in snow wouldn't match what had already been shot. John not only worked on, but highlighted the snow in panoramic long shots of the valley. Later he gave stage driver Andy Devine an explanatory line: "I took the high road because those breech-clothed savages don't like snow."

Although *Stagecoach* is remembered as an action classic and is very closely associated with the name John Ford, the film was in fact much more important to John Wayne. It was the vehicle that lifted him out of the Republic sweatshop and launched him as a romantic lead in "A" pictures. But the transition was not easy for Wayne. John had gone out on a limb for him, had fought to cast him in his picture. Now he was going to exact his pound of flesh.

As a newcomer, and as an actor with little formal training, Wayne already felt insecure playing with such seasoned professionals as Thomas Mitchell, Claire Trevor, and George Bancroft. John made it even worse by bullying him in front of the entire company, calling him a "dumb bastard," a "big oaf," and the like. He even criticized the way Wayne moved: "Can't you walk, for Chrissake, instead of skipping like a goddamn fairy."

Beyond the sadistic pleasure John took in humiliating Wayne, there was an important political reason for it. The Ringo Kid was the key character in *Stagecoach*, as well as the romantic lead. John had given the part to an upstart actor whom everybody knew was his personal friend and drinking buddy. He knew that the veterans resented Wayne. By humiliating and harassing him, John got the rest of the company to pull for the kid, and before long they were doing everything they could to help him.

After the third week of shooting, John felt he had gone far enough, and his manner changed. Calling Wayne aside, he whispered confidentially, "Duke, you're doing just great."

The taunts were over. John could be cruel, but as a master of psychology he also knew when to be kind. He knew that Wayne was reaching deep inside himself and giving his finest performance to date, in which his best qualities—the charisma, the vulnerability, the physical grace—were shining through. John was so pleased with Wayne's performance that when the Monument Valley sequences were completed and the company returned to Hollywood, he reshot Wayne's entrance, having Wayne fire a Winchester to attract the stage driver's attention, then twirl it like a pistol as the camera trucked in for a close-up. This shot is one of the most famous scenes in the finished film, and today is usually remembered as the moment that Wayne's career took off.

Stagecoach is a true "A" western. The feelings, the relationships between the characters and particularly between Ringo and Dallas, are carefully drawn and expressed in beautiful cinematic terms. But *Stagecoach* is also a great action classic, and the action is the reason that the film remains in our memories to this day.

All that action takes place in the film's climactic chase scene, when the coach dashes across the salt flats pursued by the Apaches. Although every John Ford buff has his favorite action sequence, the chase in *Stagecoach* is almost universally ranked as among his best. Writer Bob Thomas once called it, quite aptly, a "ballet filled with danger."

The chase was the last scene actually filmed. It was shot not in Monument Valley but on a dry lake in Victorville, California, just outside Los Angeles, the same dry lake that John had used for the landrush scene in *3 Bad Men*. The tension is sustained by placing action within action, by having several "little dramas" going on within it. The gambler, Hatfield, contemplates shooting Louise Platt to save her from certain rape and indignity. An Indian jumps onto the lead horse but is shot off and takes the reins with him. Meanwhile, all around the coach, the Apaches close in, and there are several dozen of the best horse falls ever filmed. (Most of these were done with "Running W's," a technique in which a horse's front legs are shackled together and attached to a long cable anchored in the ground. When the horse runs out the length of the cable, its front legs are jerked out from under it. Although this seems a cruel technique and is rarely used today, very few horses were actually hurt with it.)

John was helped in the filming of the big chase by veteran stunt boss Yakima Canutt, who had earlier worked at Republic with Wayne. A tall, laconic man and a fine raconteur, Canutt once recalled how the chase scene was filmed:

"I had been working a lot with John Wayne, and when he got hired for *Stagecoach* he put in a good word with Mr. Ford. When I first went to see him, Ford said, 'Well, Enos, how are you?' That set me back on my heels—hardly anyone in Hollywood knew my real name was Enos. I said, 'I see Wayne's given you the inside dope on me.' 'That's right,' said Ford. 'In fact, he's said so much about you that you're going to have trouble living up to it all.'

"I knew that Ford liked to shoot fast and didn't want any delays, so I planned the chase as closely as possible. We had the saddle and horse falls to do first, so the night before, I hired a farmer to dig up twenty acres of the lake bed with his tractor. That way we'd have soft ground to land on and get the job done safer and faster.

"After he shot the falls Ford said, 'We're going to do that Indian gag of yours.' He was talking about a transfer, a stunt I had first done in a Republic serial and had repeated two or three times. The idea was to have an Indian jump from his pony onto the lead horse and try to take the reins. Duke shoots the Indian, who drops to the tongue, drags awhile, then lets go, and the horses and coach pass over him. There were only two or three feet between the horses and about four feet under the coach. It was a tricky stunt. First I did the transfer. The pinto I was riding shied away from the team, and I had to make a long jump. Then Wayne shot me, and I dropped to the tongue. It was kind of spooky dragging along and looking back at those flyin' horses' hooves. But they were running straight, so when Wayne shot me again I let go. I kept my legs together and my arms flat against my body and nothing hit. As soon as the coach passed over me, I did a little roll and got up, then I fell back down and lay still. That was an added touch of my own."

The chase scene—and indeed the entire picture—was superbly cut by John and editors Dorothy Spencer and Walter Reynolds. By using a subtle and steady increase in montage, they built an ominous feeling of dread until the moment when the coach must make its dash across the dry lake. In dubbing the chase scene, they used only the sound of thundering horses' hooves—no war cries or whoops—which adds greatly to the feeling of speed. The score, by Richard Hageman, W. Franke Harling, John Leipold, and Leo Shuken, consisted of traditional American folk songs put to full orchestration. It served beautifully to define a sense of time and place.

As he was putting the final touches on *Stagecoach*, John showed it to Merian Cooper, Jim McGuinness, and Gene Markey, among others, to get their reactions. To a man, each raved about the film's Monument Valley scenery, its superb pacing, and most of all its hair-raising chase scene.

As *Stagecoach* came together, John began to sense that he had a real winner on his hands. He told Walter Wanger that the picture was going to "clean up at the box office" and that it was going to "make Zanuck look like the idiot he is." He told John Wayne to start thinking beyond Republic. "You may get some real parts from this one," he predicted. "If this picture is half as good as I think it is, you're actually going to have to go out and buy some clothes."

John's hunch that *Stagecoach* was a winner was first confirmed when Walter Wanger previewed it at the Village Theater in Westwood. During the first hour, as the characters are delineated and the tension mounts, the audience sat quietly without a stir or a cough. Then during the chase scene, when the film explodes into action, they went wild. Wayne, who was there, remembers that "the audience yelled and screamed and stood up and cheered. They loved it."

Stagecoach opened March 2, 1939, to fantastic business and absolutely superb reviews. Variety called it "A display of photographic grandeur," Newsweek acclaimed it as "A rare screen masterpiece," and The Nation dubbed it "The best western in years."

Thanks to John, the "A" western was suddenly alive and well, and John Wayne was an "A" -picture star. The score won an Academy Award, as did Tommy Mitchell as best supporting actor. John himself was honored by the New York Film Critics for his direction. His prestige had never been greater.

11

1939

It has been said many times by many people that 1939 was Hollywood's greatest year—the year the studio system hit its peak. The big picture, of course, was *Gone With the Wind*. Out of seventeen Academy Awards it captured ten, including best picture, best actress, best director, best screenplay, and best supporting actress. But 1939 was also the year of *Mr. Smith Goes to Washington, Good-bye Mr. Chips, Dark Victory, Ninotchka, Wuthering Heights, The Wizard of Oz, Intermezzo, Gunga Din, Destry Rides Again, Juarez,* and *The Hunchback of Notre Dame*. It was a year of great performances by Clark Gable, Bette Davis, Laurence Olivier, Irene Dunne, Jimmy Stewart, Greta Garbo, Thomas Mitchell, and Charles Laughton, and it was a year of superb direction by Victor Fleming, Frank Capra, Ernst Lubitsch, George Stevens, George Marshall, and William Wyler.

Whatever else it was, 1939 was the year of John Ford. Between October 1938 and November 1939 he made four films—*Stagecoach, Young Mr. Lincoln, Drums Along the Mohawk,* and *The Grapes of Wrath*—that together stand as the greatest collective achievement in the history of the cinema. With them, John established himself as the premier director of American motion pictures.

Without taking away from the magnitude of John's accomplishment, it should be said that three of these films—*Young Mr. Lincoln, Drums Along the Mohawk,* and *The Grapes of Wrath*—were "studio projects," films made on that marvelously efficient and immensely profitable assembly line called Twentieth Century-Fox. The real story behind these three is not so much John's genius as an *auteur* director as his ability to work within the confines of the studio system and his volatile and sometimes quarrelsome relationship with Darryl Zanuck.

Judged by any standard, Zanuck was one of the most important figures in John Ford's life. Zanuck steered him toward his greatest work, created an atmosphere that was supportive and creative, and brought the fine edge of discipline to his films. Perhaps more than any other man (and certainly more than John himself) he understood the kind of films that John was really good at. Yet there was always a considerable amount of tension in their relationship.

Even by Hollywood's standards, Zanuck was one of the most outlandish moguls in the history of motion pictures. At the studio he surrounded himself with flunkies, cronies, and yes-men, alter egos who were never far from Zanuck at screenings, premieres, and story conferences. They included a French tutor, the man who ran the studio commissary, and the studio barber. Their function was to provide Zanuck not with sound advice but rather amusement. Away from the studio, Zanuck lived with the same flamboyant style. His socializing, for the most part, was an extension of his work, and the cast of characters was always the same: a cross-section of collaborators, employees, Hollywood society, and national and international celebrities. Conspicuously absent among them was director John Ford.

While John had a grudging respect for the way Zanuck had streamlined Fox, he also thought that he ran the studio like a "Versailles Court" and refused to become one of "Zanuck's flunkies." He once told Gene Markey, perhaps pointedly, that "any jerk willing to kiss Zanuck's ass long enough could become a producer." He was not entirely wrong.

But John's negative feelings about Zanuck went way beyond his contempt for the studio chief's flamboyant life-style. John thought that Zanuck lacked "artistic integrity," that he was more interested in rubbing elbows with celebrities and playing "Hollywood big shot" than he was in making good pictures. In John's mind, Zanuck had lost the brashness and drive that had got him where he was and now was only interested in making "safe commercial pictures."

John's feelings about Zanuck were to a certain extent justified, but most of John's dislike was simply sour grapes. The studio chief had turned down *Stagecoach* and wouldn't let him make the occasional small, noncommercial films that he wanted to do. There was still a seed of bitterness left over from the Warner Baxter incident and from the studio chief's encroachment upon John's autonomy. Most important of all was Zanuck's insistence on recutting John's films and eliminating the slapstick humor, the broad sight gags, that John liked so much.

While John openly called Zanuck any number of four-letter words, the studio chief was much more circumspect in his handling of John. He had a healthy respect for John's explosive Irish disposition and usually handled him as gingerly as he would a vial of nitroglycerin. But there was more than fear behind Zanuck's careful treatment. He knew that John was his best director and, after Shirley Temple, his most valuable corporate asset. Zanuck was very much aware that the real measure of the man was in his work, not in his personal style.

Nunnally Johnson once recalled two incidents that seemed to set the tone of the Zanuck-Ford relationship. When they were preparing *Submarine Patrol*, Zanuck invited John to dinner to discuss "story," but the director refused to meet him anywhere except at the studio.

"You have a contract," snapped Zanuck.

"There's nothing in it that says I have to have dinner with you," John replied.

"Okay, okay," said Zanuck. "Then come *after* dinner." John arrived at Zanuck's Santa Monica home in time for coffee, and from his arrival to his departure he pointedly refused to talk about *anything* but the script.

Some months later, after the picture's very successful opening, Zanuck and his wife, Virginia, threw a party for John. Most of the Fox hierarchy and all the key people associated with the picture, including its producer, Gene Markey, its cinematographer, Arthur Miller, and its stars, Richard Greene, Nancy Kelly, and Preston Foster, were there. But John, the guest of honor, didn't show up. He later told Zanuck that he had been aboard the *Araner* and couldn't get back from Catalina because of "engine trouble."

But whatever John's feelings, Zanuck had built up a stable of some of the best writers in Hollywood—Nunnally Johnson, Lamar Trotti, Dudley Nichols, Philip Dunne, Ernest Pascal, and Sonya Levine, among others—and instead of stars, he relied on the quality of his material. Although John was too bullheaded to admit it, Zanuck's efforts had resulted in an exceptionally creative atmosphere, and in January 1939 his years of consolidation at Fox were about to come to fruition. While John was busy decrying Zanuck for taking away his freedom ("ruining my pictures"), Zanuck was, in fact, steering him toward his best work.

As pointed out earlier, John's contract at Fox paid him $75,000 a picture and was nonexclusive. Although this certainly was an enviable arrangement, particularly the nonexclusive clause, there was one major disadvantage: John had no right to select his own material, and at least on paper had to accept whatever Zanuck assigned him.

John, of course, had a well-developed story sense and extremely good hunches about which of Zanuck's various projects had any real merit, and when he sensed a bomb, he simply refused to accept the assignment. Zanuck could put him on suspension and cut off his salary, but this meant nothing to John, who was wealthy enough to go off on the *Araner* for months at a stretch, secure in the knowledge that he could work any time and any place he wanted. While Zanuck could sue him for breach of contract, the studio chief also knew that a lawsuit would risk a permanent break, and John was too valuable an asset to lose. It was better to suspend him and take him off salary until a better picture could be found for him to direct. It was even better to try and keep him happy by offering him projects that he would be sure to like.

In December 1938, as John was putting the finishing touches on *Stagecoach*, Zanuck sent him an original screenplay by Lamar Trotti called *Young Mr. Lincoln*, the story of Abraham Lincoln's formative years. Asked to consider it as his possible next assignment, John's first reaction was negative. In the last two years there had been two Broadway plays dealing with Lincoln's early days—*Prologue to Glory* and Robert Sherwood's Pulitzer Prize-winning *Abe Lincoln in Illinois*—and John felt that young Lincoln had been "worked to death." But Zanuck kept after him with bulldog persistency, telling him that this was the best screenplay he'd seen in years and insisting that John at least read the script. When John finally did, he realized that Trotti's *Young Mr. Lincoln* was a great bit of writing: subtle, graceful, sensitive, and imaginative, with suggestions of this tall, bumbling young lawyer's destiny for greatness implicit in every scene. Enormously impressed, John told Zanuck that he'd gladly accept the assignment.

Unlike *Stagecoach*, which had been an *auteur* project in every sense, *Young Mr. Lincoln* was a studio project in the assembly-line tradition. The script had been written under Zanuck's personal supervision, and the production planned by one of Fox's most respected producers, Kenneth MacGowan. The role of Lincoln was of course the key one, but Zanuck was having problems filling it. He wanted to use a little-known actor named Henry Fonda, in whom he perceived a unique blend of integrity, simplicity, and subtle strength—perfect qualities for Lincoln. But there was a problem: Fonda felt overawed by the prospect of playing Lincoln, and he told Darryl Zanuck that he couldn't take the job.

I spoke to Henry Fonda at his Bel Air home two days after his seventieth birthday, and he recalled for me how John eventually persuaded him to change his mind:

"They had sent me the script, and I told them, 'Forget it. I can't play Lincoln.' I sent it back. But Darryl Zanuck and Lamar Trotti kept after me, and finally I agreed to make a test. A few days later we screened it, and when I saw this big tall character up there with the big nose, the hair, the wart and everything, it just didn't seem right. 'No way,' I said. 'I am *not* going to play Abraham Lincoln.'

"In the meantime, Jack had been assigned to the picture. I had never met him, but I had admired his work for years. He called me into his office. He was sitting behind a desk with a hat pulled down over his eyes, and was chomping on a pipe and a handkerchief all at the same time. He looked at me for a long while. I remember feeling like a sailor, a bluejacket, standing in front of an admiral. I didn't know how I was going to explain that I just couldn't play Lincoln. Suddenly he sprang up and said, 'What's all this bullshit about you not wanting to play Abraham Lincoln? You're not playing The Great Emancipator. You're playing a jacklegged lawyer from Springfield, Illinois, a gawky kid still wet behind the ears who rides a mule because he can't afford a horse.' I couldn't believe it. How could he talk about Abraham Lincoln in such a way? But he was right. He was making me see the character for what he was. I had him on too high a pedestal, and he was shaming me into playing him."

Young Mr. Lincoln began shooting in February 1939, and from the very first day a special kind of rapport began to grow between John and Fonda. John appreciated the actor's integrity, his formal training, and the seeming ease with which he worked. Fonda, in turn, appreciated the sure-handed way in which John took charge of the picture. Although their backgrounds were very different, the two men were in fact very much alike, and a relaxed, easy camaraderie developed. As Fonda says today:

"I had never met anyone remotely like him. Pappy was full of bullshit, but it was a delightful sort of bullshit. He liked to claim that he was just a lace-curtain Irishman from the State of Maine who had come out here to do stunts for his brother, and that they had made him a director because he could yell loud. But that was bullshit. He had great instincts, fantastic, sensitive, and keen in every way. He did everything intuitively.

"It didn't take me long to discover that there was a unique aura on a John Ford picture. He was rough, heavy-handed, often cantankerous, but he also was a sentimentalist. We just got along great, and from the very first day it was a love story between us."

Although *Young Mr. Lincoln* was an assembly-line picture, John was still able to give it his own special touch. He shot it with the same graceful technique he had used on his Will Rogers films and filled the picture with communal feeling and romantic vignettes of America's past. Throughout, John focused on the common, every-day aspects of Lincoln's early life, demythologizing the legend to find the real flesh-and-blood man underneath.

To emphasize the pastoral setting, John carefully and deliber-ately kept the dramatic tempo slow and often stopped the action to focus on a face or study an attitude. Predictably, John and Zanuck disagreed over the pacing. The studio chief continually was telling his director that he thought the picture needed more verve. But John felt that the mood of *Young Mr. Lincoln* depended on the leisurely pace he had given it, that to speed it up would destroy the whole climate of the picture. Knowing that he would be going on immediately to another picture, John did everything he could to "lock in" *Young Mr. Lincoln*. He printed only one take and destroyed the negatives of any others. He "camera cut" by surrounding his scenes with built-in dissolves (made by stopping down the camera and thus gradually eliminating the light). There was little that Zanuck could do. Editor Bob Parrish, who was the sound effects cutter on *Young Mr. Lincoln*, once recalled that when John finished it there was so little film left over that there was no way it could be altered. "We just cut the slates off," he said, "and spliced it together."

As soon as John finished *Young Mr. Lincoln*, he went on to his next assignment, an adaptation of the Walter Edmonds novel, *Drums Along the Mohawk*. This was a fitting sequel to *Young Mr. Lincoln*. Indeed, many of the same people worked on it. Lamar Trotti had done the screenplay, Bert Glennon was the cinematographer, and, most important of all, Henry Fonda was cast in the lead role with Claudette Colbert opposite him.

Drums Along the Mohawk was a big picture with a big cast and crew. Filmed at a remote location in Utah's Wasatch Mountains, it was an exceptionally difficult picture to make. From its first day it was a picture beset with problems. There were difficulties between John and his leading lady, Claudette Colbert. "Froggy," as she was called, was a strong and demanding woman. A perfectionist and a self-styled expert, she fretted and complained about everything from her lines and wardrobe to the angle from which she was photographed. John, never known for his patience with women, resented having to accommodate her.

There were also problems with the weather. Summer storms hit the location, and it was overcast for days on end. Bert Glennon had a very hard time making the light match, and John fell badly behind schedule. In the administration building back at Fox, meetings were held and memos were written. Executives flew out from New York. The telegraph wires that stretched between Utah and California hummed with the production office's heated words.

Darryl Zanuck had originally planned to make *Drums Along the Mohawk* the following year, but because of commitments from his distributors, he rushed it into production in the summer of 1939. Lamar Trotti had been forced to do a hurried adaptation, and John hadn't been involved in the story sessions. When shooting began, the script was still rough and John was not really familiar with it. Even more ominous than the script problems, however, was the fact that Zanuck and John had different ideas on the form the picture should take. Zanuck wanted John to pick up the pace and give it more drive. John was worried that Zanuck's preoccupation with a fast tempo would upset the film's symmetry. On June 17, with the location scenes halfway completed, he wrote the studio chief:

"I think the production office is a bit sanguine in expecting us to finish on the fourteenth. This is a terrific task up here, and despite Technicolor and some adverse weather —I believe we will finish ahead of schedule. Secondly: this is an important picture costing a log of dough. It is a pictorial story dealing with two people against the background of the revolution. I wonder sometimes if we have hit it perfectly in the script. I feel that when we return there will be adjustments to be made. Your letters and wires about tempo frighten me. Both the script and the story call for a placid pastoral simple movement which suddenly breaks into quick heavy dramatic overtones. All this requires care."

But the biggest problem of all was with John himself. He had made three pictures in the last ten months, two of them at remote locations. Bent over by the work load, numbed by sheer exhaustion, he didn't put what he might have into the picture, and it never was what it could have been.

Drums Along the Mohawk may not have been terribly important to John, but it certainly was to Henry Fonda. The actor had been working with John since the preceding February, and he was thriving under his sympathetic, intuitive direction. A close personal and professional bond was developing. As though to cement the Ford-Fonda relationship, *Young Mr. Lincoln* opened to outstanding reviews, while they were still shooting *Drums Along the Mohawk*.

The success of the John Ford–Henry Fonda team was not lost on Darryl Zanuck. In the spring of 1939 he had purchased John Steinbeck's great and controversial best-seller, *The Grapes of Wrath*, and Zanuck felt that Ford and Fonda were just the director–actor team for the picture. In July 1939, while they were still in Utah, he offered it to them, explaining that production was to begin immediately after they finished *Drums Along the Mohawk*.

Fonda was ecstatic about the opportunity to play Tom Joad, the hero of the Steinbeck novel, and he immediately told Zanuck yes. But John did not relish the idea of moving directly on to another picture. Though *The Grapes of Wrath* was great material, he had made three films without a break. *The Grapes of Wrath* would be his fourth. Moreover, *Drums Along the Mohawk* had been a very difficult picture to make and had exhausted John to the point of despondency. He desperately needed a rest. From the location he wrote, "If I were assured of a month off I would leap at the chance of doing 'Wrath' . . . Could you leave it this way, wait until I return from location? By then you will have seen the stuff and will know if we are on the right track. Then let us make a decision. I am working like hell up here, averaging eighteen hours a day. There is so much to do . . ."

While Darryl Zanuck could have assigned *The Grapes of Wrath* to another director, he knew that John Ford, with his feeling for Americana and his compassion for simple people, was the only man for the job. He postponed production until September 15, giving John the month off he wanted.

Drums Along the Mohawk, was assembled by Zanuck and released in November to fairly good reviews and moderate commercial success. John, however, was indifferent to the film's reception. Immediately after finishing it, he had sailed over to Catalina for a much-needed rest. The Isthmus was filled with Hollywood's boozy nautical set that summer, and the Emerald Bay Yacht Club was well represented. Gene Markey and Preston Foster were there, and John made his gregarious rounds. In time, Catalina performed its therapeutic function: John started to unwind, and to come back from the brink of exhaustion.

But Catalina offered no haven from world events, and in the summer of 1939 the news was dismal. On September 2, John was sitting in the *Araner*'s deckhouse playing cards with Mary, Ward Bond, and Preston Foster when they heard on the radio the awful news from Europe. Hitler's armies were crashing into Poland. Britain and France had declared war. While the news depressed the others, John was strangely fascinated by it. He knew that it was his destiny to become involved in this war. A few days later he told Gene Markey, who was also an officer in the naval reserve, that time was running out; they had better get to work and make good pictures while there was still time.

Although *The Grapes of Wrath* would always be remembered as among John's greatest and most respected films, it was not an *auteur* project. From its inception to its final cut, it was a studio product, a film molded on the assembly line, and it owes its greatness to many people.

Although its setting was contemporary and the production itself presented no real obstacles, it should be pointed out that, from a corporate and a political point of view, this was an exceptionally difficult film to make. The Steinbeck novel was much more than the story of one uprooted farm family; it was a scathing indictment of American society, and many conservatives (including most of Fox's board of directors) considered it a radical text, subversive material not suitable to put on the screen. On the other hand, many liberals (including most of the critical establishment) saw *The Grapes of Wrath* as holy writ, and if Zanuck muted the book's tone of moral outrage they were ready to pounce on him. Zanuck was walking on a tightrope.

In July 1939, Zanuck had assigned the script to Nunnally Johnson and ordered him to work in complete secrecy. While John rested aboard the *Araner*, Johnson put the final touches on the script. As a conservative Southerner, Johnson emphasized the personal and dramatic side of the story rather than the political. "I thought the politics were secondary to the story of the Joads," he once told me. Instead of dramatizing Steinbeck's bitter critique of America, Johnson filled the script with New Deal homilies. Johnson also made two major structural changes: he dropped the "inter chapters," in which Steinbeck generalized the Plight of the Joads and wrote about all uprooted "Okies"; and he ended the script at a point only two-thirds of the way through the novel, with a powerful scene in which Tom Joad says good-bye to his mother and goes off to become a labor organizer.

The Grapes of Wrath was cast entirely from the ranks of Fox's contract players. In addition to Fonda as Tom Joad, there was Jane Darwell, a warm, wonderful woman and a great favorite of John's, as Ma Joad; John Carradine as Casey, the defrocked preacher; Russell Simpson as Pa Joad; and Charley Grapewin as Grampa Joad. Tom Collins, who had run migrant camps for the Farm Security Administration and to whom Steinbeck had dedicated his novel, served as technical advisor to the production.

One of the most important men in shaping The Grapes of Wrath was art director Richard Day. A tall, elegant man with gray hair and distinguished features, Day visited John aboard the Araner and proposed that they imitate the work of Thomas Hart Benton, a Missouri-born artist whose subjects were the simple people of his native Midwest. Day had made a number of production sketches in which he had copied Benton's style and he showed them to John, who was very impressed.

Another guest aboard the Araner was the man Zanuck had selected to photograph The Grapes of Wrath, cinematographer Gregg Toland. A tall, handsome, high-strung man with an erratic and sometimes difficult temperament, Toland was one of the best cinematographers in Hollywood. (His work would later culminate with Citizen Kane and The Best Years of Our Lives.) In 1939, Toland was under contract to Sam Goldwyn, and Zanuck had paid $50,000 to get him. Toland and John poured over Richard Day's design sketches and decided to emphasize the contrasts, to go for a stark, almost documentary effect: murky silhouettes against light skies, and grim figures bent against the wind.

The Grapes of Wrath began shooting in September 1939 on locations in the San Fernando Valley, which was then a pastoral citrus-growing area outside Los Angeles. From the first day, John shot with tremendous concentration and intensity, determined to do justice to the Steinbeck book. Working extremely fast, he shot only 40,000 feet of film where most directors would have shot upwards of 100,000. John was after a straight, hard effect, and to accomplish this he submerged his actors so completely into the overall style that the finished film looks and feels like a documentary.

By any definition *The Grapes of Wrath* is a classic film. While the book is remembered as a political and social document, the film is remembered for its austere and tender beauty. Its focus, first and last, is human; however strident the political implications, it is the *people* who ultimately count. The characters are bathed in an idealizing light and presented with love, compassion, and human dignity. One of the great strengths of the film is Jane Darwell's Ma Joad, the matriarch who holds the family together. Wearing a pair of man's shoes and wardrobe two sizes too large, she bring great compassion and dignity to her part. The story is told through her eyes, and through her we feel the nostalgia for the old ways, for the values of the family and the land.

There are the faces that fill all of John Ford's films: John Carradine, who brings just the right demonic edge to Casey; the young-old face of Russell Simpson; and John's brother Francis, who plays to perfection the same inarticulate old comrade that he does in so many other films.

Yet greatest of all is Henry Fonda as Tom Joad. He is a tough, simple, straightforward son of the American heartland, a cunning survivor who is driven to violence and finally to social commitment. Today Fonda looks back on *The Grapes of Wrath* as a milestone in his career, and a key point in the evolution of his relationship with John Ford: "The thing that sticks in my mind about *The Grapes of Wrath*, and my favorite story about Pappy, was when we were shooting the scene where I say good-bye to Ma at the Government camp. The shot started inside the tent. I go in, shake her and whisper that I want to talk to her, then go out and wait while she pulls on a robe. She comes out, and we walk around and sit on this dance floor where they've had a dance the night before. We don't go into our dialogue until we sit down. Most directors would have shot this scene in two or three different setups. But Pappy wanted to do all of it in one shot. That made it technically very difficult because it meant that the camera had to be mounted on a track and they had to pull back from the tent, then dolly over to the bench with it.

"We rehearsed it and rehearsed it so that the camera crew could get the moves down. Every time we got to the bench and were about to go into our lines, Pappy would say 'cut.' He didn't make a big deal out of it. He just said 'cut.' Well, as actors we were very much aware of the emotion in this scene, and we really wanted to run it. We were like race horses chomping at the bit, but he wouldn't let us go until the camera was ready. When we finally did run the scene we were *ready*! I mean the emotion was built up inside of us, and it was working for us. It was there in the face and in the eyes, and we had to fight to hold it back. It was a great, great scene and we knew it right then.

"After it was over, Pappy just got up and walked away from it. He didn't say anything. He just got up and walked away. Everybody knew we could print that take."

Beyond its performances, *The Grapes of Wrath* stands out as a visual masterpiece. Gregg Toland's photography gives the film a unique texture, bringing to life the world of the migrant camps. Likewise, the music consists of simple folk songs, primarily "Red River Valley," played by Danny Borzage on his accordion. Muted, nostalgic, and a little off-key, the sentimental song beautifully sets the tone for the picture.

On November 8, 1939, after forty-three shooting days, John turned *The Grapes of Wrath* over to Zanuck to edit and assemble. The studio chief made only one change: Zanuck felt that Tom Joad's good-bye speech was too morbid an ending. To reinforce the populist theme of the picture and to fade out on a more upbeat note, he added the film's famous epilogue. After Tom says good-bye, the Joads leave the camp and head out looking for work. As they drive off, Ma Joad says, "For a while it looked like we was beat ... Rich fellas come up and they die, an' their kids ain't no good an' they die out. But we keep a-comin. We're the people that live. Can't nobody wipe us out. We'll go on forever 'cause we're the people."

In the fall of 1939, as *The Grapes of Wrath* was being prepared for release, there was much speculation in the liberal press that Zanuck had "laundered" the novel's political content. Six weeks before the picture opened, Fox mounted a publicity campaign aimed at countering that notion. The film was called a "faithful adaptation of the Steinbeck novel," and the studio claimed that the writer had given his "unqualified approval" to the script. They called it a courageous picture that would usher in the age when motion pictures would become a much greater and much more respected medium.

The Grapes of Wrath opened in January 1940 at the Rivoli Theater in New York, where 12,917 people jammed the theater on the very first day, and in even greater numbers on the second and third. For weeks the lines around the theater caused a traffic snarl so severe that police ordered the Rivoli to open its inner turnstiles so that the lines could move faster.

Frank Nugent in a famous review in *The New York Times* wrote, "In the vast library where the celluloid literature of the screen is stored there is one small uncrowded shelf devoted to the cinema's masterworks, to those films, which by dignity of theme and excellence of treatment, seem destined to be recalled not merely at the end of their particular year but whenever great motion pictures are mentioned. To that shelf of screen classics Twentieth Century-Fox yesterday added its version of John Steinbeck's 'The Grapes of Wrath' adapted by Nunnally Johnson, directed by John Ford..."

The Grapes of Wrath went on to become a great success on every level, and today it stands as one of John Ford's most admired films. Yet it was not a film shaped by one man alone; it was the product of many talents working together in a remarkably successful system.

12

Prelude
to
War

John missed all the commotion and hoopla surrounding the release of *The Grapes of Wrath*. The push to get the picture finished had left him exhausted, and as soon as he handed it over to Zanuck he boarded the *Araner* and set sail for Mexico. On board were the usual companions: John Wayne, Ward Bond, Preston Foster, Wingate Smith, and John's cameraman from his early days at Fox, George Schneiderman. While George Goldrainer and a crew of six stood the watches and ran the ship, they sat in the deckhouse, played cards, drank, and talked fishing. Though the same frivolous atmosphere prevailed now as on previous trips, there was a sense of urgency, of impending crisis, about this voyage—as though it might be their last for a while. For this was the fall of 1939, and Europe had gone to war.

John had his own reasons for returning to Mexico. Ellis Zacharias, now chief intelligence officer in the 11th Naval District, had asked John to make a detailed report on Japanese activity. John had asked for military orders but Zacharias refused, on the grounds that there were too many "diplomatic complications." But lack of official orders didn't deter John. Zacharias' enthusiasm and unofficial support were all that he needed; in his mind, he had carte blanche to organize his own semiofficial mission. As with his 1936 and 1938 "expeditions," John's motives were half patriotic and half adventurous. There was the lure of secret planning, the prospect of being on the "inside" of an intelligence operation, and the chance of advancing himself in the naval reserve.

The *Araner* made its usual stops in Magdalena Bay, Cabo San Lucas, and Mazatlán, where John and the others on board found time to explore the local bars.

From Mazatlán, the *Araner* motored up into the Gulf. The weather was hot, the sky overcast, and the sea flat and oily. To pass the time, John and George Schneiderman loaded a 16-millimeter camera and made an "art film" in which they photographed beer bottles from unusual, dramatic angles.

As they approached Guaymas, at the northern end of the Gulf, they still hadn't seen any signs of Japanese activity and John was beginning to grow genuinely concerned about his mission for Zacharias. He had been willing to go to great lengths to gather what he believed to be valuable information and never doubted that his "mission" was completely worthwhile.

Then on December 16, the *Araner* pulled into Guaymas harbor, and the entire mood of the trip changed. Inside the bay were dozens of Japanese fishing trawlers. As the *Araner* eased into the harbor and anchored, John studied the vessels through powerful binoculars. He was certain that these weren't fishing boats—that they were spy ships engaged in some sort of espionage activity. While George Schneiderman took still photographs through a powerful telephoto lens, John studied the ships and took notes on their size and displacement. After gathering all the information he could, he went ashore and studied the crews on liberty, taking copious notes that he later distilled into a detailed report to Ellis Zacharias. I found a copy of the report among my grandfather's papers:

"When entering Guaymas harbor, I thought for a moment I was in the Moji straights. The Japanese shrimp fleet was lying at anchor. Fourteen steam trawlers and two mother ships. The small trawlers looked very much like those used by the British for patrol work during the World War. It is my opinion that they were built in Great Britain. I believe the company that owns them is Nippon Kaisha, the majority of the stock is owned by the Imperial family, the remainder by Matsui.

"The following facts are no doubt familiar to you, but for the sake of accuracy, I humbly submit my impressions:

"The most striking thing concerning the fleet is its personnel. This has me completely baffled. The crews come ashore for liberty in well tailored flannels, worsted and tweed suits, black service shoes smartly polished. The men are above average height, young, good looking, and very alert. All carry themselves with military carriage... They are straight as ramrods, high cheek boned with aquiline features, definitely aristocratic. I cannot compare them to any ratings in our service unless possibly to the University Naval Reserve units such as the one at the University of California. For want of a better word, I would call them Samurai or Military Caste. (During trips to Japan I have studied this type very closely. I am positive they are Naval men.)

"Aboard each trawler three or four young officers were stationed who never went ashore unless in uniform. The uniform, with the exception of the cap, badge and stripe, was the regulation braid-bound Imperial Navy uniform smartly cut and well pressed. The cap and badge, while not regulation, had the rising sun motif.

"I beg to submit the following opinion: It is my belief that the crews and officers of this shrimp fleet belong to the Imperial Navy or Reserve. The crews are not the same class of fisherman that I have seen many times in Japan. It is my opinion that their young men are brought here from time to time to make themselves absolutely familiar with Mexican waters and particularly the Gulf of California ... It is plausible to assume that these men know every bay, cove and inlet in the Gulf of California, a bay which is so full of islands and so close to our Arizona borderline that they constitute a real menace. Although I am not a trained intelligence officer, still my profession is to observe and make distinctions. I have observed well in Japan, and I will stake my professional reputation that these young men are not professional fishermen."

Were they really cadets, Japanese midshipmen? Or was my grandfather fantasizing and reading between the lines? I think he was fantasizing. The report reads like a spy thriller, but it leaves you with the conclusion that he was too aggressively looking for information, too aggressively jumping to conclusions. Certainly he was a man with astute powers of observation, but he was also a dreamer and a storyteller and a man with military ambitions, who was quite capable of exaggerating to suit his own ends.

When the *Araner* left Guaymas she sailed back down to Mazatlán, where John disembarked and returned to Los Angeles by train.

Today it's not really important whether the crews were Japanese fishermen or if my grandfather had stumbled across an espionage ring; for the record, the area was extensively fished by the Japanese during these years. What is important is the fact that he was looking, that he followed a spectacular thirteen months' burst of creativity with a privately financed espionage expedition in Baja California. It suggests the importance of the military to him, and the extent of his ambitions. He spared no expense, no amount of effort. Even more incriminating is the fact that if he was exaggerating (as I suspect he was), then he had no *real* concern for accurate intelligence and was only concerned with his own ends— that is, with advancing himself in the navy.

Back from Mexico in February, John found that the war was the least important thing in most people's minds. The motion-picture industry was enjoying unprecedented prosperity; production was at an all-time high, salaries were skyrocketing, and studio schedules were jammed. People were oblivious to the fact that German divisions were crashing through Europe and that English soldiers were dying on the beaches of Dunkirk. This obtuseness seemed unreal to John, who more than ever was concerned by the darkening international situation and convinced that America was about to enter the war. Not even the news that he had won a second Academy Award for his direction of *The Grapes of Wrath* could shake John out of his preoccupation with the war. When Dudley Nichols wired his congratulations, John wrote back, "Awards for pictures are a trivial thing to be concerned with at times like these."

John's feelings about the war (and his desire to participate in it) went from strong to passionate in March 1940, when he learned that Merian Cooper had walked out on a $100,000-a-year vice-presidency at RKO to help his old friend Claire Chennault organize The Flying Tigers, a quasi-mercenary band of pilots who flew for Chiang Kai-shek. John told Cooper that he was "green with envy," but his feelings went beyond that. Since the Spanish Civil War, he had secretly envied all those who had taken a stand against fascism. While others had contributed time and money, his only contribution had been a vicarious one, through his nephew, Bob Ford. Moreover, he had been late joining the liberal causes of the 1930s. There was a residue of guilt because he had stayed in Hollywood and prospered while others had joined the struggle to save the world. Now here was a chance to get on the bandwagon, to join hands with liberals, intellectuals, and all progressive people, and get involved in the fight against the most destructive force the world had ever known. It was a chance that he wasn't going to let pass by.

In April 1940 John set out to create a naval reserve unit made up of professional film makers. His plan was to recruit the best people he could, mold them into a military unit, present them to the navy as a *fait accompli*, then hope that the brass hats in Washington could see the value of such a unit. John called his outfit the Naval Field Photographic Reserve or, more simply, the Field Photo. Even though he was operating without authorization and without official sanction, the credibility of his name allowed him to sign up some of the biggest names in motion pictures: cinematographers Gregg Toland and Joe August, sound man Sol Halprin, special effects wizard Ray Kellogg, editor Bob Parrish, and writers of the caliber of Garson Kanin and Budd Schulberg.

To mold his cameramen, mixers, editors, and writers into a military unit, to teach them the fundamentals of military discipline,

John recruited actor Jack Pennick an ex-marine and veteran of both the Peking Garrison and World War I, who had worked in scores of his films. To assist Pennick and help him with the paperwork, John recruited a retired Chief Petty Officer named Ben Grotsky. A dark, heavyset native of Brooklyn with an enormous nose, Grotsky was straight out of the pages of Damon Runyon.

Since the Field Photographic was unrecognized, it had no source of supply. To get the equipment they needed to train with—lights, reflectors, Mitchell, Eymo, and DeVry cameras—John cultivated a clerk named Mark Armistead at Faxon Dean's motion-picture supply house, promising him a commission as soon as the navy sanctioned the unit if he would let the Field Photo use Dean's equipment.

From a purely military point of view, the Field Photographic was a joke, a ragtag little band that looked more yacht club than navy. Drills were held on a sound stage at Twentieth Century-Fox; weapons were borrowed from the property department; uniforms came off the racks of the Western Costume Company.

From the very outset, John loved the theatrical side of the military, the pageantry and ceremony, and if nothing else, everybody in the Field Photographic learned all the drills. Mark Armistead remembers: "The Field Photographic wasn't the navy, but it ... was John Ford's navy. Jack hated regulations and paperwork, but he loved all the ceremonies. He did everything his own way. He ran it like it was one of his pictures. At one point he decided that all the officers were going to wear swords and learn the navy sword drill. I was always afraid that he was going to kill someone the way he waved his sword around. He was always saying to me, 'I've got arthritis in my thumb and can't get the damn sword back in the holster.' I'd have to help him with it, and he'd manage to stick me and draw blood every time. Every pair of white gloves I ever owned had blood all over them. One day, during a sword drill, Jack pointed his sword toward the ground and leaned on it. The ground was soft, the sword was sharp, and it went into the ground until he fell over."

But there was also a serious side to the Field Photographic. John was a bonafide Lieutenant Commander, and by 1940 he was well established and widely connected in the Naval Reserve. Moreover, the unit was made up of skilled professionals and included some of Hollywood's most able people in its ranks. The

152

unit was also making technical advances and developing documentary equipment suitable for field use. In the summer of 1940, the Field Photographic developed a lightweight 35-millimeter camera mounted on a rifle stock. It was designed by a camera engineer named Harry Cunningham and called the Cunningham Combat Camera.

For much of 1940 the Field Photographic continued to meet and train without authorization from the navy. John's repeated appeals fell on deaf ears. Then in October, John met a career naval officer with the smooth good looks of a matinee idol, whose name was Jack Bolton. He was a "ring knocker," an Annapolis graduate, who was serving in a liaison role between the navy and the Hollywood studios. Bolton knew how to get things done in the navy. He went to Washington and within a few weeks the unit was officially recognized.

It was a sweet moment for John. For the last eight months he had been laughed at, called a "warmonger" and an "overage sea scout" by his detractors. But now, with the unit recognized, he was able to enjoy the fruits of his labor. In 1941, when the draft began to be felt in Hollywood, "John Ford's navy" was bombarded with applications.

John's "spy missions" in Mexico and his experiences with the Field Photographic fueled the fires of his obsession. More than ever before he sensed the stillness before the gathering storm and heard the ghostly drum taps from distant battlefields. Like a minuteman with a loaded musket over his hearth, he was ready for war. But it would be an injustice to the man to say that he saw only the glory of war and none of the madness. There was a strange duality in him: the war was his middle-age quixotic adventure, yet he dreaded it and saw the insanity of it as well.

In the spring of 1940, a time when most of Hollywood was closing its eyes and ears on reality and concentrating on escapist pulp, John set out to make a film that would remind them of the madness and folly of war. As a vehicle he proposed a remake of *Four Sons*, his silent classic about the destruction of a Bavarian family, and update it to the present war. John managed to sell Darryl Zanuck on the idea, but after some preliminary work had been done on the script, Zanuck canceled it when he learned that MGM begin production on *Mortal Storm*, which was also set in modern Germany.

It was at this point that Dudley Nichols suggested taking four of Eugene O'Neill's one-act plays—*In the Zone, The Moon of the Caribees, Bound East for Cardiff* and *The Long Voyage Home*—and weaving them into a single screenplay. Nichols had long thought that these plays, all set aboard an English freighter during the First World War, were among the playwright's best and most underrated works. Though their emphasis was more personal than political, more about the rootless wandering men aboard a tramp steamer than about the war, John decided to go ahead with them, and he and Nichols went to work shaping them into a screenplay. They updated the plays to the present, emphasized the antiwar theme, and called their screenplay *The Long Voyage Home*.

While working on the script, John and Nichols made a number of trips to Eugene O'Neill's home in Danville, California. Both men, and particularly Nichols, were mesmerized by the crusty playwright. The most eminent playwright in the American theater, he was an icon, a hero to them. As a playwright with a solid string of hits behind him, he enjoyed a freedom and an independence that a Hollywood screenwriter like Nichols could only envy. Nichols' exposure to O'Neill rekindled his long-dormant desire to break away from Hollywood, and he made up his mind that as soon as *The Long Voyage Home* was finished he would return to his native New England, far from the glitter of Hollywood and a world gone mad with war, and write, really write.

Still upset over Zanuck's cancellation of *Four Sons*, John decided not to present *The Long Voyage Home* to him. He told his agent, Harry Wurtzel, to present it instead to Walter Wanger, "one of the few producers in Hollywood," John explained, "who might appreciate a work of this caliber." Wanger was ecstatic about the project and quickly gave John the go-ahead.

John made *The Long Voyage Home*—with Thomas Mitchell, John Wayne, Ian Hunter, Barry Fitzgerald, Mildred Natwick, Ward Bond, and Jack Pennick—in the summer of 1940. He strove, whenever he could, for realism and a sense of being at sea. The set was an iron deck that rang when walked on; and every member of the crew looked like a sailor on a freighter, from the tough, dirty firemen in their sweat rags to the deckhands who reeked of rust chips.

The Long Voyage Home, made under the lengthening shadow of World War II, is a lean and uncharacteristically grim John Ford film reflecting the darker side of his thinking about the war. One of the crew, Yank (played by Ward Bond), dies and is buried at sea. A forlorn and tattered group of seamen huddle on the heaving deck for the burial service. The captain's reading is lost in the wind and the crash of the heavy seas. Then the prayer book is snapped shut, the ship is slowed, and the shrouded body of Yank is dumped over the side. There is one long blast on the ship's whistle. That is all. Within thirty seconds the ship, with its living, goes plowing on.

Though *The Long Voyage Home* was widely hailed by critics and is accepted today as one of John Ford's most distinguished pictures, it was not successful commercially. Perhaps it was too grim; perhaps it reminded people of events that they were trying to forget. It never recovered its costs.

When *The Long Voyage Home* was finished, Dudley Nichols kept the promise he had made to himself: he left Hollywood and returned to Connecticut, where at an isolated farmhouse he settled into a writer's strict routine. Perhaps more than anyone else, Dudley Nichols admired *The Long Voyage Home*. When he saw the final cut, he wrote John a valedictory tribute:

"I got a terrific belt out of the film. I know you've got a magnificent picture, and I think you know it too. Another 16-inch shell into the MGM glamour empire. I agree with Condon, all you need is the phone book and the contents of the office wastebasket— then get on the set. I didn't think any picture could ever be as good as 'Grapes,' but I have a feeling that this one is better...

"I shan't be doing any more Hollywood work for a long time, and it's a fine thing to be connected with a picture like 'Voyage' on going away. It leaves a sweet taste in the mouth. You're a thorny guy, but a grand thorny guy, the O'Neill of the picture makers. Trouble is, that nobody who works with you ever wants to work with anyone else. In that sense, you've deprived me of an easy living. I can no longer sit on my ass with a fat contract and turn out crap. I don't want to be a screenwriter any more—I want to be a writer.

"I want to thank you for many things, you will know what; and not the least is for what I've learned about screenwriting. You're so far ahead of the rest of Hollywood that they'll never catch up. Good luck and God bless you."

Richard Llewellyn's *How Green Was My Valley*, a surprise best-seller in 1939, was a bittersweet novel about the dissolution of a Welsh coal-mining family. A beautifully written novel, it was also the story of how the black coal, wrung so perilously from the earth, darkens the lives of those who dig it and fouls the verdant valley in which they live.

Darryl Zanuck bought *How Green Was My Valley* in February 1940 and first assigned the script to Liam O'Flaherty, who he felt would have a great sympathy for the characters. But the Irish novelist had an even greater sympathy for the politics in Llewellyn's novel—for the battle of labor against capital—and he lost sight of the story of the Morgans. After two months, Zanuck decided that O'Flaherty was on the wrong track and took him off the picture. He next gave it to Ernie Pascal, who toned down the politics but still failed to emphasize the family. In May, Zanuck switched again, this time to Philip Dunne.

A gifted playwright, screenwriter, and director, a smooth, articulate survivor of the Hollywood wars, Dunne lives today in a massive wood and glass cathedral behind an electric gate in Malibu. He recalled for me that when Zanuck assigned him to *How Green Was My Valley*, he told him to forget about the other two screenplays and work directly from the book. "Zanuck didn't want a sociological diatribe or an English *Grapes of Wrath*; he wanted to capture what Llewellyn had captured in the book, a great human drama about the dissolution of a family. Length was no problem. This was going to be a big-budget, four-hour picture, Fox's *Gone With the Wind*. So when I went to work I had everything in it—the family, the strike, love affairs, the mine cave-in, everything."

William Wyler, not John Ford, was originally to have directed *How Green Was My Valley*, and Dunne and Wyler went off to Lake Arrowhead to work on the script together. "The script was tuned exactly to Willy's satisfaction," says Dunne today. "He loved it. He still talks about it. There were wonderful relationships on every level, the strong bond between the brothers, between the father and the sons, the mother and Huw."

After they finished the script, Wyler, Dunne, and Lew Schreiber, the head of casting at Fox, started looking for someone to play young Huw Morgan, the boy through whose eyes the story is told. They looked at tests of dozens of English child actors who had been evacuated to America because of the blitz. They saw dozens of little Eton-collar types, but no one good enough to play Huw. Then one day they saw a knock-kneed, wall-eyed, gangly-looking kid with big hands and feet. Schreiber turned to the projectionist and said,

"OK, kill it. I've seen enough."

"Wait a minute," said Wyler. "I want to see this kid. I think he's terrific."

His name was Roddy McDowall.

Wyler also cast the other principal roles. As Huw's father he chose Donald Crisp; as his mother, Sara Allgood. Walter Pidgeon was set as the minister, Mr. Gruffydd; Maureen O'Hara and English actress Anna Lee were cast as the two Morgan daughters.

How Green Was My Valley was to have begun production in the summer of 1940, but just before shooting began, Fox's New York front office, for various reasons, delayed the picture. Several months went by before it was rescheduled. But by then William Wyler had gone on to another project, and Zanuck decided to assign it to John Ford.

How Green Was My Valley finally began shooting in June 1941 at the Fox Ranch in the Malibu hills, where the studio had built a beautiful replica of a Welsh coal-mining village. Though the picture had been prepared by William Wyler, John was still able to make subtle changes and reshape it in his own way. Richard Llewellyn's story evoked recollections of the rich family life he had known as a child, and he infused it with a special glow of domestic warmth. He modeled the principals on his own family, making Mr. Morgan as proud, strong, and sentimental as his own father had been. Sara Allgood was modeled on his mother, and the three brothers were copied after Patrick, Francis, and Eddie.

John's relationship with Zanuck was unusually harmonious during the making of *How Green Was My Valley*. Zanuck, who had battled his New York bosses to make the picture, wrote John daily memos that were almost euphoric in their praise of the film: "I have every confidence that this will be one of the greatest pictures of the year, and if it keeps up like it is going, it will be the greatest directorial job you have ever turned in . . . Don't let anything stop you. This is going to be a masterpiece, not only in a classical sense, but a masterpiece of sure-fire commercial entertainment."

Philip Dunne looks back on *How Green Was My Valley* with a great deal of sentiment for the Hollywood that was, but the two other principals with whom I have talked, Roddy McDowall and Anna Lee, remember the film in even more personal terms.

"I was twelve years old when we made *How Green Was My Valley*," McDowall told me, "much older than the child I played. I had already made about twenty films in England, and I wasn't naive. I knew what was going on. What stands out in my mind is that I never remember being directed. It all just happened. Ford played me like a harp.

"I remember him as very dear and very gentle. He was like a friend who never appeared ruffled. He was an authority figure, but in the best possible sense of the word.

"It was the easiest film I ever worked on, a total delight. Ford created an atmosphere that was unique. He forged a unique sense of family with all of us. Everyone who worked on *How Green Was My Valley* became very emotionally connected to one another. I don't say this through the pink haze of childhood recollection. I still see a number of people who worked on that film, and I see the picture quite often."

Anna Lee says today that when John took over from William Wyler, she was afraid that he would replace her because she was English. To get on his good side she invented a fictitious Irish grandfather whom she called Thomas Michael O'Connell: "When I met Pappy, I immediately started talking about my grandfather, and we got along very well. He called me 'Limey.'

"John Ford was perhaps the most unusual man, and certainly the most unusual director, I had ever met in my life. He had a clairvoyance, an almost mystical way of manipulating your emotions that's really hard to describe. He could put you in almost any state of mind he wanted to. He used to take his scarf and tie it around my waist or put it in my hand for a good-luck talisman, and it would change my mood entirely. He'd get you in a corner and start talking—not about the scene—but about something entirely different—and instinctively you knew he was trying to tell you something. It was like magic; it was as if there was some kind of thought transference. That's the only way I can describe it."

Because of an incident that occurred during the filming of *How Green Was My Valley*, Anna Lee became of very special interest and concern to John. Unbeknownst to him, Anna was pregnant when the picture began shooting. Midway through it she had a scene in which she learns that her husband has been killed in a mine; she walks to her cottage, calls out his name, then stumbles down a flight of stairs. When John shot the scene he told her it was an easy fall, that she didn't need a double. Anna went ahead and did it but landed hard and started to bleed. She was rushed to a nearby hospital and had a miscarriage. John was tremendously upset. For the rest of his life he would blame himself for this accident.

John completed *How Green Was My Valley* in August 1941. Edited and prepared for release by Zanuck, the film premiered at New York's Rivoli Theater in late October 1941, a gala affair complete with sky-sweeping searchlights, disrupted traffic, dignitaries, movie stars, and a gawking public. *How Green Was My Valley* went on to become a very successful picture on every level, critically, commercially, and artistically. Opening on the eve of America's entry into World War II, it was greatly helped by a flood of pro-British sentiment.

Though *How Green Was My Valley* was a studio "assembly line" project that had been prepared by William Wyler and edited by Darryl Zanuck, it was John Ford who gave it its emotional flavor, its feeling for family, its domestic warmth. Anna Lee says, "Pappy always told me that this was his favorite film because it was about a family and we were all like a family." He filled it with the same love for humanity that he had lavished on the Joads in *The Grapes of Wrath* and on the sailors in *The Long Voyage Home*.

Philip Dunne, Roddy McDowall, and Anna Lee were all deeply touched by this film. All three spoke of a marvelous chemistry that developed within the company and of an almost reverential feeling for John. Deep and lasting friendships were formed on the set. For years afterward the women held an annual party and called themselves "the women of the green valley." Maureen O'Hara named her daughter Bronwyn after Anna Lee's character. Many of the principals still see each other socially. Today, thirty-seven years after it was made, the spirit of *How Green Was My Valley* is kept alive by those it touched.

13

The
Battle
of
Midway

On September 11, 1941, immediately after he had finished *How Green Was My Valley*, recently promoted Commander John Ford, U.S.N.R., was ordered to report to Washington, D.C. Without fanfare or publicity and with only Jack Bolton to see him off, he boarded the Union Pacific Streamliner and headed east. As he zipped across the country, past high desert rangelands and the dim lights of small western towns, John sat in his compartment and chewed on a cigar. He was quiet and introspective, lost within himself. In Green River, Wyoming, a porter entered his car with a sudden rush of cold and noise and brought John a telegram on a silver tray. It was from Darryl Zanuck, who had just shown a rough cut of *How Green Was My Valley* to the New York front office. "Picture went over marvelously. Everybody crazy about it," the telegram read.

As John studied the telegram he asked himself why in God's name he was going into the navy. Why was he giving up money, career, security, family, and freedom for the iron regimen of the military? Why was he trading success, prestige, and glamour for a khaki work shirt with a maple leaf on the collar? Was he being quixotic? A fool? Was he an old man playing a young man's game? As he sat back in his chair, John knew one thing: the years ahead were going to bring great changes in his life.

As the train rattled east, past the Rockies and into the midwestern grain lands, John mulled over the events in his life that were taking him away from his lucrative, rewarding life in Hollywood and launching him on this new, uncertain adventure. In a way, this was not unlike his 1932 trip to the Far East with George O'Brien. There was a Byronic poet in him who needed to experience life firsthand, who craved experience for its own sake. He had done everything there was to do in the world of motion pictures; he had scaled every peak, earned fame and fortune and heard the world applaud as he took his bows. The very best that lay in store for him was more of the same—more pictures, more awards, more money. He wanted a change, for its own sake. He wanted to shake up his life, to move on to new conquests, new adventures. John had turned forty-six that year. He was old enough to know that he wasn't immortal but still young enough to take bold steps and change his life.

When John arrived in Washington, he found the city hot, sticky, and seething with office seekers and entrepreneurs. Every huckster with a tool kit or a machine shop was trying to land a government contract. Rooms were at a premium, and apartments were out of the question. It took John's best efforts at cajoling, browbeating, and arm twisting, to land a fourteen-by-eight-foot broom closet in a corner of the Carlton Hotel—room number 501. It had a narrow plank of a bed, one dusty shelf, one dirty window with crude wavy glass that distorted an already distorted Washington. For the next four years this room would be home.

Almost immediately John's men from the Field Photographic—Mark Armistead, Gregg Toland, Ray Kellogg, Jack Pennick, Ben Grotsky, Bob Parrish, and Carl Marquard—followed him to Washington. With a lot of help from Grotsky and Pennick, his two "major domos," John settled into the routine of being a unit commander, arranging for quarters and mess facilities, uniforms and equipment, requisitions, triplicate, and governmentese. The Field Photographic set up shop in the south wing of the Department of Agriculture Building, a long, low government monolith on the corner of 25th and E streets. They built a lab and studio in the basement.

The Field Photographic had been ordered to Washington under circumstances that John had never expected: the unit had been scooped up intact not by the navy but by one of the most dynamic, mysterious, and visionary men in the first half of the twentieth century—William J. "Wild Bill" Donovan. The head of a powerful Wall Street law firm and the winner of a Congressional Medal of Honor in World War I, Donovan had recently been appointed Coordinator of Information by President Roosevelt and had been given orders to reorganize and enlarge his unit into the Office of Strategic Services—the O.S.S.

Donovan was recruiting men from all walks of life, from ten-goal polo players and America's Cup yachtsmen to professors and academicians, diplomats and bankers. He was bringing some of the ablest men in America—the flower of the American Establishment—into the O.S.S. The roster of names he recruited reads like a "Who's Who" of postwar America: David Bruce, the distinguished diplomat; John W. Gardner, later Secretary of Health, Education and Welfare, and head of Common Cause; Arthur Goldberg, later Supreme Court Justice and ambassador to the United Nations; Arthur Schlesinger, Jr., the distinguished historian; Allen Dulles and Richard Helms, future heads of the Central Intelligence

Agency (which was an outgrowth of the wartime O.S.S.). Believing that film could be an effective tool for propaganda and intelligence gathering, Donovan snatched up John Ford and his Field Photographic unit from under the navy's nose.

To John, being part of the O.S.S. was a great honor. As a navy unit assigned to the O.S.S., the Field Photographic was outside the navy's regular chain of command: John was accountable only to Donovan and, beyond that, to the President himself. Being part of Donovan's new "super agency" helped instill a pride, an *esprit de corps*, in the Field Photo that it might not have otherwise achieved. John, who for years had operated on the fringes of naval intelligence with his privately financed "spy missions" in Baja California, was ecstatic at being so close to the top. He began telling Mark Armistead, Ray Kellogg, and others that, "We're going to be involved with a hell of a lot more than photography." This was shaping up as a grand adventure, and he was having the time of his life.

Most eager to advance his fortunes in the O.S.S., John never hesitated to use his status as a Hollywood celebrity to achieve his own ends. Bob Parrish once recalled that one of John's favorite tricks was to invite O.S.S. and navy bigwigs to screenings of his recent films, *Stagecoach, Young Mr. Lincoln, Drums Along the Mohawk*, and *The Grapes of Wrath*. Before each film began he would announce that he'd been wanting to see this picture himself because "I never did get to see the final cut." This, of course, was pure fabrication, but Ford liked to project the image of a freewheeling Irishman who could effortlessly knock out one great film after another. When the picture was over and the lights came on, he would brush an invisible tear aside and announce that "the picture came out a lot better than I had thought." Says Parrish, "For Ford, the O.S.S. was no different from Twentieth Century-Fox. You manipulated whom you had to, and if you didn't get what you wanted through channels, you simply went around them. He had no more respect for bureaucrats and professional military types than he had for producers or production managers back home."

Not only was the Field Photographic outside the military chain of command, but part of its mission was to monitor the effectiveness of army and navy units. In November 1941, Donovan gave the Field Photographic its first mission. He ordered John to make a film report on the condition of the Atlantic fleet, which was then escorting convoys between the U.S. mainland and Iceland and fighting an undeclared war against German U-boats. The film was made by Ray Kellogg. A straight factual accounting, it was shown by Donovan to the President.

Though it was part of the O.S.S., the Field Fhotographic was still "John Ford's navy," and its commander's style soon became famous in Washington. Columnist Jerry Klutz of the *Washington Post* once caught John conducting training exercises while wearing "a tropical khaki army shirt and trousers [and] a tan Hollywood pullover sweater with the insignia of an Army Lieutenant Colonel hung from one collar point. He was tieless and hatless. His friends attributed his attire to the 'Hollywood influence.'"

Everyone alive at the time remembers where they were on December 7, 1941. John was enjoying a Sunday afternoon with Mary and their daughter, Barbara, who had come East, and Merian Cooper, who had left Chennault's command in China and was awaiting reassignment to a regular Air Force unit. They were at the two-hundred-year-old Alexandria, Virginia, home of Admiral and Mrs. William Pickens. At two o'clock in the afternoon they were seated at the dinner table when the phone rang and was answered by the Pickens' maid.

"It's for you, Admiral," she said. "It's the War Department."

"Tell them I'm at dinner."

"I did, but they said it's urgent."

Pickens took the phone and listened silently. John could see the blood drain from his face. He hung up the receiver and said,

"There's been an attack on Pearl Harbor by the Japanese. We are now at war." Nobody could think of anything to reply. Finally, Admiral Pickens' wife, Darrielle, got up and showed them a hole where a musket ball had gone through the wall during the Revolutionary War. "I never let them plaster over that hole," she said.

As the awful details of Pearl Harbor came in, America was grieved, shocked, and scared. In the Far East the Japanese were on the march, invading Thailand, the Malay Peninsula, Hong Kong, Borneo, and the Philippines. As the year drew to a close, the news kept getting worse: Wake Island, Guam, the Borneo oil fields. By Christmas the Japanese had made seventeen amphibious landings

165

on the Philippines, and on December 27, General Douglas Mac-Arthur abandoned Manila and withdrew his army to the Bataan Peninsula. When Manila fell to the Japanese, John thought back nostalgically to his 1932 and 1933 trips there. He had a mental picture of the Army-Navy Club being looted by Japanese troops, and of the Manila Hotel being sacked and burned. (Later he would learn that his niece Cecile and her husband, Larry DePrita, still manager of Fox's Manila film exchange, had been captured by the Japanese and interned at Santo Thomas Prison.)

In those first days of the war, nobody knew where the Japanese might strike next, and there was concern that they might try to knock out the Panama Canal, a vital waterway in a two-ocean war. Donovan ordered John to fly to Panama and, without reporting to the military brass, make a film revealing the state of the canal's defenses that he could show the President. On December 30, John and two Field Photographic cameramen, Al Jolkes and Al Zeigler, flew to the Canal Zone, where over the New Year's holiday they photographed the area's key installations.

When John returned to Washington he assembled the film with Bob Parrish, wrote the narration, and spoke it himself. John's script—personal, emotional, and theatrical in tone—concentrated on the men who manned the canal's defenses. The *Canal Report*, as the film was called, was shown to President Roosevelt a few days after the New Year. According to Bob Parrish, who attended the screening, Roosevelt was "very pleased not only with the film, but with the ability of the O.S.S. to cut through red tape and give him accurate reports on what was really going on. No army or navy unit could have made such a report. By the time it got through channels, all the flaws in the canal's defenses would have been covered up. But Ford was a pragmatist who just went ahead and did things without worrying about the consequences."

The year 1941, one of upheaval and change, ended on a sweet note for John. After he returned from Panama he received a wire from Leo Mishkin, chairman of the New York Critics Committee, informing him that he had won the New York Film Critics' Award for his direction of *How Green Was My Valley*. Mishkin invited him to attend a small dinner on January 10 in honor of the award winners, to be held at Leone's Restaurant in New York.

John attended the dinner, accepted the critics' award, then traveled up to Maine for a brief reunion with his son, Pat, then a senior at the University of Maine at Orono. Having just been accepted into the navy's Officer Candidate Program, Pat would soon be reporting for active duty.

Pleased by the success of the Atlantic fleet and Panama Canal films, Bill Donovan next ordered the Field Photographic to make a top-secret report on the Pearl Harbor attack. He wanted a film that would tell the story of the attack and try to determine whose fault the debacle there was. It was a ticklish assignment. The navy didn't want Donovan's collection of eggheads and spies snooping around Pearl Harbor and asking embarrassing questions. Secretary of War Henry Stimson had personally warned Donovan that any motion picture purporting to tell the story of Pearl Harbor had to be approved by him before it could be released. But Donovan was undeterred and ordered the Field Photographic to go ahead with the project. John put Gregg Toland in charge of it; the veteran cinematographer had long wanted to direct, and John saw this as a good opportunity for him to do so.

In January 1942, Toland and Ray Kellogg flew to Pearl Harbor and went to work. Toland assembled film of the actual attack that had been shot by navy photographers, as well as footage of the navy's salvage operations. Kellogg then restaged the attack with miniatures. Toland approached the project with great enthusiasm, and forged ahead with complete disregard for military protocol. But when he should have been working circumspect and quietly (as John had done in Panama), Toland was brash and arrogant, operating with little regard for political consequences.

In mid-February John flew to Pearl Harbor to see how Toland was progressing. He had heard rumblings that the cinematographer was stepping on a lot of toes, and he warned him to be careful, "to be inky" and not to let anyone know what he was up to. But John's warnings fell on deaf ears. Toland forged arrogantly ahead.

While John was at Pearl Harbor, he got wind of the Doolittle raid—the scheme whereby Army B-25s under the command of Colonel Jimmy Doolittle would be launched from the aircraft carriers *Enterprise* and *Hornet*, bomb the Japanese home islands, then fly on to mainland China. Leaving the Pearl Harbor project in Toland's hands, John and several photographers wangled their way into joining the fleet and set off to cover the attack. John himself was aboard the flagship cruiser, the U.S.S. *Salt Lake City*.

On the morning of April 14, 1942, while plowing west through heavy weather, the *Salt Lake City*'s wireless equipment monitored the Academy Awards broadcast from Hollywood, and John learned that he had won his third Academy Award for his direction of *How Green Was My Valley*. His feelings were a mixture of pride that he was off in the service and "too busy" to accept the award, and nostalgia for the Hollywood he had left behind. Perhaps sensing his mood, the officers of the *Salt Lake City* made up a flag, a gold likeness of the Oscar on a blue field, in honor of the Academy Award-winner in their midst. It flew from the masthead throughout the raid.

In the end, John paid a high price for going on the Doolittle raid. When he returned to Pearl Harbor he learned that the navy had confiscated Gregg Toland's film and locked it away in a vault. It was a bitter blow to John, but an even bigger blow to Toland. A volatile and high-strung man, he went into a deep depression, then asked to be sent overseas as far from Washington as he could get. John sent him to head up the Field Photographic station in Rio de Janeiro.

Washington was hot and muggy, with unseasonable thundershowers, when, in May 1942, John returned from the Doolittle raid. After a month of "the clean life" at sea, the city seemed noisy, crowded, and rushed. His tiny room at the Carleton Hotel seemed a sweatbox.

The navy's confiscation of the Pearl Harbor film had been a bitter blow to the entire Field Photographic. Morale, which had been very high only a few months before, was suddenly very low. John's first order of business was to get his men busy on other projects and get their minds off the film. Besides posting Gregg Toland to Rio de Janeiro, he sent Mark Armistead and Ben Grotsky to open a branch office in London and Lieutenant Guy Bolte to open one in New Delhi, India.

John's own stay in Washington was to be short-lived. After only a few days back in the capital he was told by Bill Donovan that something very big and very hush-hush was going on out in the Pacific. Navy cryptographers, working under John's old friend Ellis Zacharias, had scored a major intelligence coup: they had broken the Japanese code system and learned that Admiral Yamamoto was trying to provoke the remains of the American Pacific fleet into a major battle at Midway Island, a tiny atoll 1,100 miles northwest of Pearl Harbor. Admiral Nimitz was reinforcing Midway with every available plane and deploying the aircraft carriers *Enterprise*, *Hornet*, and *Yorktown*. John was conversant enough with military strategy to realize that this just might be the most important battle of the war, perhaps even the turning point, and after only a few days in Washington he turned around and headed back out to the Pacific. If there was going to be a showdown battle at Midway, he wanted to be there to photograph it.

Hopscotching across the country on a military DC-3, John arrived in San Francisco on May 14. There he waited at Treasure Island Naval Station for sea transportation to Pearl Harbor. While laying over in San Francisco, John called on Eugene O'Neill and enjoyed a warm reunion with the playwright at the Officers' Club at Treasure Island. O'Neill told John that *The Long Voyage Home* was the best film that had ever been made from his work. Moved to the point of tears, John said, "If there is any single thing that explains either of us, it's that we're Irish." A few days later John was on board a destroyer on his way to Pearl Harbor. He spent the four-day passage reading, sleeping, and pacing the wet decks, wondering what lay ahead at Midway.

It had been less than two weeks since John had last passed through Pearl Harbor, but even in that brief period the change in the big Pacific base was remarkable: new buildings, repair sheds, and dry docks were going up everywhere. Salvage operations were underway, the hulks around Ford Island were being raised, and many ships thought to have been destroyed were already back in service. John was more than a little awed by the way the navy had bounced back from the attack.

A day after arriving in Honolulu, he was in a navy patrol plane on his way to Midway. With him was photographer's mate Jack MacKenzie, a red-haired, freckled, twenty-year-old whose father was a veteran cinematographer at Columbia Pictures. After a four-hour flight they reached Midway, and as they circled overhead John could see the island's deep blue water, brightly colored reefs, and white sand beaches. From the air, it was obvious that Midway was braced for a fight. Sandbags were stacked everywhere, and all available space around the airfield was jammed with navy and marine fighters, over which mechanics and ground crews swarmed like honeybees. On landing, John and MacKenzie found the island's defenders moving with a sense of urgency and purpose.

A few days later, on the morning of June 3, a patrol plane from Midway spotted the Japanese fleet. Last-minute fortifications were dug and ammunition was handed out. John and Jack MacKenzie got ready to photograph the attack. John took a position in the airfield control tower and put the young photographer's mate on the island's generator plant, telling MacKenzie not to worry about photographing airplanes. "Photograph faces. We can always fake combat footage later."

At dawn on June 4, the Japanese attacked. Wave after wave of planes bombed and strafed the island in a holocaust of explosions, concussions, and flying debris. John saw one enemy plane coming up the runway toward him, two lines of holes popping up in the asphalt 100 yards in front of it. The pilot made a sharp banking turn around the tower, and, as he did so, John could see his face behind the canopy only a few yards away. He gave John a toothy grin, then went skidding back down the runway. Never in John's life had his adrenaline pumped so hard. Never had he experienced anything so terrifying, or so intoxicating. Several planes attacked the control tower, stitching the wooden structure with machine-gun fire. Wood splinters and ricochets were everywhere. John received a grazing wound in his left forearm. It felt hot, and at first John thought he had burned himself until he looked down and saw blood on his arm.

John continued to photograph the attack. Even under fire his sense of theater remained intact, as he photographed the faces of the men around him with their expressions of intense excitement, terror, and fear; time stands still in these pictures. He photographed one scene in which a group of marines raised the flag against a background of smoke and fire. The shot was so dramatic, looked so perfectly staged, that in the narration John would feel compelled to write, "This actually happened."

The battle of Midway, fought on June 4, 1942, was a great victory for the United States and the end of the defensive phase of the war in the Pacific. The initial attack on Midway was only a small part of the actual battle; most of it was fought by carrier-based aircraft hundreds of miles from the island. After the first raid, American dive bombers caught three Japanese carriers rearming and refueling their planes and sank them. Later, planes from the *Enterprise* sank a fourth enemy carrier and Admiral Yamamoto ordered a general retreat.

John and young MacKenzie spent the days after June 4 photographing the battle's aftermath: fires and wreckage and bodies of young soldiers being lifted into ambulances; flyers returning and climbing out of their planes; a memorial service beside a bomb crater; a line of PT boats going out through iridescent blue water carrying the flag-draped coffins of the navy's dead; a shot of the President's son, Marine Corps Major Jimmy Roosevelt, who had served at Midway, paying homage to the marine dead.

Quietly and without fanfare John gathered up his film and slipped back to Pearl Harbor and boarded a transport ship for the mainland. Gregg Toland's problems with the Pearl Harbor film were still very much on his mind. Back in Los Angeles, John had a rush print of the film made. Rumors were flying through Hollywood that he had somehow been involved at Midway, and his presence in the film capital (aided by the fact that he had been wounded) was attracting a great deal of attention. The *Hollywood Reporter* picked up the story and on June 18 carried the headline, "Ford Filmed Battle of Midway." The feature story said that "the director had been wounded as he made his greatest film aided by a Hollywood boy." But John wasn't looking for publicity—he was trying to avoid it; and as soon as he had his film back from the lab he wrote "Priority One" orders, signed Bill Donovan's name to them, and commandeered a seat on the first civilian airliner for Washington.

Back at the Field Photographic's headquarters, John immediately went to work breaking down the Midway film with editor Bob Parrish. "I don't want you to work here in Washington," he told Parrish. "As soon as the brass gets wind of this they'll assign nine or ten high-ranking public relations men to supervise it. It'll be like having nine or ten producers on a picture. The four services will start bickering over it, and the goddamn thing will get so bogged down in red tape that we'll never get it released. I want you to get on a plane and take this film to Hollywood and work on it there."

"Should I report to the navy barracks there?" asked Parrish.

"No," said John. "Report to your mother."

"What about orders?"

"Fuck 'em. Just get going."

Parrish flew home to California without orders and began assembling the film. He lived at home, wore civilian clothes, and worked on the Fox lot. But he was convinced that the FBI, Naval Intelligence, and the Shore Patrol were right behind him and that he was going to wind up in Leavenworth. When Parrish had the film assembled, John had him show it to Dudley Nichols, who wrote a narration. When it was ready John flew out to California. Nichols had written a beautiful piece; it was intense, patriotic, and emotional, but he had gotten carried away and had overwritten it. When John saw his material, he picked up the phone and called Jim McGuinness at MGM.

"Seamus, what are you doing?" he asked.

"Well, right now I'm producing five pictures."

"Oh," said John. "Then you've got plenty of time to do a little something for the war effort. It'll do your character some good. Get over to Fox right away, will you? I need your help on something."

McGuinness arrived a half hour later and John screened the film for him.

"Will you write me something?" he asked.

"Sure, but I'll have to think about it," answered McGuinness.

"Well, don't think too long. There's a war on, and it's about this war. Can you give me something by this afternoon?"

"What kind of approach do you want to take?" McGuinness wanted to know.

"Give me something that will interest the mothers of America."

McGuinness sat down and rewrote Nichols' narration, making it more personal and emotional. In the footage of the battle's aftermath there was a scene in which two men, obviously suffering from exposure, are being helped into an ambulance, which then whisks them away. Over this McGuinness wrote: "Get those boys to a hospital, please do! Quickly! Get them to clean cots and cool sheets! Get them to doctors and medicine and nurses' soft hands. Hurry, please!"

John took McGuinness' material and went onto the set of *The Ox Bow Incident*, which was then in production. He gathered up Henry Fonda, Jane Darwell, Donald Crisp, and Irving Pichel and took them to a sound-recording booth. With Bob Parrish operating

172

the sound equipment, John fed them their lines and they recorded the script.

By this time John's presence in Hollywood was starting to attract a lot of attention. The navy's Public Information Office was becoming very nosy. Worried that they might be closing in, John had Parrish move to an obscure lab in the San Fernando Valley and had him lay in the voices and sound effects there.

"If anybody from the navy comes snooping around and asks what you are doing, tell 'em it's none of their business."

"But suppose they're officers?" protested Parrish.

"If they're officers, they'll be no problem. They'd never expect an enlisted man with no orders to be working on a classified project. If anybody knocks on your door, just tell 'em to go fuck off."

"What if they get the Shore Patrol?"

"The Shore Patrol won't bother you if you stay in the cutting room where you belong."

As they were putting the final touches on the film, John and Parrish had intense arguments over it. Parrish thought that the personalized narration and the conversations were too maudlin. John listened to his arguments, then said, "You have a mother, don't you?"

"Of course."

"Well, how do you think she'd feel if she saw *you* in that ambulance?"

With their completed film, John and Parrish flew back to Washington, as Parrish says, "one step ahead of the Shore Patrol." There, John showed the film to Donovan, who was so impressed that he arranged to have it screened at the White House. But John wasn't taking any chances. He was going to make *sure* that Roosevelt paid attention to this film. On the day of the screening he handed Parrish the clip of the President's son Jimmy that he had taken at Midway. "Put this in the memorial service sequence near the end of the picture," he told him.

"We've already got a composite print. If I put this in, it'll cause a bump in the sound track and the music will go silent while his picture is on."

John thought for a minute. "Good," he said, "that'll help get the audience's attention."

John and Donovan took the film to the White House to run for the President. Mrs. Roosevelt, Harry Hopkins, and Admiral Leahy, Roosevelt's senior naval aide, were all there. Roosevelt was talking and joking with Harry Hopkins all through the picture and not really paying any attention. Then they got to the funeral sequence where "My Country 'Tis of Thee" is played during the burial services. Irving Pichel intones, "We buried our heroic dead. The last salute for their comrades from their officers, Captain Simar of the Navy, Colonel Shannon of the Army, and Jimmy Roosevelt of the Marine Corps." The President froze when his son's picture came on. He became perfectly silent and remained so until the end of the film. When it was over and the lights came on, Roosevelt was ashen, and Eleanor was crying. Finally FDR turned to Admiral Leahy and said,

"I want every mother in America to see this picture."

Bob Parrish then took the negative to Technicolor in Hollywood and had 500 prints made. They were turned over to Twentieth Century-Fox, which handled the distribution. Within a month, *The Battle of Midway* was playing throughout the country.

John ordered Bob Parrish to attend the first public screening at Radio City Music Hall in New York. "My official assignment," Parrish recalls today, "was to attend the running in New York and report to Ford, who by this time had gone on to London. On reflection, there have been so many changes in combat film. It's so much more realistic now, and it's not unusual to see people get shot, particularly after Vietnam. But *The Battle of Midway* was the first film of its kind. It was a stunning, amazing thing to see. At Radio City women screamed, people cried, and the ushers had to take them out. And it was all over the material that we had fought about, the stuff I thought was too maudlin, like when Jane Darwell says, 'Get those boys to the hospital, please do! Quickly!'

"The people, they just went crazy."

14

Ford
of the O.S.S.

Immediately after the screening of *The Battle of Midway* for the President, John took off for London in a Pan American flying boat. Traveling with him was Jack Pennick, who by the summer of 1942 had become his unofficial aide. In deference to the neutrality of Ireland, where they were to change planes, they traveled in civilian clothes. After a long, sleepless flight they touched down on the Shannon River, and John celebrated a brief homecoming: while most of the passengers sat down to a full Irish breakfast at Foynes, he opted instead for a little "liquid repast" before boarding the connecting flight to London. During the layover John made jokes about Irish neutrality. "There are only two neutral countries in all of Europe," he said. "The peace-loving Irish and those cowardly Swedes."

In London they checked into Claridge's, which, despite three years of war, bombing, and blitz, still managed to keep its sense of luxurious comfort. The city was muggy and hot, but the trees in Hyde Park were in fresh leaf, and there was the pleasant smell of English greensward in the air. John settled into his room with its wide foyer, tiled bath, and rug-sized bath towels.

John's room at Claridges soon became a mecca for new acquaintances and old friends. Sitting propped up in his bed, he received a string of guests and enjoyed boisterous reunions with Mark Armistead, Ray Kellogg, Brian Desmund-Hurst, David Bruce, and his old boss from Twentieth Century-Fox, Darryl Zanuck. When John saw Zanuck, who was now a colonel in the Signal Corps, he quipped, "If I ever get to heaven you'll be standing there under a gate that says 'Produced by Darryl F. Zanuck.'"

John's official mission in England was to organize Field Photographic camera crews to cover the invasion of North Africa—"Operation Torch"—which was coming that fall. All the film they shot was to be turned over to Zanuck for distribution into newsfilm pools. Working through the summer, John divided his men into teams and sent them to commando schools in Scotland for special training and conditioning.

"Operation Torch" was one of the most complex military operations ever undertaken. It began at dawn on November 8, when a combined British and American task force landed troops at Oran, Algiers, and Casablanca; Field Photographic camera crews covered all three landings. John himself waited in Gibraltar during the first phase of the invasion, but he was itching to get to the front

176

lines and see action. On November 14, he left for Algiers with Jack Pennick and photographer's mate Robert Johannes, a Hollywood cameraman and veteran of the original "unauthorized" Field Photographic. There they commandeered a jeep and attached themselves to "D" Company, 13th Armored Regiment, 1st Armored Division, which was commanded by Captain J. E. Simmerman of Richmond, Virginia. They were loaded onto a British transport ship, taken up the Tunisian coast, and put ashore.

After the Tunisian landing, the 13th Armored Regiment proceeded to Bone, where John was reunited with Darryl Zanuck. Following the war in a commandeered Chevrolet coupe, Zanuck had a Thompson submachine gun, a half dozen grenades, two .45 automatics, and a bandolier of ammunition across his chest; he was so heavily armed that he could hardly move.

Though the studio chief and John spent several days together, John was less than enthusiastic about the reunion with his old boss. Zanuck was making his own film, a documentary that would eventually be called *At the Front*, and was keeping a diary which he planned to publish. John was upset about Zanuck's "private projects." While his own work had to remain anonymous and disappear into news-film pools, Zanuck was free to write a book publicizing his exploits as a "combat soldier." John had been willing to assume the same risks and hardships as the men of "D" Company, but Zanuck came and went as he pleased, traveling in the comparative luxury of a civilian car. Moreover, Captain Simmerman and the men of "D" Company quickly became contemptuous of Zanuck, whom they called "the littlest colonel," and John was afraid that they would start to resent him as well.

Fortunately, the monotony of life in the field didn't sit well with Zanuck, and after a few days with "D" Company he returned to the rear echelons. John was glad to see him go.

A few days later, at a place called Soul El Arba, Tunisia, John had a personal encounter with the enemy. German dive bombers were everywhere that day, attacking everything that moved, and Captain Simmerman sought refuge for his armored company in a grove of eucalyptus trees. But they were spotted and attacked. John, Pennick, and Robert Johannes huddled in a foxhole; explosions, concussions, and flying debris were everywhere. Then a flight of British Spitfires arrived on the scene and took on the dive bombers, John watching and photographing a fierce dogfight right over his head. He saw a Spitfire shoot down a German JU-88 and a tiny speck emerge from the German plane. Quickly a parachute trailed out and filled.

"Come on! Let's take him prisoner," John said. He and his two men jumped into their jeep and lurched across ditches and gullies to where the German airman had landed. When they got to him, he threw up his hands and surrendered. The prisoner, who spoke some English, told them that he was the bombardier and that he was the only one of four crewmen who had gotten out. He asked John to take him to where the plane had crashed, which was about a mile away, to see if any of the others had survived. John said he would.

When they got to the plane, they found a jagged, burning wreck. Picking through the debris, they found the charred bodies of the crew. The German bombardier was very upset, explaining that these had been his only friends. Before they left the crash site, a Free French lieutenant drove up and claimed jurisdiction over the prisoner. John turned the German over to him, and the Frenchman immediately began slapping him about while interrogating him. "OK, that's enough," said John. "The prisoner stays with us." The Frenchman exploded into a tirade of epithets in English and French, but the prisoner stayed with John and was turned over to Captain Simmerman. The German airman never knew that the man who had captured and been so kind to him was Hollywood's greatest director.

After six weeks in the field John, Jack Pennick, and Robert Johannes flew to Gibraltar, where on December 19 they reported aboard the destroyer U.S.S. *Samuel Chase* and sailed for the United States the next day. They celebrated Christmas with a pint of Scotch that Pennick had smuggled aboard, docked in Norfolk, Virginia, on New Year's Eve, and were driven to Washington that evening.

Between January 1943 and the following August, John worked in Washington attending to the administrative details of the Field Photographic and fighting what he called "the paper war." During this period he became very adept not just at the "paper war" but at the entire Washington game. Although he liked to think of himself as a brash, crusty, two-fisted naval officer in the Bull Halsey mold, he was, in fact, quite capable of being a smooth Washington manipulator who could skillfully use his Hollywood name and celebrity status to advantage. Like Zanuck, he bragged shamelessly about his exploits as a "combat soldier." (He once told Garson Kanin that he had filmed *The Battle of Midway* from the airport control tower because he was "too shot up to move.")

John cultivated important contacts at all levels of government—senators, congressmen, military officers, and high-ranking bureaucrats. In March 1943, Jimmy Roosevelt, who had inadvertently played an important part in getting *The Battle of Midway* released, was awarded the Navy Cross. John sent him a congratulatory letter:

"Been thinking a lot about you and the wonderful job you are doing. Stay in there and pitch fella. Was especially delighted about your Navy Cross. I hear from numerous Marine files that not only did you deserve it, but you should have gotten a hell of a lot more. Good work!

"Things by me are not so good. With 32 of my boys, I covered the North African landing. I personally covered the landing at Bone which was really tough. From Bone we went to Tunisia. We were under dive, horizontal, bombing, artillery, and machine gun fire twenty-four hours a day for six weeks and subsisted on tea and English biscuits. Was I hungry! Lost 32 pounds, but I got my outfit out with minor casualties. The Navy threw a Purple Heart at me so now I guess I'll have to buy a uniform, as all my personal gear was blown up..."

When Darryl Zanuck returned to the States, his projects in North Africa, the film *At the Front*, and the book called *Tunis Expedition*, backfired on him. The press and Harry Truman's Senate War Investigating Committee took after him and other "Hollywood Colonels" who they claimed, had obtained commissions based on grounds other than military merit. Zanuck in particular was singled out, and political pressure eventually forced him to go on inactive status.

From Washington, John followed Zanuck's troubles closely. To make sure that the same thing didn't happen to him, he went to great lengths to authenticate his own service record. He had Robert Johannes detail his experiences in North Africa, including the capture of the German airman, and arranged to have all the data entered into his records. Though most of the Field Photographic's work had little to do with national security, John made it a point to classify everything so he could keep it out of the hands of a potentially hostile press.

But John was able to enjoy some of the fruits of his labor. *The Battle of Midway* had enjoyed a phenomenal reception while he had been in North Africa, and in March 1943 the film was awarded an Academy Award as the best documentary of 1942.

This was a moment of sweet triumph for John. It was his fourth Oscar and his third in three years, after *The Grapes of Wrath* in 1940 and *How Green Was My Valley* in 1941. He was not only combining his two great ambitions—the military and motion pictures—but he was riding a phenomenal string of successes that even the war hadn't been able to stop. The Academy Award for *The Battle of Midway* was another badge of the legitimacy of the Field Photographic, and helped to place the unit above criticism.

The Academy Award for *Midway* encouraged John to try to resurrect Gregg Toland's Pearl Harbor film. When the navy had confiscated it, they had only picked up Toland's work print; the negative was still in the Field Photographic's offices. John put Bob Parrish and Budd Schulberg to work on it. Jim McGuinness also contributed to the narration. They scaled it down from a feature-length film to a two-reel short, eliminated the "finger pointing" of Toland's film, and changed it from an investigation of the attack to a pure propaganda film. They kept the footage of the actual attack and Ray Kellogg's special effects, but emphasized the navy's comeback. The film finished with a burst of glory as the big battle wagons put back out to sea.

The recut film, called *December 7th*, was never released publicly. Rather, it became part of what was called "The Industrial Incentives Program." Shown to workers in key defense industries, its purpose was to spur them on to greater heights of production and encourage them to avoid strikes and absenteeism by appealing to their patriotism.

Since being ordered to active duty in September 1941, John had been to Panama, Pearl Harbor, Midway, and North Africa. Events had moved so quickly that he had had little time for his personal affairs. Now, however, between January and August 1943, he had time to concentrate on them. Going into the navy had been an enormous financial sacrifice. In the years before the war, John had averaged $225,000 a year. Now he found himself trying to live on the $4,000-a-year salary of a navy commander. While he had some savings and a substantial interest income (over $36,000 in 1941) it was nevertheless a big adjustment to make. His biggest single fixed expense was the *Araner*; there was no way he could afford to maintain her. Rather than let her sit and deteriorate from lack of use, he offered to turn her over to the navy, which was then leasing large yachts for a dollar a year and using them as offshore patrol vessels. John wrote his business manager, Fred Totman, who was still with him on a part-time basis, that "under the circumstances, it is the only thing we can do, and, as a matter of fact, I am happy and proud to have the *Araner* in service."

In January 1943, the yacht *Araner* became the U.S.S. *Araner*, and for two years she was used as an antisubmarine patrol vessel off the coast of California.

John's going into the service and the subsequent loss of income also meant an abrupt change in Mary's standard of living. She cut back on all frills and entertainment, put her car in storage, and closed off part of the big Odin Street house. To keep herself busy and keep her mind off her loneliness she became involved with the Hollywood Canteen, the World War II landmark that gave servicemen a chance to meet movie stars and see and hear the big bands of the day. But even with her volunteer work the war years were a time of desperate loneliness for Mary, a time of Christmases and holidays spent worrying about John.

Mary got some help from Pat, who had been commissioned in the navy, but because of poor eyesight was confined to shore duty and was working as a public information officer in Los Angeles. She also got some support from John Wayne and Ward Bond, both of whom were draft-exempt (Bond because he was an epileptic, Wayne because he had four children and was over the draft age). While there wasn't any question about Bond's deferment, there did seem to be some about Wayne's. Many of the top actors in Hollywood—Jimmy Stewart, Clark Gable, and Robert Montgomery, to name just a few—were as old as he was, had as many dependents, and still managed to find their way into the service. Wayne's status didn't sit well with him; in the winter of 1943 he tried to get a commission in the Marine Corps and get attached to the Field Photographic.

But the Field Photographic's billets were frozen by 1943, and John couldn't get Wayne in as an enlisted man, much less as an officer. Wayne tried other avenues but couldn't get a commission. The only way he could get in the service was to enlist in the army as a private. He says today: "I felt that it would be a waste of time to spend two years picking up cigarette butts. I thought I could do more for the war effort if I stayed in Hollywood and did an occasional tour. In the summer of 1943 I toured the South Pacific and Australia for the U.S.O. This was MacArthur's theater, and because there was a lot of animosity between the O.S.S. and MacArthur, Donovan's people weren't allowed there. Jack asked me to keep my eyes open, write down what I saw, and make a report to Donovan when I came back. I was overseas for about four months. I guess I got to go places the average entertainer wouldn't get to go. I saw Merian Cooper and General Whitehead, but I never did catch up with MacArthur. When I got back to the States I made my report, and they gave me a plaque saying that I had served in the O.S.S. But it was a copperhead, something that Jack had set up. It didn't mean anything."

As the war progressed, Wayne's career skyrocketed and he became less and less enthusiastic about leaving Hollywood.

John Wayne and Ward Bond went through divorces in 1943, and both were spending a lot of time at John's house. While their presence was good for Mary and eased her loneliness, their antics sometimes got out of hand. Once Bond was asleep in John's bed and Wayne tried to wake him up to go drinking with him. When he wouldn't get up, Wayne poured vodka on his chest and lit him on fire. On one of their better drunks, Bond bet Wayne $100 that he could stand on a newspaper and Wayne couldn't knock him off it. Wayne took the bet, and Bond laid a newspaper out on the floor in an upstairs doorway. Then he closed the door. "Ok, you dumb son of a bitch, now hit me," he said from behind the door. Wayne drew back and hit Bond *through* the door—knocking him off the newspaper.

But even with Pat, John Wayne, and Ward Bond around her, the war years were still a hard time for Mary. On Christmas Day, 1942, while John was crossing the Atlantic on the *Samuel Chase*, she wrote:

"Guess you'd like a picture story of our Christmas. I'll have to start by telling you we were really out there with you all day long.

We had a beautiful tree and big fires in the fireplace and Christmas carols in the music box. Ward and Duke were over generous. A new uniform for Pat from Duke, gorgeous bags for Barbara and Ward filled the house with flowers and perfume bottles, and in return we spent the night before Christmas helping Josie and Doris keep their chins up.

"Three of Pat's fraternity brothers spent their furlough with us. Nice big strapping fliers and a medico. Swell kids we have in this generation. The family dropped by and are swell. We missed you like anything and the kids all went to mass Christmas morning and said a prayer for you.

"I've done my 100% best this Christmas. Maybe I've succeeded, who knows. The house looks so pretty in its Christmas finery. Fires in all the fireplaces, the wind outside blowing like heck makes it seem even more homey. Your brother Frank is drunk and telephoning every few minutes, but no one is letting him come up. We all feel we will see you soon. We love you so awfully much and miss you so."

In April 1943, John's brother Francis, sixty-five years old, dyed his hair, went on the wagon, and enlisted in the army. Before he left he came by to see Mary in his new uniform and apologized for the fact that he didn't have any World War I campaign ribbons, "because I was too old to get in the service at the time." He reported for basic training at Fort Ord, California, with men young enough to be his grandsons.

When John heard about Francis' enlistment he wrote that he was "truly delighted and proud." But Francis' army career was short-lived. During basic training he tried to cash a Social Security check at the Fort Ord Enlisted Man's Club and his real age was discovered. He was drummed out of the service for the second time—the first time having been in 1898, when he had been too young.

As the war progressed, the O.S.S. grew from a fledgling agency into a vast global intelligence network. From its Washington headquarters a vast espionage web was woven around the world with sensitive strands that reached deep into Axis territory. By 1943 there were agents operating behind enemy lines in Italy, France, Albania, Baghdad, and Borneo. At its wartime peak there were

30,000 names listed on the agency's roster. There were also countless partisans in occupied countries who were paid and supplied by the O.S.S., and whose names will never be known.

There had never been anything quite like the O.S.S. in American history. It was a quasi-military organization that operated outside the military chain of command and was immune from congressional scrutiny; it had unprecedented power and authority—but, as Gregg Toland had found out, traditional military leaders were suspicious and resentful of the new super agency, and throughout the war Donovan's organization had trouble gaining footholds in certain theaters. General Douglas MacArthur never did allow them in the southwest Pacific.

In the summer of 1943 Bill Donovan wanted to get the O.S.S. established in the China-Burma-India theater, where a coalition of Nationalist Chinese, British, and Americans were fighting the Japanese. The theater was rife with political intrigue. The British, hard-pressed to protect their own home island, were fighting the Japanese in Burma and trying to keep India, the crown jewel of their empire, from working loose from its setting in the Imperial crown. In China, Chiang Kai-shek was fighting the Japanese with his right hand and the Communists with his left. Some of his American advisers thought he was doing a tremendous job; others thought he was brutal, repressive, and corrupt. Donovan, a man of great vision, believed that the outcome of the battle between Chiang and the Communists was as important as World War II itself, and that it would affect the postwar world for decades, possibly for centuries. He was determined to establish an O.S.S. base there and gain accurate information. Yet Donovan knew that this wasn't going to be easy. If American military leaders were suspicious and resentful of the O.S.S., then foreign leaders were much more so. This was true in India, where the British suspected that the Americans supported Indian independence, and even more so in China, where a history of exploitation by outsiders made all foreigners suspect.

To help pave the way, Donovan proposed that the Field Photographic (which already had a small station in New Delhi under Lieutenant Guy Bolte) make a propaganda film celebrating the British effort in Burma—one that would make the theater commander, Lord Mountbatten, a household word in the United

184

States. Donovan felt that if he could establish an atmosphere of trust between Mountbatten's staff and the O.S.S., they would allow him to set up bases in India and Burma. They would be his entree into the theater and his springboard into China. In May 1943, John sent Irving Asner, a veteran Hollywood director, now an army major attached to the Field Photographic, to New Delhi to begin work on a film to be called *Victory in Burma*.

Meanwhile, on the other side of the globe, Mark Armistead was developing a technique for making aerial photographic surveys with Mitchell 35-mm motion-picture cameras. The filmstrips were put together and used for intelligence surveys in a process called the Intelligence Documentary Photographic Project, or "Ippy Dippy Intelligence" for short. By the summer of 1943, teams from the Field Photographic were busy all over the world teaching the aerial reconnaissance wings of the army and navy how to mount and operate Mitchell cameras and how to put the filmstrips together. In the summer of 1943, John decided to go to the China-Burma-India theater to help put the "Ippy Dippy" technique to use and to check the progress of Asner's Mountbatten film.

In August 1943, John, Jack Pennick, and Field Photographic cameraman Jack Swain boarded a civilian airliner in Washington and flew to San Francisco. From there they flew the long legs of the Pacific in a succession of military planes. Four days later they arrived in New Delhi.

John took a few days to get over the time changes and get into the rhythm of British-ruled India. He found little evidence of war there. The racetracks were open and thriving; there were rugby and cricket matches nearly every day, and association football on weekends.

One of the first people John looked up was Gene Markey, who was with a Naval Intelligence unit attached to Lord Mountbatten's staff. The Fox producer was living in his accustomed style: in a Rajah's palace surrounded by high walls and iron gates, with platoons of liveried servants gliding about.

Always gregarious, Markey knew every important American and British officer in India, and he took John on the social rounds to all the clubs and messes. John boasted of his exploits and praised the O.S.S. at every opportunity, claiming that Bill Donovan had created "the most fantastic organization in the world." It was "filled with men who thought nothing of parachuting into France, blowing up a bridge, pissing in Luftwaffe gas tanks, then dancing on the roof of the St. Regis Hotel with a German spy."

John was an oddity in India. He was an O.S.S. man but also a celebrity, and even more important, a Hollywood celebrity. He was colorful, charming, and tremendously interesting to the British officers he met. They clustered around him to hear his anecdotes and enjoy his wit. Whether he knew it or not, John was performing an important diplomatic function for Bill Donovan: he was making contacts that would help get the O.S.S. operational in India.

Markey introduced John to the senior American in New Delhi, General A.C. Wedemeyer, a ramrod-straight West Pointer with steel-gray hair. John and Wedemeyer hit it off immediately. In John's eyes he was the very essence of the word "soldier," and a strong personal bond was forged between them.

At the end of September, John, Irving Asner, Jack Pennick, Guy Bolte, and Jack Swain left New Delhi for Rangoon, Burma, to begin shooting documentary footage for *Victory in Burma*. There John was reunited with his boss, Bill Donovan, who had come to Burma to inspect a group of Kachin tribesmen who had been organized into a guerrilla band by one of the most amazing characters of World War II: a priest named Father James Stuart.

Father Stuart had been a missionary among the Kachin for nine years before the war. Then, in 1942, he had watched the Japanese burn down his church and torture his parishioners. He swore vengeance.

Operating out of an isolated tea plantation at Nazira, Assam, Burma, in the heart of Kipling's jungle-book country, he organized the Kachin into a guerrilla army and appealed to the O.S.S. for support and modern weapons. The Kachin were uncanny jungle fighters, and even with primitive weapons they had been wreaking havoc on the Japanese. Donovan decided to support Father Stuart and his Kachin unit, which came to be called the 101 Detachment and went on to become one of the most successful O.S.S. units in World War II.

While Donovan saw Father Stuart's quasi-mercenary band from a military point of view, John Ford saw it from a theatrical one. This was exciting and dramatic material, and he decided to incorporate it into the Mountbatten film. He put Guy Bolte in charge of gathering documentary footage on the Kachin and assigned him two cameramen: Bob Rhea, one of the original members of the Field Photographic, and Arthur "Butch" Meehan, a handsome twenty-year-old whose father, a Hollywood camera-man, had worked on a number of John's pictures. Bolte, Rhea, and Meehan were to live with the Kachin guerrillas, go on raids behind the Japanese lines with them, and film them in action. It was the most dangerous project that the Field Photographic had ever undertaken.

In time, Bolte, Rhea, and Meehan became very close to their Burmese subjects and transcended their functions as combat photographers. Often they were the only Americans with the Kachin, and they became vital links to the O.S.S. as communica-tors, suppliers, administrators, and paymasters.

John's success as an O.S.S. "advance man" in New Delhi was not lost on Bill Donovan. When John finished in Burma the intelligence chief decided to take him on the next and more difficult leg of his trip—to China. On December 2, 1943, John, Bill Donovan, and Jack Pennick left Rangoon and flew "over the hump" to Chungking, Chiang Kai-shek's wartime capital. High in the mountains, Chungking contrasted sharply with the sordid humidity of Burma and India, and John luxuriated in the clean, cool air. He hadn't been to China since the S.S. *President Cleveland* had stopped in Shanghai in 1933. War had been raging there in the country all these years since and Chungking was bomb-splattered and fire-gutted, with heaps of rubble and barbed wire everywhere.

Establishing an O.S.S. base in China was one of Bill Do-novan's top priorities, but he was having a very hard time doing so. Chinese intelligence was controlled by a general named Tai-Li, a cold, brutal hatchet man who was sometimes called "The Chinese Himmler." Tai-Li was fearful of American involvement in Chinese internal affairs, and despite Bill Donovan's promises of money and material, he remained adamant that the O.S.S. should stay out of China.

But there was a way around this impasse, and John proved to be an important contact man. The only American unit in China completely independent of Chiang Kai-shek was the 14th U.S. Air Force, which was commanded by the former head of the Flying Tigers, General Claire Chennault. Through his long friendship with Merian Cooper (who had served as Chennault's chief of staff), John knew the tough, leathery, swashbuckling general well. He introduced Donovan to him and, more important, helped establish a working rapport between the two men.

Donovan asked Chennault to let him set up an O.S.S. station within the command structure of the 14th Air Force and bring his agents into the country disguised as airmen. After some lengthy negotiations in which John served as an intermediary, Chennault agreed, and a unit with the unwieldy name of the "5329th Air and Ground Forces Resources and Technical Staff" was created. It was an O.S.S. cover; within six months O.S.S. agents were spread throughout China.

Late in December, with his mission accomplished, Donovan returned to Washington. John, however, stayed on for two more months teaching the "Ippy Dippy" technique to the men of the 14th Air Force. He personally photographed the terrain between Chungking and Kunming, the northern terminus of the Burma Road—Chaing's vital supply link from the south. John flew aerial reconnaissance flights between Kunming and Chabua and west to Chengtu at the base of the Himalayas. In Chengtu, outside the city's ancient high walls, the camel caravans were still coming down from Tibet, slowly and imperturbably, as they had for untold centuries. In Kunming, John watched an army of 50,000 workers build entirely by hand an airfield capable of accommodating huge four-engine B-17s.

John's experience in China and the Far East made a great impression on him. Besides the visual and sensual impact of the place, which in itself was staggering, he had been affected in subtle ways that he himself did not completely understand. He had spent a lot of time with Donovan, Wedemeyer, and Chennault, all great American names; he had sat in on the councils of power and had been an important link, a contact man, whose fame, notoriety, and celebrity status had helped to establish an important O.S.S. operation. His perception of himself, his sense of who and what he was, and some of his most basic values were undergoing a change. Increasingly he was adapting the attitudes of the professional military men around him. He was beginning to see himself as an O.S.S. operative first, a naval officer second, and a Hollywood

188

director third. More and more he was looking at Hollywood with scorn and distaste.

The China-Burma-India trip had been an unqualified success; John had helped Donovan in China, had implemented the "Ippy Dippy" project, and had begun work on *Victory in Burma*. But there were other things going on in other theaters that John wanted to take part in. On January 14, 1944, he and Jack Pennick flew back to New Delhi, where John enjoyed warm reunions with Gene Markey and Al Wedemeyer. After a few days they began their long journey home, flying to Karachi, Aden, Karthoum, and Accra, then across the Atlantic to Natal, Brazil, and north to Miami. The trip took seven tedious days; John was gloomy, cranky, and tired when it was over. His first order of business was to call Mary, whom he hadn't spoken to in seven months. Then, after a brief layover, he and Pennick flew on to Washington.

Back in the capital, Bill Donovan called John into his office and told him that he greatly appreciated the work he had done in the Far East, that he had been a great asset to the organization. He told John he was recommending him for an out-of-line promotion to captain. Then Donovan dropped a bombshell. He told John that the Allies were preparing to invade the European continent in June. The landing would take place somewhere on the Normandy coast and was going to be the biggest single invasion in history. It would involve more ships, more men, more guns than had ever been assembled before. And, Donovan said, John was going to be in charge of all Allied photography.

John was stunned and elated. This was the operation that would decide the fate of the war, the ultimate military adventure. That Donovan had selected him for such an important assignment was the greatest honor of his life.

But with the good news came the bad. A few days later John learned that young Butch Meehan had been killed while filming the Kachin guerrillas behind enemy lines. John was deeply upset: young Meehan was a "hometown" kid and one of his favorites. He expressed his sorrow in a letter to the boy's father:

"Dear George: It is with the deepest sorrow that I write to you and Mrs. Meehan about Arthur. By now I understand you have been informed officially of his heroic death. George, it is hard for me to put it in words—he was such a wonderful lad, one of the finest I've ever known. I am heartbroken to think he has gone. He had volunteered to take the place of one of his buddies who was down with fever, it was a dangerous mission and Butch went down with his machine gun blazing.

"We are stunned with grief back here, but of course our sorrow is nothing compared to yours. He was such a swell kid—brave, considerate, hard working, always thinking of the other guy, never of himself—it is so ironic that fate should cause him to go that way doing the other guy's job.

"I am trying to get several days leave so I might come to the Coast and see you and your wife, if you wish. Perhaps I could tell you better in words what I'm trying to say on paper, but I know nothing I can ever say or write will ease the cold fact that our country, our Navy, and our home town Hollywood has lost the bravest, cleanest, most lovable boy that ever made the supreme sacrifice for the things he loved and for which he fought."

Such was the price of John's military adventures.

15
They Were
Expendable

Set in the opening days of World War II, W. L. White's *They Were Expendable* was the nonfiction account of a squadron of PT boats in the Philippines that battles the invading Japanese, evacuates General MacArthur, and then, after a series of defeats, becomes directionless and breaks up. The book was made up of interviews with the squadron's commander, Lieutenant John Bulkeley, who had been awarded the Congressional Medal of Honor, and three of his officers. Timely, terse, and exciting, it was a best-seller in 1942 when MGM bought the film rights. Jim McGuinness was put in charge of it, and he assigned the screenplay to the crippled maverick screenwriter, Spig Wead.

To Spig Wead, *They Were Expendable* was more than just another war story; it was an homage to the professionals, the unsung heroes who fought the delaying action that gave the nation time to gear up for war. As an Annapolis man whose career had been cut short by a tragic accident, he brought a great empathy to the script, and gave it a tragic quality, a grandeur, an intensity, and an epic sweep that W. L. White's book didn't have.

Both Wead and Jim McGuinness knew that there was only one man who could breathe real fire and life into this picture: John Ford. In April 1943, they flew to Washington and offered it to him. McGuinness told John that MGM could get him a leave of absence if he would direct *They Were Expendable*, that it would be at least as significant a contribution to the war effort as anything he could do with the Field Photographic.

John was torn. He liked the story, which evoked his deepest feelings for the navy as well as his nostalgic memories of the Philippines. But he was reluctant to leave his unit at a time when his men were involved in projects all over the world. Moreover, Darryl Zanuck was just then coming under fire for his activities in North Africa, and John was very sensitive about such criticism. He told McGuinness that if he made a commercial picture while still in uniform, "every congressman in America would be after my ass." But McGuinness and Wead kept after him, emphasizing the heroic quality of the story and its importance to the war effort. To avoid criticism, they suggested, John could donate his salary to Navy Relief. Gradually they swung him around.

By the summer of 1943 all the pieces seemed to be falling into place and John was set to take a leave of absence to do the picture.

The Portland High School
football team, 1912.
John Feeney, fullback,
stands beside coach.

Francis Ford in 1917.

A *Peg o' the Ring* poster, 1916. At center foreground is Francis, to his right, Jack.

A still from *Marked Men* (1919), an early Harry Carey film based on the Peter B. Kyne short story "Three Godfathers." Carey, at right, played a part that John Wayne would play in John's 1948 remake, *3 Godfathers*.

Mary McBride Smith in 1920.

John in 1920.

John, center
foreground,
and Harry Carey,
kneeling above
him, pose with
the cast and
crew of an
early Ford-
Carey western.

John on location in
Wadsworth, Nevada,
during work on
The Iron Horse (1924).

John with his father in 1927.

In 1934, John bought the *Faith*, a 100-foot John Hanna-designed ketch, for $30,000. He rechristened her the *Araner*, after the Aran Islands off the coast of Galway from which his mother's ancestors had come.

John in the then Dutch East Indies, 1932.

John, with pipe, and George O'Brien, standing at center, at a local boxing match in Manila, 1930.

John with John "Duke" Wayne and two unidentified companions aboard the *Araner* at Catalina, 1935.

Four Ford men: (from left) John, Eddie O'Fearna, Francis' son Phil, Francis.

John aboard the *Araner* in the late 1930s.

Pat and Barbara in 1936.

Kate Hepburn aboard the
Araner in 1936, with
John's foot well in hand.

Henry Fonda, fisherman, aboard the *Araner*, 1938.

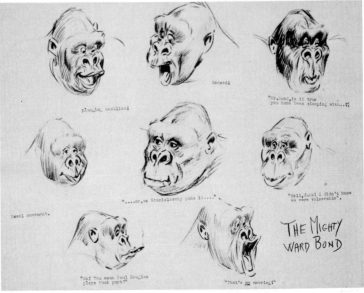

"The Mighty Ward Bond," as caricatured by John.

The Emerald Bay Yacht Club, with reserve uniforms, in 1938. It was hard to tell where Hollywood stopped and the navy began.

John aboard the *Araner* during a training session of the Field Photo Reserve, 1940.

John with Gregg Toland, the great cinematographer
who photographed *The Grapes of Wrath*.

"The Joad Family." From left: Charles Grapewin, Dorris Bowdon,
Jane Darwell, Russell Simpson, Henry Fonda, Darryl Hickman, Frank Sully,
Shirley Mills, Frank Darien, O. Z. Whitehead, Eddie Quillan, John Carradine.

The Joad Family wish you a Merry

The opening scene in *How Green Was My Valley.* *(Copyright © 1941 Twentieth Century-Fox Film Corp. All rights reserved. Courtesy of Twentieth Century-Fox)*

John in June 1944.

The Sons of the Pioneers perform at a gathering at the Field Photo Farm.
(Official Naval Reserve Photograph)

John, at center, prepares to shoot a scene in *She Wore a Yellow Ribbon* (1949).
(Courtesy of RKO General Pictures)

John with Lord Killanin in Dublin during work on *The Quiet Man* (1952). *(Photo by G. A. Duncan)*

John directing Clark Gable in *Mogambo* (1953). *(Courtesy of MGM Studio)*

John at West Point, 1954.

John in London in spring 1953, while shooting interiors for
Mogambo. About this time he developed cataracts in both eyes.
Following surgery, he began to wear an eye patch.
(Photo by John B. Prizer)

John's vitality is still evident on location for
The Searchers (1956). (© *1956 Warner Bros. Pictures, Inc.*)

In *The Wings of Eagles* (1957), Ward Bond played a
director named "John Dodge"–really John Ford. *(Photo by Gene Trindl)*

John on location in Natchez, Mississippi, during work on
The Horse Soldiers (1956).

John with John Wayne and Ward Bond during filming of
The Colter Craven Story, an episode of Bond's *Wagon Train*
television series. Bond died before it was aired. *(NBC photo by Gerald Smith)*

A scene from *Cheyenne Autumn* (1964), John's "film of atonement"
to the Indians. Here Richard Widmark leads cavalry column to a spot in
Monument Valley known locally as "Ford's Point."
(*©1965 Warner Bros. Pictures, Inc.*)

John dockside in Honolulu, 1962.

John late in life, photographed by Brick Marquard on the set of Howard Hawks' *Rio Lobo*, Tucson, Arizona, 1971.

At this point, however, MGM chief Eddie Mannix decided that Wead's script had too many rough edges and brought Sidney Franklin in to polish it. Franklin was a graceful stylist, but he knew nothing about the navy. The intensity that Wead had given the script was lost on him, and while smoothing it out, he took away much of its real power. When John learned of Mannix's move he was incensed, and in early August he decided to back out of the project. He told Jim McGuinness so in a letter dated August 5, which went on to explain that in any case Bill Donovan had a new secret assignment for him that would make him unavailable for some time.

On August 14, John left on that assignment for the China-Burma-India Theater. Eight months later, when he returned, he came home to California on a fifteen-day leave. It was a long-overdue respite from the war, and he was delighted with the home-coming that Mary had prepared for him, filling the Odin Street house with family and friends. But every day of John Ford's life was touched by his work--even those precious few when he was on leave from the war, for Jim McGuinness was constantly at his house trying to get him to reconsider *They Were Expendable*. McGuinness, an elegant, polished man, argued forthrightly and directly.

"This isn't another war movie," he said. "The story of John Bulkeley and his PT squadron is part of America's heroic tradition. It's like the Alamo or Valley Forge. It would be like recreating a great moment of history while it's still fresh in people's minds. It would be available for our youth, generation after generation."

But John was impervious to his arguments and kept putting him off. His heart was in the navy, and his mind was on the forthcoming Normandy invasion.

"I'm committed to a major operation," he told McGuinness, "one that would probably decide the outcome of the war. Your film will have to wait."

"But we've got no picture without you."

"Tell that to Eddie Mannix."

War or no war, when you're hot you're hot, and in March 1944 John Ford was hotter than boiler plate. He had the tide of history, the wind of fate, and the luck of the Irish all working for him at the same time when *December 7th* won an Academy Award as the best documentary subject of the year. It was John's fourth Oscar in four years and the second time the Academy had honored the Field

Photographic. Beyond boosting the unit's morale and serving as yet another symbol of its legitimacy, the Oscar strengthened John's resolve not to return to Hollywood until the war was over.

"Get yourself another boy," he told McGuinness, "or forget the whole goddamn thing."

On April 5, 1944, freshly promoted to captain, John took off for London on a military transport plane, and for the next two months he worked furiously getting ready to cover the invasion. As he had done prior to the North African landings, he sent most of his men to commando schools to get in shape and used to living in the field.

The invasion was the day of reckoning for the London branch of the Field Photographic; they had been preparing for it for more than eighteen months. Mark Armistead and his men had photographed the entire coast of Europe from low-flying B-25s. They had collected information on the French coast from photographs and old books. Armistead had interviewed everybody who knew the waters, the beaches, the roads, and the surrounding terrain.

Ironically, one of his best sources of information on the Normandy coast was the real-life hero of *They Were Expendable*, John Bulkeley, who was now in charge of a squadron of PT boats in the English Channel. Bulkeley's boats had been running agents and commandos in and out of Normandy, and he knew the waters well—particularly where the mine fields and the underwater obstacles designed to rip props and rudders off boats were. He knew all the inlets because on damp, foggy nights he had idled his PT boats into them. Bulkeley had furnished Armistead with invaluable data not available on charts or maps.

In the course of their many meetings Armistead and Bulkeley had become quite friendly, and thinking that John would enjoy meeting the man who had gotten Douglas MacArthur out of the Philippines, Armistead brought him by Claridge's one morning. They knocked on the great man's door for some minutes before a gruff voice ordered them in. John was still in bed, but when Armistead introduced Bulkeley to him he insisted on getting up and saluting the Medal of Honor winner—even though he was stark naked.

After two months of frantic work the invasion was now at hand. On the night of June 5, with his camera crews dispersed throughout the Allied army, John reported aboard the invasion command ship, the battleship U.S.S. *Augusta*. Mark Armistead went with his friend Bulkeley on his PT boat, which was to be patrolling off the beach. By 2:00 A.M. the *Augusta* was churning through the choppy, blue-gray water of the English Channel, leading the greatest armada ever assembled: 4,600 ships carrying 176,000 men. John was much too excited to sleep and spent the night pacing the decks.

At first light John could see the silhouettes of the armada. The destroyers and the cruisers looked low on the horizon, the troop transports heavy and swollen. Huge battleships swung broadside and began hurling salvos at the French coast, the shells sounding like freight trains going overhead. John could see the landing barges come alongside the transport ships, and men scurrying down the rope nets until they were packed shoulder to shoulder in the open holds like medieval pikemen.

Through his binoculars John studied the coast, which loomed gray and hostile, a jagged wilderness of iron stakes and barbed wire. The bluffs behind the beaches looked insurmountable. The invasion was going badly in this sector. German machine guns in concrete pillboxes were laying down a murderous crossfire. Although he was too excited and too caught up in the invasion to think about it, John was taking part in another great moment in history, a day that would be remembered for centuries to come: the time 0800, June 6, 1944. The place: Omaha Beach.

As the day wore on, John grew restless aboard the *Augusta*, which was some distance from the actual combat. He radioed Mark Armistead on Bulkeley's PT boat and told them to come over and pick him up. At first Bulkeley was reluctant to do so. As a true fighting man he didn't want any rear-echelon types—and particularly rear-echelon types that outranked him—looking over his shoulder. But Armistead assured him that John was all right and wouldn't get in the way, so Bulkeley brought his PT boat alongside the *Augusta* to pick up the director. Although he had found Ford eccentric on their first meeting, he was completely unprepared for the crusty, disheveled figure that was lowered down in a bosun's chair. He looked more like one of the infantrymen ashore than a navy captain.

"Captain Ford," said Bulkeley, holding out his hand, "welcome aboard."

"Jack Ford," said the visitor.

Bulkeley briefed John on the day's operation. They were patrolling off the beachhead, looking for submarines, and he showed John the charts. Bulkeley was surprised at how quickly and accurately his guest absorbed naval information. His questions were intelligent and his manner quietly deferential. Bulkeley was a movie buff, but every time he tried to turn the conversation to Hollywood, John fended off his questions. Bulkeley found John simple, direct, gentle, and unaffected. His sole purpose, it was plain, was to get closer to the war.

John spent the next five days aboard Bulkeley's PT boat. To Mark Armistead he seemed oddly happy and very much in his element standing on the little bridge, looking through his binoculars, and snatching bits of sleep cramped in the boat's small places. At one point they came in contact with a group of German E-boats off Cherbourg and, bumping across the channel at forty miles an hour, they engaged in a running machine-gun duel. Lines of red tracers streamed overhead and the decks were covered with the spent brass rounds. One burst stitched across Bulkeley's hull at the waterline. When it was over, John jokingly accused Bulkeley, who had a camera at his side, of standing by to take the first picture of the famous director's dead body.

This was one of the most ironic moments in John Ford's life. Here he was at Normandy with John Bulkeley, the subject of a best-selling book that half the people he respected in Hollywood wanted him to make into a film. But he wasn't making that film because he was too busy fighting the war—with Bulkeley!

"If Jim McGuinness or Eddie Mannix knew where I was, they'd die," he told Mark Armistead.

Beyond the irony of their being together, something more was happening: a genuine rapport was developing between the two men. John watched Bulkeley handle his boat and lead his squadron with a calm, easy professionalism. He was mesmerized by the rough but always cool and unassuming hero. When he asked him about the campaign in the Philippines and the evacuation of MacArthur, Bulkeley told him that W. L. White had exaggerated the whole thing in *They Were Expendable*, and that he hadn't deserved the Congressional Medal of Honor.

"The whole thing happened at a time when the country was looking for heroes. Frankly, I've already had too much publicity. I'm a professional navy man. Nothing more, nothing less. With all due respect to both your rank and your accomplishments as a director, I hope they never make the goddamn thing into a movie."

John was delighted with the man's candor and modesty. In his mind they were the true marks of his greatness, and he realized that Spig Wead and Jim McGuinness had been right. John Bulkeley would be a great subject for a motion picture, and he, John Ford, was the only man to tell his story, the only man in Hollywood who really appreciated the professional navy man. John's contact with Bulkeley—the five days they spent together off the Normandy coast—did what the beguiling and smoothly persuasive Jim McGuinness couldn't do. It convinced him that he had to return to Hollywood and film the story of John Bulkeley.

New York was sweltering through a heat wave, and a limpid humidity hung like a fog over the city when John landed in La Guardia Field. He caught a cab into the city, checked into the Plaza Hotel, and immediately undressed and soaked himself in a cool bath. Then he crawled into bed naked and slept for twelve hours.

A few days later, back in Los Angeles, he called Jim McGuinness at MGM and announced that he was ready to begin *They Were Expendable* on the condition that he and Spig Wead make a final revision of the script. The producer agreed. John and Wead immediately went to work.

John surprised everyone when he cast Robert Montgomery, a gentle, boyish-faced actor, to play John Bulkeley (who had become "John Brickley" in the script). Although he wasn't an action type, Montgomery was uniquely qualified for this part: he was a navy officer who had commanded a squadron of PT boats in the Solomon Islands; John had arranged for the Navy to release him from active duty. John Wayne was cast as the executive officer, Lieutenant Rusty Ryan; Donna Reed was cast as Sandy Davis, an army nurse that Ryan falls in love with; Jack Pennick, on leave from the Field Photographic had a big part. Ward Bond had been set for a big part as a navy chief, but just before the picture began he was seriously injured in an automobile accident; John rewrote his role so that he gets wounded early, and Bond played his part on crutches.

MGM was paying John $300,000 to produce and direct *They Were Expendable*, and the question of his receiving that much money while still on active duty was potentially an embarrassing one. Earlier, Spig Wead had suggested that John donate his salary to

Navy Relief, but John had ideas of his own. He wanted to buy a clubhouse for the veterans of the Field Photographic and dedicate it as a "living memorial" to the men of his unit. He wanted a place that would help preserve the communal feeling of the unit, where the men could gather on Sundays and bring their families for picnics, barbeques, and softball games; where they could gather on Memorial Day to pay tribute to their fallen comrades. John had Harry Wurtzel and Fred Totman draw up corporation papers for "Field Photo Homes, Inc." as a nonprofit charitable corporation, and made arrangements to have his salary paid directly into it.

Just as John was about to begin *They Were Expendable* he learned that Al Wedemeyer was going to assume the number-one job in the Far East, replacing "Vinegar Joe" Stilwell as Chiang Kai-shek's chief of staff. Pleased that Wedemeyer had been so honored, John wrote and congratulated him. Then he summed up his feelings about *They Were Expendable*:

"My militaristic ego has been somewhat deflated. I have been ordered to make a commercial picture called *They Were Expendable*. While I will at least get a chance to spend Christmas with the folks and play with my grandson's electric train, still I'm a bit ashamed that a great warrior like me should be in 'movie land' while the good people are fighting. However, the picture won't last forever while the war seems a bit indefinite yet. I am getting a big chunk of dough for the picture, which I am turning into a trust fund for Pennick and the boys. That at least clears my conscience a bit. It will give Pennick a place to store his loot."

After nearly two years of vacillation, script changes, false starts, and delays, *They Were Expendable* began shooting on John's fiftieth birthday, February 1, 1945, in Key Biscayne, Florida. There an army of art directors, carpenters, and set dressers had recreated the look and feel of Manila before the war. Since it was a big-budget action picture with a lot of propaganda value, the navy was generously supporting *They Were Expendable*. They had lent MGM several squadrons of PT boats, and second-unit director Jim Havens (who was also a captain in the Marine Corps and a demolitions expert) put them through their paces on Biscayne Bay. He photographed some superb action scenes of the boats attacking mock-ups of Japanese cruisers and destroyers.

Just as shooting began, John received some sad news from the war front. "Junior" Stout, the son of his old colleague Archie Stout, had been killed when an unarmed DC-3 transport plane in which he was riding had gotten lost in the fog and accidentally landed on the German-occupied island of Jersey. Stout had jumped out carrying his Cunningham combat camera—which looked something like a machine gun—and had been gunned down by the German guards. John also learned that Kim and Rosina Wai's oldest son, Francis, an All-American running back at UCLA before the war, had been killed at Leyte, in the Philippines.

As a result of these tragedies John began the picture with a heightened awareness of the cost of war. Today John Wayne says, "Jack was awfully intense on that picture and working with more concentration than I had ever seen. I think he was really out to achieve something." *They Were Expendable* was the culmination of four years of the most intense personal experience. At every opportunity John tried to elevate it above the level of a propaganda film. As he had done on *The Grapes of Wrath*, he went after stark documentary effects and kept the interiors dark and realistic. Reunited with Joe August, his cameraman on *The Informer*, he went after a visual style of great simplicity and strength, with compositions of monumental force, yet never grandiose. He also went after the most delicate touches of human feeling. Half-way through the film, there is a scene in which Douglas MacArthur reports aboard Brickley's PT boat to be evacuated from Bataan. Wayne remembers that when the scene was filmed, "there were a number of top navy brass at the location, and there were quite a few disparaging remarks like 'This is where the old bastard ran out' and that sort of thing. But by God, when the scene started and the guy who was playing MacArthur walked out and Danny Borzage was there with his little music box, you could see the look in their eyes change. Jack had created such a sense of awe that even among these navy men there was a feeling of respect for this man."

They Were Expendable is the story of a defeat, the rout of American forces in the Philippines and the dissolution of a small and closely knit military unit. John was at his most effective in conveying this sense of loss. Although the film has a complicated plot, John filled it with grace notes, and the story unfolds at an almost leisurely pace. Time and time again he halted the action to concentrate on a face or an attitude. In one instance, an old trader (Russell Simpson), who has spent a lifetime building up a shipyard, refuses to desert it to the Japanese.

"I've worked forty years for this, son," he tells Brickley. "If I leave they'll have to carry me out." He is last seen in a wordless shot, sitting on the steps behind a shack. He shifts a keg of whiskey to his side, lays a shotgun across his knees, and waits. And the film waits with him.

Because he was putting so much personal feeling into *They Were Expendable*, John was also setting himself up for some major disappointments. He had wanted his crew to come from the ranks of the Field Photographic but had been blocked at every turn. He had wanted to keep the music sparse and limit it to one song, "Marquita," which had a hint of Latin rhythm and helped capture both the flavor of the Philippines and the elegiac feeling of loss he was after. But John was overruled on this and the studio later added a heavily orchestrated score.

But most of all, John had trouble adjusting to what he thought of as the commercial and self-serving attitudes of everyone else on the picture. He was, after all, "working for free," and he expected the same sort of dedication from his actors and technicians. He was upset to learn that not everyone was as altruistic as he was.

Today John Wayne says that John was particularly hard on him during the making of *They Were Expendable*: "Bob Montgomery was his pet on that picture. He could do no wrong. I guess it was because he had been in the navy. Jack picked on me all the way through it. He kept calling me a 'clumsy bastard' and a 'big oaf' and kept telling me that I 'moved like an ox.' Now if I couldn't do anything else, at least I *moved* well.

"We almost got into a fistfight at one point. It was while we were shooting a process scene where my boat is strafed by an airplane. A special-effects guy was shooting ball bearings at my boat, and he had forgotten to replace the windshield with a nonbreakable plexiglass one. Real glass went flying into my face. In a rage I grabbed a hammer and went after the guy. But Jack stepped in front of me and said, 'No you don't. They're my crew.'" 'Your crew, goddammit, they're my eyes,' I said."

John did not see *They Were Expendable* through to completion. During the final days of shooting he slipped off a camera scaffolding and fell twenty feet to the cement floor below. He suffered a compound fracture in his left leg. Robert Montgomery took over the picture and directed the last few days. Although John's injury was not life-threatening, it was painful, and he had to spend two weeks in traction at Cedars of Lebanon Hospital.

For the first time since reporting to active duty in 1941 John had time to reflect on the events of the last four years. As he lay in his hospital bed he thought of his clandestine trip to Panama, of Gregg Toland's Pearl Harbor film, the Doolittle Raid, the filming of the Battle of Midway. There was the North African campaign, the encounter with Darryl Zanuck, and the capture of the German airman. There was the "paper war" period in Washington and the six months he had spent in the Far East. There was the landing at Normandy and the days aboard Bulkeley's PT boat. A hundred names and faces flashed by John as he lay in his room: Bill Donovan, Mark Armistead, Jack Pennick, Bob Parrish, Butch Meehan, Bob Rhea, Al Wedemeyer, Claire Chennault, Spig Wead, Eddie Mannix, Junior Stout, John Bulkeley.

As he thought about the war, John realized that the four years he had spent with the Field Photographic had been the most eventful, rewarding, and satisfying period in his life. He had turned his back on the glitter of Hollywood and had found a comradeship, a fulfillment, and a sense of purpose that he had never known before. He made up his mind that after the war he was going to take the experiences of the last four years and carry them forward into civilian life; he was going to do everything he could to preserve the idealized communal life he had experienced in the military.

When John was released from the hospital in April, he made the Field Photo home his first priority, putting it ahead of even the postproduction assembly of *They Were Expendable*. After looking at scores of properties, he decided to buy a twenty-acre estate in the San Fernando Valley from Columbia executive Sam Briskin. It had a large wood-frame house, a barn, corrals, a tennis court, and a swimming pool. There were pepper trees, white picket fences, and rolling lawns. With its wide spacious grounds and recreational facilities, John felt that it was ideal. The price: $225,000.

In April 1945, when John returned to Washington, events in Europe were moving dramatically and rapidly to a climax. Allied armies were rolling into Germany, Austria, and Poland. As they did so, they came upon one torture camp after another: at Buchenwald,

Dachau, Belsen, Auschwitz, Linz Lubin, and many more. The Allies were totally unprepared for the revelations of human depravity that they saw there.

When Germany collapsed in May, the surviving Nazi leaders—Goering, Doenitz, Keitel, Hess, and the rest—were rounded up to be tried at Nuremberg. The O.S.S. was given the mission of gathering evidence to be used against the war criminals, and it fell to the Field Photographic to collect photographic documentation. John assigned Ray Kellogg and a group that included Budd and Stewart Schulberg, Bob Parrish, Joe Ziegler, and Bob Webb to the project, and sent them to Germany, where they began scouring through archives. Although John planned to go to the Nuremberg trials, he never made the trip. Through the summer of 1945 he was busy with the administrative details of disbanding the Field Photographic and commuting to Los Angeles, where he was overseeing the postproduction of *They Were Expendable* and the work on the Field Photo home.

On July 16, 1945, the first nuclear device was exploded at Los Alamos, New Mexico, and ten days later President Harry Truman presented the Japanese with an ultimatum: surrender or face annihilation. On August 6, an atomic bomb was dropped on Hiroshima, and three days later another one was dropped on Nagasaki.

On September 2, General Douglas MacArthur and the Japanese foreign minister, General Umezu, signed the instruments of surrender aboard the battleship *Missouri*. The war was over.

On September 27, John was called into Bill Donovan's office and presented with the Legion of Merit. It was a strange moment for John. He was more aware of the regret he felt at leaving behind the most rewarding years of his life than he was of the pride surging through him as Donovan pinned the medal on his chest and, with an uncharacteristic display of emotion, embraced him.

The next day, except for the small contingent at Nuremberg, the Field Photographic was officially disbanded and John Ford joined the millions of other American men in uniform making their way home.

MGM had originally planned to release *They Were Expendable* in September, but because of the Japanese surrender the studio delayed the opening until December 1945. MGM was worried that the picture wasn't going to be timely, and they were right. After four years of war Americans were tired of the military, of shortages, rationing, and the loss of loved ones.

Released on December 7, 1945, *They Were Expendable* opened to a good critical reception but small audiences. It did not make money, and after a few short months it was pulled out of release.

It was some years before its great qualities were appreciated; it is still not fully recognized as one of its director's greatest achievements.

16

The
American
Kipling: I

Christmas 1945 was the Fords' happiest and gayest holiday in years. Mary went all out to decorate the Odin Street house, and once again, after four long years, it was redolent of John's pipe tobacco mixed in with the smell of holly and pine. She put on party after party; there were boisterous reunions with Henry Fonda, just discharged from the navy, Wingate Smith, home from the army a Lieutenant Colonel, and Merian Cooper, who had retired from the air corps a Brigadier General.

Over the holidays John got the *Araner* back from the navy and made putting her back into "yacht trim" one of his first priorities. He also re-established the Emerald Bay Yacht Club and appointed Ward Bond club secretary. Bond drew up a list of the original members of the Young Men's Purity Total Abstinence and Snooker Pool Association and they became charter members of the group's postwar version. Soon after the New Year Gene Markey married actress Myrna Loy, and the membership gathered to celebrate the occasion in grand style.

To a casual observer John might have seemed to be picking up the pieces of his old life, to be slipping back into his old routine. But the truth was that the war had profoundly changed him. After four years with the O.S.S., after having served with the likes of Bill Donovan, Al Wedemeyer, and Claire Chennault, Hollywood seemed seedy, shoddy, and full of hucksters.

Before the war, the military had been an avocation, something John had played at for his amusement and used as a way of gaining social status. Now it became the centerpiece of his life. He now became a remote, paternal figure who presided over his aides and ruled his stock company in an almost military manner.

The military shaded his personal style.

There was a new military aspect to his personal style. At work he started wearing his fatigues and his navy baseball cap with the captain's eagle perched proudly on it. He kept a closet full of uniforms; perfectly tailored and carefully maintained, they stood in marked contrast to the casual work clothes he usually wore. John gleefully donned them at every opportunity—weddings, christenings, social gatherings of any kind. He joined every veterans' organization that would have him: The American Legion, the motion picture chapter of the Military Order of the Purple Heart, The Veterans of the O.S.S., The Veterans of the 101 Detachment.

Having developed a virtual obsession with military glory, John tried to milk his accomplishments in the navy for all they were worth. He was constantly maneuvering to get more medals, decorations, and awards. He tried to get a second Purple Heart, claiming that he had been injured in a buzz bomb incident in London, and he shamelessly wrote letters describing in detail how a civilian doctor (whose name he had forgotten) had treated him. John talked Bill Donovan into recommending him for a Silver Star for filming *The Battle of Midway* in actual combat, but he still didn't manage to get the award. John also cultivated a man named Jean DeBetz, a wartime O.S.S. agent and member of the Belgian underground who had emigrated to America after the war. DeBetz had connections with the Belgian royal family and made arrangements to have John presented with a Belgian Croix de Guerre.

While John went to great lengths to enhance his own military record, he was also willing to go to great lengths to help others who had been in the service. He couldn't do enough for Francis' son, Billy Ford, who had spent three and a half years as an infantryman in the South Pacific. Proud of his nephew's war record, John made arrangements to put him to work as an assistant director. He was also materially helpful to Larry and Cecile Deprita, who had spent three and a half years in a Japanese prisoner-of-war camp.

Deep down, beneath the cutting tongue and the acerbic wit, he was a kinder, more charitable man. John Wayne says, "It took me a while to realize it, but a big change had come over Jack. Before the war there had always been an edge to him. But after the war, after he had been out there, he was a lot kinder and a lot more sympathetic." Henry Fonda concurs: "The war changed Pappy. He was just as difficult, just as egomaniacal, but the sweet side of him was a lot more pronounced. He was a lot easier man to be around."

The most revealing thing he did, of course, was to create the Field Photo Home, and it more than anything else reflects the changes that had gone on inside the man. During the first few months of 1946 he was preoccupied with putting the final touches on the farm. He immersed himself in dealings with carpenters, contractors, and landscapers. He poured the remaining $75,000 from his *They Were Expendable* salary into improving the property. More important, he poured the same emotions, the same love for military tradition and service, into the Farm. Off from the main house he built a chapel, of wood frame construction, white with a green roof and miniature porticoes. Inside, the setting was non-denominational: on the altar was a Protestant cross, a Catholic crucifix, and a Star of David. Inscribed above it were the words of A. E. Housman:

"Here dead lie we because we did not choose
   to live and shame the land from which we sprung."

John also had the main house extensively redecorated. The master bedroom was permanently reserved for Bill Donovan's personal use. A den, furnished with Early American antiques, hooked rugs, and richly paneled walls, was added on. In this room were thirteen glass cases, one for each member of the Field Photographic killed in the war. Inside each case were the medals of the fallen.

John wanted the Farm to be both a living memorial to the men of the Field Photographic and a recreational facility where the veterans would *want* to come. It had a feeling of family about it that was very special. In 1946 there were 176 active members and their families. They held picnics, square dances, barbeques, and put on rodeos and exhibitions of movie stunt work. There was a bar called The Starboard Club, and it was jammed every night. There were annual Chrismas, Saint Patrick's Day, and Founder's Day parties.

In a very real way my grandfather recreated the world of his pictures at the Farm; the gatherings had the same sense of community that his films had. Everyone that was close to him, whether they were veterans of his unit or actors from his troupe, became involved with the Farm. It was a cult, a true community, and one of the most unique institutions ever created in Hollywood.

Some of my own most vivid childhood memories are of the Farm. It was a child's paradise. I remember the barn, dark, musty with the smell of salve, oats, and damp hay. I remember the tack room with its halters and bridles and the smell of saddle soap being worked into leather. There was a cannon, an old French 75, on one of the lawns. Even though its breach had been welded shut and its trails anchored in concrete, I fought and won hundreds of child-hood battles with that cannon.

At the annual Christmas Party there was a zany tradition that could have happened only in Hollywood. Santa Claus rode up in a stagecoach with a bag full of toys. We children—Waynes, Careys, Fords, Boltons, and Armisteads—would gather in the thin shade of a pepper tree, straining our ears, listening for the sound of the steel-edged wheels running over gravel. Santa Claus, a huge rotund actor—Charles Kemper, Alan Hale, or Burl Ives—would emerge laughing and hand out the gifts.

The most important day on the Farm's calendar was May 31, Memorial Day, when the veterans of the Field Photographic gathered to pay tribute to their fallen comrades. My grandfather, with his love of pageantry and military ceremony, took great delight in organizing the services down to the smallest detail. A typical service would be called to order at 11:00 A.M. sharp. The men would stand in formation, and the flag would be flown at half-staff; an invocation would then be read as a choir softly sang "America," following which there would be a reading of some sort of patriotic literature, a traditional folk hymn, and a speech by a visiting military dignitary. In closing, the names of the thirteen fallen members of the Field Photographic would be read, with a muffled drum roll and the utterance in unison of "Died for his country" after each name. The services closed with a bugle sounding taps, and the lonely sounds would echo hauntingly among the Farm's eucalyptus trees.

For years John and Merian Cooper had talked about forming their own production company. Now, after both men had been through the war and had been touched by it in similar ways, they decided to go ahead with the idea. In March 1946, they filed incorporation papers for Argosy Productions.

Argosy was a closed corporation and its backers were all close associates from the O.S.S. There were four principal investors: Bill Donovan, Ole Doering (an O.S.S. veteran and Donovan's right-hand man at his Wall Street law firm), David Bruce, and William Vanderbilt, another O.S.S. man and scion of a famous family. The company was built on three cornerstones. The first was an aristocratic disdain for some of the gaudier aspects of the picture business. The second was a sincere desire to make films of genuine merit. The third was an international orientation. Donovan, Doering, Bruce, and Vanderbilt, as former O.S.S. men, were all well connected abroad, with access to information--and financing—that few people in the picture business enjoyed. They wanted to use their contacts and expertise to make films all over the world.

As president of the company, Cooper was the financial head of Argosy Productions. But John, as chairman of the board and creative head, was clearly the dominant partner. He decided what properties to buy, what pictures to make. Foremost on his list was an unusual love story called "The Quiet Man," which had first been published in a February 1933 issue of *The Saturday Evening Post*, and which John had owned since 1936. But because the story line was thin, and most of its appeal was in the writing rather than in characters or plot, he had never been able to interest a studio in backing the project.

John wanted to make *The Quiet Man* in the west of Ireland, and in March 1946 he began working with Lord Killanin, a big, cherub-faced Irishman whom he had known for years. (He is famous today as the head of the International Olympic Committee.)

While Killanin was working out the details that would permit Argosy to produce a film in Ireland, Merian Cooper put together a deal with RKO for financing it. Argosy would make three pictures for RKO; they would share the costs and the net profits 50–50, while Argosy would retain complete creative control. Its key provision was that if the first picture made money, then RKO would let John make *The Quiet Man*.

For the initial project, John decided to film the Graham Greene novel *The Power and the Glory*—the story of a priest being hunted down in a brutally anticlerical Latin American police state. He finds refuge in a mountain village where he gets involved with a prostitute and waivers between the sins of the flesh and the call of Christ. The flesh wins, and they become lovers. Why John chose to film a seemingly noncommercial and antireligious story at a time when he needed a money-maker is difficult to say. According to Henry Fonda, John had first read the novel aboard the *Araner* in Mexico in 1939, and had tried to make it then. Says Fonda, "It had been rejected all over town because there were too many censorship problems, but Jack felt that if he took out the love affair he could make the story acceptable to them and be left with a beautiful Christ allegory." Quite probably the decision to make *The Power and the Glory* was prompted largely by reasons of convenience. Working through producer Emilio Fernandez, Bill Donovan had already raised money for a picture to be made in Mexico, and they needed a property with a Latin American setting.

John went to work with Dudley Nichols blocking out the script, which they called *The Fugitive*. They performed major surgery and took out all the sex. Then, to keep the story logical, they changed the character of the priest from an anguished but very strong man to a weak and hunted one. Henry Fonda was cast as the priest and Dolores Del Rio as the prostitute. Shooting was scheduled to begin May 1, at the Churubusco Studios in Mexico City.

But before John could venture into independent production he was still obligated to make one more Fox picture. In April 1946, Darryl Zanuck called the contractual note due, and John turned the preproduction of *The Fugitive* over to Merian Cooper. Then, grumbling all the way, he moved back into his old offices at Fox.

While John's reunion with Zanuck was friendly enough, it was strained by the fact that the studio chief wanted him to renegotiate his Fox contract. Zanuck's offer was tempting: a guarantee of $600,000 a year, plus continuation of John's nonexclusive clause, the little loophole that gave John freedom to go elsewhere and make the "noncommercial" pictures he liked so much. But John was adamant about going into independent production. This was a time when most of the major directors in Hollywood—Frank Capra, William Wyler, and George Stevens, among others—were leaving the studios, and he told Zanuck that his days as a "piece goods worker in the Hollywood sweatshops" were over.

Since Zanuck only had John's services for one picture, he wanted to put him on one with surefire commercial appeal. After considering half a dozen properties, he assigned to John the remake of a 1940 Randolph Scott vehicle called *Frontier Marshal*, the often-told story of Wyatt Earp and the gunfight at the OK Corral. Zanuck had a new script by Sam Engel and Winston Miller called *My Darling Clementine*. With Henry Fonda as Wyatt Earp, Victor Mature as Doc Holliday, Walter Brennan as the heavy, and Cathy Downs as Holliday's girl friend, Clementine Carter, John began shooting *My Darling Clementine* in Monument Valley in May 1946. Working with a generous budget and an ample shooting schedule, John shot the picture at a relaxed, easy pace. Because this was to be his last picture as a contract director he took considerable liberties in shooting it, throwing out whole passages of detailed exposition that he found "too dull." He concentrated instead on grace notes, character touches, and bits of impromptu comedy. But *My Darling Clementine* was not a fun picture for everyone concerned. Throughout the filming Victor Mature had to endure such epithets as "Greaseball," and "Liverlips," and similar examples of John's crude wit. He was understandably uneasy and on edge, but he was also working harder than he ever had before and giving a fine, tightly controlled performance. Nor was *My Darling Clementine* an enjoyable project for Walter Brennan. For whatever reason, the veteran actor and John did not get along,and after one particularly bitter exchange he told John that under no circumstances would he ever work for him again. And he never did.

John brought *My Darling Clementine* back to Fox early in June and two weeks later handed a rough cut over to Darryl Zanuck. When the studio chief screened it, he liked it and thought that some of the character touches rivaled John's best work. But he was very upset with the way in which John had freely discarded whole passages of detailed exposition. The story line, said Zanuck, was not clear and (the old argument again) the pace was too slow.

Zanuck took *My Darling Clementine* and dissected it frame by frame. He cut thirty minutes out of John's version, eliminating the weak points—the unrestrained sentimentality, the boozy, rowdy humor, the low comedy—while leaving the visual flow and the rugged action intact. He clarified the exposition and made the story line clear. In recutting *My Darling Clementine*, Darryl Zanuck, the editor supreme, markedly improved it.

Released in November 1946, *My Darling Clementine* was well received by critics and audiences. It recovered its costs within six months and went on to gross $4.5 million.

John had meanwhile turned his back on *My Darling Clementine* and returned to Argosy, where he immersed himself in *The Fugitive*. In reaction to the tight discipline and commercial considerations of *My Darling Clementine*, he set out to make *The Fugitive* a bold, sweeping artistic statement, an art-house picture of the caliber of *The Informer* or *Four Sons*. Working with an all-Mexican crew and free at last from the restrictions of Hollywood, he went after dramatic angles, shadows, backlights, stylized compositions, and ravishing pictorial effects. John's enjoyment took him over the edge of self-indulgence. In spite of protests by Nichols and Henry Fonda, he departed from the script as the whim took him, and the picture suffered accordingly.

The Fugitive was released in November 1947, exactly one year after *My Darling Clementine*. Many critics liked it, including Bosley Crowther of *The New York Times*, who called it "a symphony of light and shade, of deafening din and silence, of sweeping movement and repose." But *The Fugitive* was not popular with the public. John had gone too far with his new freedom. The photography was so stunning that it distracted the audience from the story, and for most viewers just watching *The Fugitive* was an exhausting experience. The picture was a commercial failure and a major financial setback for Argosy Productions. Most important of all, it prompted RKO to cancel, indefinitely, *The Quiet Man*.

Bitter as it was, the failure of *The Fugitive* taught John an important lesson: the price of liberty was having to work under the economic gun. A big studio could afford an occasional artistic experiment to give breadth to an actor and add prestige to its program, but a small independent company couldn't afford such luxuries. If it was to survive, Argosy Productions was going to have to make commercial pictures. Taking a lesson from the success of *My Darling Clementine*, John and Merian Cooper turned to the wide open spaces of the American West and planned their raid on the American box office there.

Between 1947 and 1950 John made five westerns under the Argosy banner: *Three Godfathers*, *Fort Apache*, *She Wore a Yellow Ribbon*, *Wagonmaster*, and *Rio Grande*. All enormously popular, they helped spark a renaissance in western films. Though they were all commercial pictures, they represented more than a retreat to a proven format. Three of the five—*Fort Apache*, *She Wore a Yellow Ribbon* and *Rio Grande*—celebrate the tradition of the United States cavalry and are among the most famous films that John ever made. They reflect his wartime experience and his fascination with the heightened sense of community among fighting men. To understand them, one must go to their source. They were all based on short stories of James Warner Bellah, a romantic chronicler of the cavalry during the Indian Wars and the most fascinating writer that John ever worked with.

I spoke to Bellah a few months before his death in 1976. A tall, gray-haired man, he was trim, blustery, and profane, carrying himself with a stiff-backed mid-Victorian air that suggested his roots in the old WASP aristocracy. His father had been a major in the army, and he had grown up on the cavalry posts of the vanishing frontier. It had ingrained in him a love for the west and the military that he never forgot. Bellah would be an interesting subject for a doctoral dissertation in American literature. He, more than John (though John has been so named), was "The American Kipling." Bellah's novels and short stories echo in American terms Rudyard Kipling's call to empire. His work speaks of conquest and the white man's burden; his stories are vigorous, energetic, and like Kipling's, given more to vivid expression than to careful logic. They are heavy on rape and racism, and their message about the Indians is clear: the only good one is a dead one. But there is also a softer side to Bellah's stories. They speak of an honor, spirit, tradition, that is largely gone in America, and they are rife with the aristocratic watchwords of duty, honor, and country.

In the winter of 1947 Bellah began publishing a series of superbly researched and beautifully descriptive short stories in *The The Saturday Evening Post*. The first of these, which appeared in the February 22, 1947, issue, was called "Massacre." Lean, bloody, and vivid, it was the story of a Civil War general named Owen Thursday who, after the war, is reduced to his former rank of major and banished, or so he feels, to a remote frontier outpost. There he feels that glory will pass him by, that he will die a forgotten man. Serving under Thursday is veteran Indian fighter Lieutenant Flint Cohill. The two men come into conflict when Thursday underestimates his Apache adversary, Cochise. They have a bitter fight, and Cohill is relieved of his command. Thursday then leads his men into a deadly trap where they are surrounded and shot down. When he realizes his tragic error, Thursday commits suicide. Later Cohill finds his body, and to protect the honor of the regiment, he removes the revolver from the dead man's hand. The story ends with Cohill fictionalizing Thursday's death for a painter to immortalize in a work to be called *Thursday's Charge* which is to hang in the Capitol dome.

From the first time John read "Massacre" he was drawn to it. Beyond its vigorous prose and its spirit of aristrocratic militarism, it seemed to articulate all his wartime emotions, his fascination with the American military tradition, and the special nobility he felt was born of combat. In March 1947, Argosy Productions bought the story outright.

Developing "Massacre" into a screenplay presented some unusual problems. The story needed to be expanded and the romantic elements needed developing. Much of its appeal was based on Bellah's prose and his hard-hitting imagery, all of which would be lost in translation. Although Bellah was a brilliant stylist, he was also a blatant racist, and his nineteenth-century attitude toward the Indians would have to be softened.

To accomplish this formidable task, John turned to a man who in many ways was Bellah's antithesis; former *New York Times* critic Frank Nugent. A ruddy man with a crew cut and thick glasses, Nugent had been brought to Hollywood by Darryl Zanuck in 1941. While Bellah traced his ancestry in America back eleven generations, Nugent was half-Jewish and half-Irish, a man whose immigrant origins seethed just beneath the surface. While Nugent could appreciate the mood, flavor, and traditional atmosphere of Bellah's story, his liberal, outsider's view of America ensured that he would have a natural sympathy for the Indians, that he wouldn't be seduced by the power of Bellah's prose.

In John's mind, one of the great attractions of "Massacre" was its depiction of life on a frontier outpost, and he was determined to preserve the same authentic spirit in the film. A great amount of research went into preparing the script. Before one word of dialogue was written, John had Nugent research the period extensively. Among other things, he had him devise intricate fictional "biographies" for each of the major characters.

Only when all the characters had been carefully researched did John let Nugent begin his script. For love interest he added the characters of Philadelphia, Owen Thursday's daughter, and Lieutenant Michael O'Rourke, a West Point graduate whose father is the post Sergeant Major and whom Thursday detests because he is a "ranker's" son.

Unlike *The Fugitive*, which had been designed as a low-budget artistic experiment, *Fort Apache*, as the script was now called, was a commercial picture with a generous $2.5 million budget. To ensure that it earned back its costs, John wanted major stars in both principal roles; he thus cast Henry Fonda and John Wayne as, respectively, Owen Thursday and Kirby Yorke (the new name of the Flint Cohill character). As Philadelphia Thursday, John cast Shirley Temple, who by now, of course, had grown up. Casting her was more than the sentimental gesture that some have suggested. John thought enough of the box-office value of her name to pay her the same $100,000 he paid John Wayne and Henry Fonda. The other roles in *Fort Apache* went to Ford regulars Anna Lee, Ward Bond, Victor McLaglen, and Jack Pennick. John's old friend George O'Brien was set with a big supporting role, while John Agar, Shirley Temple's real-life husband, played Lieutenant O'Rourke. John cast Pedro Armendariz, a handsome Mexican actor whom he had used on *The Fugitive* and had become very fond of, to play Sergeant Beaufort, the regimental interpreter.

Fort Apache had a lot of complex action, and to handle it John hired Cliff Lyons, a heavyset man with blond hair and almond-shaped eyes. He had come onto the scene immediately after the war when the SPCA, the Society for the Prevention of Cruelty to Animals, succeeded in banning the "Running W"—the tripping of horses with hidden wires. Lyons had developed a safer, more humane way of staging horse falls by training them to fall on cue for the rider. As a stunt boss Lyons introduced John to a whole new generation of stuntmen and bit players who would appear in all of his postwar westerns. There was a little gamecock of an Irishman named Frankie McGrath, who wasn't afraid of anything—including John Ford. There was Terri Wilson, a tall limber athlete. (Wilson and McGrath would later become famous as regulars on Ward Bond's *Wagontrain* TV series.) There were Chuck Hayward, nicknamed Good Chuck because he didn't drink and was a devout family man, and Chuck Robertson, nicknamed Bad Chuck because he was none of the above. There was Ben Johnson, a part-Cherokee Indian from Pawhuska, Oklahoma, who was absolute poetry on horseback.

John could think of only one place to shoot *Fort Apache*— Monument Valley. After having shot part of *Stagecoach* and most of *My Darling Clementine* there, he knew every inch of its beautiful terrain. His generosity toward the valley's Navajo Indians had also paid off, and he had built up a large and loyal repertory company among them. Even more important, both *Stagecoach* and *My Darling Clementine* had been successful box-office pictures. Now, with the future of Argosy Productions on the line, he needed a hit more than ever. Always the superstitious Irishman, John believed that Monument Valley was his "lucky spot."

Shooting began in late June 1947.

Despite John's enthusiasm for the material, and the careful preparation that had gone into it, *Fort Apache* proved a difficult picture to make. In those years facilities were limited in Monument Valley, and most of the company had to live in tents pitched outside Goulding's lodge. It was midsummer and temperatures reached 115 degrees at midday, cooling down to 90 degrees at night. Actors and crew suffered alike in the searing heat. The shooting was continually delayed by high winds and desert storms. Forced to shut down the picture time and time again, John fell badly behind schedule. He was under a tremendous amount of pressure to keep the film within its budget, and found himself working eighteen-hour days trying to catch up. His mood was brittle, his temper short, and his sharp, barbed tongue spared no one. His principal target was Shirley Temple's husband, young John Agar. John chastised him for his halting delivery and his awkardness on horseback, and delighted in calling him "Mr. Temple" in front of the cast and crew.

At one point Agar rebelled and stormed off the set, vowing to quit the picture, but John Wayne took him aside and convinced him to stick it out. He explained some of the pressures John was under and said, "You're the whipping boy now, but give him time. He'll get around to the rest of us soon enough." Agar didn't have long to wait. A few days later Ward Bond was flown up to Monument Valley. He announced his arrival by having the pilot buzz the company which was set up out in the middle of the valley. He destroyed one take and forced John to wait until he landed before he could resume shooting. Wayne turned to Agar and said, "Well, you can relax now, he's found another whipping boy."

During these years, John liked to make jokes about the size of Ward Bond's rather pronounced posterior. He and Wayne often had their picture taken standing beside a horse's rear end, and they would send the snapshot to Bond with a note that said, "Thinking of you." On *Fort Apache* John carried this gag one step further. Unbeknownst to Bond, he set up his camera so that it actually featured the actor's butt, and in the finished picture there are several scenes where he actually shoots around Bond's behind rather than over his shoulder. John's willingness to hurt his picture to play a practical joke points to his more relaxed approach to his work as an independent producer. He indulged himself whenever he wanted, milking every gag for all it was worth, letting his camera linger on anything he thought poetic, and throwing out long expository scenes if he thought them dull.

John was also in complete control of the editing of *Fort Apache*, and he was able to shape it as he saw fit. The film has a complicated plot, and it continually shifts its emphasis from action to comedy to drama. *Fort Apache*'s greatest strength is its action scenes, which, except for one short chase early on, all take place in the last half hour. There is a dramatic confrontation between the arch-enemies Cochise and Owen Thursday, who meet under a flag of truce with their men massed behind them. This is followed by the climactic battle in which Thursday leads his men into the Apache trap, and to annihilation.

Fort Apache ends with a powerful ironic epilogue. As in the short story, Owen Thursday has become a hero in the public mind, and the picture closes with Wayne delivering a eulogy of Thursday and the men of the regiment to a group of newspaper men:

"They'll keep on living as long as the regiment lives. Their pay is thirteen dollars a month, and their diet is beans and hay. They'll fight over cards or rotgut whiskey, but they'll share the last drop in their canteens. Their names may change, and their faces, but they're the regiment. The regular army, now and fifty years from now. They're better men than they used to be. Thursday did that. He made it a command to be proud of."

John scored the film with traditional cavalry songs from the 1870s: "Gary Owen," "The Girl I Left Behind Me," and "Regular Army O." They beautifully enhance the story's military theme.

Fort Apache opened March 9, 1948, to mixed reviews. More important than the critical reception, however, was the fact that *Fort Apache* was the commercial success John—and Argosy—needed. It returned its $2.8 million cost in six months and eventually grossed $4.9 million, easily surpassing *My Darling Clementine*. Not only did it put Argosy Productions in the black, but in John's mind it was proof that the public shared his visions of military glory and was ready for more pictures based on the stories of James Warner Bellah.

17
Uncle Jack

In September 1947, John's old friend and mentor, Harry Carey, died of cancer. John was deeply grieved. Carey had given him his first real chance and over the years had remained one of his closest friends. Carey had gone through many rough years since his days as a silent film star and only recently had made a comeback as a character actor. To make sure Hollywood paid Carey the tribute John thought he deserved, he put on an enormous funeral at the Field Photo home. Carey's body lay in state in the newly completed chapel for two days before the service. Then, on the day of the funeral, his flag-draped coffin was put on a caisson and there was a long procession up the Farm's tree-lined drive. Carey's horse, Sonny, saddled and riderless, clomped along behind.

But the funeral alone wasn't enough to express John's affection. To pay homage to his old friend he decided to launch his son, Harry Carey, Jr., as an actor. For a vehicle he chose to remake "Three Godfathers," the Peter B. Kyne short story that he and Carey, Sr., had made in 1919. "Three Godfathers" was the story of three bank robbers, desperate hunted men, who find an infant abandoned in the desert. After two of the robbers are killed, the third takes the baby to town and surrenders, giving up his freedom to save the child. John cast John Wayne, Pedro Armendariz, and young Carey as the three bank robbers, and Ward Bond was set as the sheriff chasing them.

Today Harry Carey, Jr., or "Dobe" as he is called, is a veteran of thirty years in motion pictures. He has gone from the carrot-headed kid playing in John's films to one of Hollywood's senior western actors. Perceptive and funny, open and honest, he is perhaps the best raconteur in the old Ford stock company. He told me about the making of *Three Godfathers*, and, more importantly, about his own unique relationship with John Ford:

"Even though I had known John Ford all my life, I was scared to death of him when I first went to work for him. I had called him 'Uncle Jack' since I was a little kid, but suddenly I was afraid to call him that. I didn't know what to call him. He was so erratic—he was like quicksilver—and I never knew when he was going to jump all over me. A few weeks before the picture began shooting, we had a birthday party for my mother at the Farm. When it came time to cut the cake, Uncle Jack handed me a knife and said, 'Here, Dobe, you cut it.' I took it, and for no reason at all he started yelling at me because of the way I was holding the knife. 'Goddammit, you don't hold a knife that way.' Then he smiled and said, 'You're going to hate my guts before this picture is over.' He said that to me three or four times that night.

"We shot *Three Godfathers* in Death Valley. It was in May, and that's a beautiful time of year up there. We stayed at the Furnace Creek Inn, and Uncle Jack was in seventh heaven. He was off on location with no front-office types to look over his shoulder, and he had both Pete Armendariz and Ward Bond to pick on.

"Pete was a great favorite of Uncle Jack's. He was a very wealthy man and was a big star in Mexican pictures—the equivalent to Rudolph Valentino down there. When he came up to make *Three Godfathers* he thought he was going to be the star of the picture. He showed up at the location in a skin-tight black leather costume with silver studs and a great big sombrero, looking like Leo Carrillo in the Santa Barbara Parade. When Uncle Jack saw this outfit he took him aside and said, 'Pete, I want you to forget about the hero you play in Mexican pictures. You're playing a bandit, a rogue, a low-life, with a flock of illegitimate kids you've deserted in Mexico. Everything you have, you have stolen. Now here, put this wardrobe on.' He gave him a pair of pants with conchos on the sides, a gringo shirt with flowers on it, a Mexican vest, and an old beat-up sombrero.

"When Pete saw this wardrobe he went into a rage, but Uncle Jack just ignored him. For a horse he gave him an old swaybacked mare with a Mexican saddle and a huge bedroll tied on back. Pete was furious. He thought he should have a sorrel horse with a silver saddle and didn't think he needed a bedroll even though he was 5,000 miles from home. 'I am one of the finest horsemen in all of Mexico, surely you don't expect me to ride this goddamn burro!' Every time Pete complained Uncle Jack would go over to the prop truck and get a coffee pot or a frying pan and hang it on his saddle.

"Ward Bond also had a big part in *Three Godfathers*. Ward was a hell of an actor, but his problem was that he had a star complex. When Ward was around you could relax. He took the heat off of everyone else. He was always doing something like interrupting a tender love scene to complain about his dressing room, and Uncle Jack would get all over him. But Ward had a hide like a rhinoceros, and he could take anything that Uncle Jack could dish out. He'd answer right back and make it twice as bad.

"Ward, Duke, Pete, and Uncle Jack were all terrific card players, and every night on location they played pitch. I'm not a card player. At night after dinner, I'd go to my room and work on my lines. In those days I had a really good singing voice, a deep baritone that wasn't at all like my speaking voice. Uncle Jack always had me sing 'The Streets of Laredo' or 'Come all ye Saints' at those affairs at the farm. I always used to get a little gassed up, so I wouldn't be nervous. About nine o'clock at night there would be a knock on my door. I'd open it, and Wingate would be standing there. He'd say, 'Mr. Ford wants to see you.' I'd go over to his room. It would be full of cigar smoke and silver dollars spilled all over a green felt table. Uncle Jack would say to me, 'Sing "The Streets of Laredo."' The game would stop, and I'd sing the song. Afterwards Uncle Jack would sit there for a moment then say, 'Thanks, Ol' Dobe.' Then I'd leave.

"John Ford was a born psychologist. He could manipulate actors better than any other director I ever worked for. If you were doing a tender love scene, he was just marvelous to you; he treated you with loving care, and you wanted to kiss him after every shot. But if it was a scene that had violence in it or anything to do with your coming apart emotionally, he was just the opposite. He'd start digging and picking on you the moment you walked on the set. On *Three Godfathers* I was supposed to be real downcast. I start dying in the beginning, and I'm dying all the way through it. Uncle Jack was picking on me from the first day of shooting. He kept saying, 'Jesus Christ, I wish I'd have gotten Audie Murphy for this part.'

"I was always self-conscious and never really comfortable with him off the set, but I was completely relaxed in front of the camera. Now figure that one out. I don't care how much he picked on me or how much he chewed my ass out, I was always completely relaxed when I worked for him. He gave me tremendous confidence, and I was never more at ease. I never ate better, and I never slept better than when I was working in one of his movies. That's the God's truth.

"There was a very special feeling on every John Ford set. It was the feeling that something great was happening, a feeling of reverence. It wasn't a feeling of reverence for John Ford; it was a feeling of reverence for art. It was like being in church. Maybe the music had something to do with it. Danny Borzage was always there with his accordion. Danny had a song for everybody. Duke's was 'Marquita,' from *They Were Expendable*. Ward's was 'Wagons West,' Hank Fonda's was 'Red River Valley,' and mine was 'The

Streets of Laredo.' Danny would play that song every time he saw me, and I'm practically bawling just thinking about it now.

"My last scene in *Three Godfathers* was shot back on the lot at RKO Pathe. After we shot it Uncle Jack said to me, 'OK, kid, that's it. You're finished. You can go home now.' I said, 'Well, can I just sort of hang around for a while?' 'No,' he said, 'I'm going to shoot something I don't want you to see.' I remember thinking, what the hell's going on here. I walked out to my dressing room, and as I did a horse trailer pulled up with my father's horse, old Sonny, in it. He was all shined up and reshod and everything. I knew my being sent home had something to do with the horse's being there. Then, when I saw the picture I understood. When it opens, it shows a cowboy in silhouette that looks exactly like my father. He rides to the top of a hill, pushes his hat back on his head, and looks off. Then a title comes on, 'Dedicated to Harry Carey, a bright star in the early western sky.' That was Cliff Lyons riding Sonny and doubling my dad.

"A few days later I was called back onto the lot to do some dubbing. As I was leaving, I saw Uncle Jack sitting outside in his station wagon. I went over and reached in and shook his hand and told him what a great education the picture had been for me, and I thanked him for the opportunity. Then I said, 'Uncle Jack, I don't hate you.' 'Well, that's a hell of a thing to say,' he said. 'No sir, you don't understand. You said before we started the picture that I was going to hate you when it was over. But I don't hate you. I love you.'

"That seemed to embarrass him. He didn't know what to say. He just grunted and drove off."

The American Kipling: II

In the fall of 1947, as John was putting the finishing touches on *Fort Apache*, the House Un-American Activities Committee began its investigation of Hollywood. Much has been written about this investigation; most who have studied it agree that it was an outgrowth of cold-war frustrations and an attempt by certain members of Congress to gain power and publicity. Outside the Presidency, Hollywood was the most visible institution in American life, and news about film stars—particularly film stars in trouble—had always guaranteed widespread publicity.

Though John was more conservative-thinking, more a man of the Establishment, after his experiences in the war he saw the HUAC investigation of Hollywood as a "bully tactic" and immediately sprang to the defense of those accused. Using his influence with the Hollywood chapter of the Military Order of the Purple Heart, he had them draft a resolution condemning the investigation. He joined an organization called "The Republican and Democratic Joint Committee of Hollywood for the Preservation of Civil Liberties," and, as in the political struggles of the 1930s, he used the Screen Directors Guild as a forum, joining forces with fellow directors John Huston, George Sidney, and William Wyler. On October 20, 1947, they wired a protest to the committee:

"The following telegram is being sent this date to the chairman of the investigating committee of the Congress. Every signatory of this telegram is an American citizen, opposed to Communism. Making motion pictures is our business. Our homes and our families are in Hollywood. We are proud to belong to this industry. Now our industry is faced with a congressional investigation. We recognize the right of Congress to investigate, but we firmly believe that an American citizen should not have his reputation attacked by anyone without the rights which we believe it was the intent of the Constitution to give... We believe these rights should include the right to make a statement in his behalf, to be represented by council and have the privilege of cross-examination of witnesses against him ... If there are traitors in Hollywood, or anywhere else, let the Federal Bureau of Investigation point them out. Let the Attorney General bring them before the courts. But as citizens, let them have a fair trial, protected by the guarantees of the Constitution. Such is The Bill of Rights."

But John's liberal stand against the HUAC didn't change his basic drift to the Right. His primary interest was in celebrating the American military tradition. Beyond that, he needed to make commercial pictures that would keep Argosy afloat. He had found a winning formula in *Fort Apache*, one that both worked commercially and expressed his vision of military glory. Even before that film was released, John was busy adapting still another James Warner Bellah short story called "War Party." Written with the same vigorous intensity and the same hard-hitting imagery that "Massacre" possessed, "War Party" was the tale of Captain Nathan Brittles, a veteran of forty-three years in the cavalry, who faces an Indian uprising on the eve of his retirement.

By now there was quite a love triangle between John, Merian Cooper, and Bellah, and in June 1948 Argosy brought him to Hollywood to adapt his own story. Bellah was good at creating certain kinds of characters and writing at a high emotional pitch, but he was weak at love interests and at developing complex exposition. So, when John felt that Bellah had contributed all he could, he turned his draft over to Laurence Stallings.

A graduate of Annapolis, Stallings had been a lieutenant in the Marine Corps in the First World War and had planned a military career, but he had lost a leg at the battle of Château-Thierry. Mustered out of the corps in 1918, Stallings turned to writing and within a few years had written a best-selling novel called *Plumes*, a hit film called *The Big Parade*, and, with the playwright Maxwell Anderson, *What Price Glory?*, probably the greatest play to come out of World War I. More of a dramatist than Bellah, Stallings brought pacing, structure, and crisp dialogue to the story. For love interest he added a character named Olivia, developed an elaborate courtship between her and two young cavalry lieutenants, and gave the story a more romantic title: he called it *She Wore a Yellow Ribbon*.

Stallings' main contribution wasn't what he added, however, but what he developed. He took two scenes briefly alluded to in the short story and developed them into powerful dramatic moments. In the first, Nathan Brittles passes by the post graveyard where his wife is buried and chats with her as though she were still very much alive; in the second, Brittles is presented by his troop with a watch and chain inscribed "To Captain Nathan Brittles from the men of B Company. Lest we forget."

After Bellah and Stallings had completed their work, John turned the script over to Frank Nugent, his favorite "body and fender man," for a final polishing. Nugent tied the exposition together, reworked the dialogue and made it authentic to the period. He also added a stirring narration that tied the rambling story together.

She Wore a Yellow Ribbon cried out to be made in color, and John hired the premier color cinematographer in Hollywood to photograph it. Winton C. Hoch was a former chemist and one of the pioneers of the Technicolor process. In preparing the picture, John, art director Jim Basevi, and Hoch pored over the paintings of western artist Frederic Remington and carefully studied their hues, color tones, and treatment of the western landscape.

Although the choice wasn't obvious to everyone, John knew there was only one man to play the aging, cantankerous Nathan Brittles: John Wayne. The year before, Wayne had starred in Howard Hawks's *Red River*, and it was as important a milestone in his career as *Stagecoach* had been. Playing a character named Tom Dunson, a rough, weather-beaten, middle-aged man, an obsessed fanatic, Wayne proved that he was an actor with a much broader range than anyone had suspected. As Wayne says today, "Jack never respected me as an actor until I made *Red River*." Wayne's career was now really starting to move.

She Wore a Yellow Ribbon was assigned a budget of $1,851,290, considerably less than *Fort Apache*'s $2,252,000, but more than enough considering that Wayne was the only high-priced star.

Production began in Monument Valley in October 1948.

If John had the Monument Valley "drill down" on *Fort Apache*, by the time he made *She wore a Yellow Ribbon*, he knew everything there was to know about working there, every dramatic vista and every good road. He shot the picture at a blistering pace, averaging between eight and ten script pages a day.

She Wore a Yellow Ribbon is the best remembered of John's "cavalry trilogy," and Winnie Hoch's sweeping Technicolor vistas are the reason why. But Hoch was a laboratory man, with no real appreciation for the production end of film making. On the set he was a tinkerer and an adjuster of dials; everything was always perfectly lit, perfectly focused, and perfectly framed. But he was oblivious to actors waiting in hot lights, beads of perspiration breaking through their makeup, while he fidgeted with a lamp and fussed with a focal length.

She Wore a Yellow Ribbon marked the beginning of a long and often stormy association between John and Hoch, and some of their battles are the stuff of which Hollywood legends are made. At one point in the film John was shooting a line of cavalry when a desert storm came up and filled the sky with angry clouds. John thought it made a good dramatic background and wanted to photograph it, but Hoch didn't think there was enough light. John actually had to insist that he roll the camera. Hoch did, but then filed a formal protest with the American Society of Cinematographers, claiming that the scene "wasn't acceptable" to him and that he had only shot it because he had been "ordered" to do so. The resulting shot was one of the most beautiful in the finished picture and one of the reasons why Hoch won an Academy Award for his work on the film.

Red River had been a milestone in John Wayne's career, but *She Wore a Yellow Ribbon* was the point at which he blossomed into full professional maturity. His portrayal of the cantankerous but kindly Nathan Brittles was one of his greatest performances and firmly established him as a mature leading man, giving him a character he could play for years. His two best-remembered scenes are the ones that were developed by Laurence Stallings, in which he sits at his wife's grave watering the flowers and telling her about Custer's Massacre, and in which he is presented with an inscribed silver watch by the men of his company. Wayne says today that John added a last-minute bit of business that gave the watch scene a whole extra dimension. "He had me reach for an old pair of bifocals. I'm embarrassed and fumble with them. It was a bit of comedy that perfectly balanced the sentiment and kept the scene from becoming maudlin." Wayne's reading of the inscription, "To Captain Nathan Brittles from the men of B Company" and his choking back the line "Lest we forget" is quite possibly the finest bit of acting in his career.

The breakneck pace with which John shot *She Wore a Yellow Ribbon* paid off financially. John completed the picture in thirty-one days and nearly half a million dollars *under* budget, a figure that says a lot about his production expertise. Working with editor Jack Murray, he assembled the film in the winter of 1949. Although the film continually shifts from comedy to action to warm domestic scenes, *She Wore a Yellow Ribbon* is superbly bound together by Winnie Hoch's magnificent cinematography.

As much as any film he ever made, *She Wore a Yellow Ribbon* reflects John's own idealized vision of life on the frontier. The film builds with subtle momentum and montage until Nathan Brittles, acting without orders, stampedes the Comanche horses and thus averts an Indian War; it ends with him avoiding the retirement he dreads, instead riding off "to the new settlements of California" when his appointment as Civilian Chief of Scouts comes through.

John had composer Richard Hageman write a stirring score built primarily around the traditional cavalry song "She Wore a Yellow Ribbon," from which the picture takes its name. As in *Fort Apache*, he closed it with an homage to the cavalry which reinforced the military theme and preserved the flavor of the short story:

"So here they are, the dog-faced soldiers, the regulars, the fifty cents a day professionals, riding the outposts of a nation. From Fort Reno to Fort Apache, from Sheridan to Stark, they were all the same. Men in dirty shirt blue, and only a cold page in the history books to mark their passing. But wherever they rode, and whatever they fought for, that place became the United States."

She Wore a Yellow Ribbon was released in October 1948. From its first day of release it was a solid box-office success and went on to gross $5.2 million. Though this film is revered by John Ford buffs today, it was not generally well received by the critics of its day. A curious thing was happening to John: although he was making some of the best, most profitable, and certainly most remembered films of his life, his once-exalted reputation with the critics was beginning to fade. Critics of the day liked pictures that broke with the Hollywood tradition to deal with contemporary themes. "Realism" was the order of the day. Critics were finding John's Kiplingesque call to arms, his themes of manifest destiny and of an empire thrusting westward, particularly hard to stomach. More and more they were looking on John as one of Hollywood's grand old men, an honored has-been to be rememberd for such masterpieces as *The Informer, The Grapes of Wrath*, and *How Green Was My Valley*. Andrew Sarris summed it up in 1975 when he wrote, "To the critics of his time and even after, Ford appeared as a grizzled old prospector, who had lost his way out of Monument Valley."

If John's reputation with the critics was beginning to fade, his artistic world was becoming more and more a refuge, a region where he could create his own values, loyalties, and beliefs, and turn them into poetry. In 1950 he made a small scale western called *Wagonmaster*. The story was simple: a Mormon wagontrain sets out across the Utah desert in search of a fertile region beyond the mountains. A tale suffused with nostalgia, John cast it as though it were a family reunion: Ward Bond was the irascible wagonmaster, and Russell Simpson a censorious elder. Ben Johnson and Dobe Carey play two cowboys who guide the wagontrain and Joanne Dru is a spirited girl with a past. Once described as "an intimate epic," *Wagonmaster* is expansive and relaxed and stands as one of the most purely lyrical films John ever made. Though it is a western, its mood anticipates *The Quiet Man*.

John Wayne should have benefited more than he did from the success of *Fort Apache* and *She Wore a Yellow Ribbon*, but he wasn't able to. During these years Wayne was locked into an ironclad contract at Republic Pictures, a small studio that specialized in "B" westerns.

Republic was run by a man named Herbert J. Yates, who had made a fortune speculating in tobacco. In 1932 he had bought Consolidated Film Industries, a laboratory that processed film for small "poverty row" producers on credit. Over the years, like a long-tentacled octopus, Yates gained control of a number of these companies. In 1935 he brought a number of them together and formed Republic Pictures.

Yates was a shrewd businessman, but there was something clumsy, even comic, about the way he ran his studio. John Wayne says, simply, "He had no taste." He was a financier and a money man who had no flair for showmanship. Moreover he had a way of getting himself into ridiculous situations. For example, he was madly in love with a Czechoslovakian ice skater forty years his junior named Vera Hruba Ralston. She was stiff, awkward, and spoke with a heavy, almost unintelligible accent. But Yates thought she was the greatest thing ever to hit Hollywood, and he was determined to make her a star. He made picture after picture with her, and they were all financial disasters.

Wayne was understandably restless at Republic. On the one hand he was making pictures of the quality of *Fort Apache*, *Red River* and *She Wore a Yellow Ribbon*, but on the other he still had to come back to Republic to make pictures of a far inferior quality. Since he couldn't get out of his Republic contract, Wayne was determined to do something to improve the quality of the pictures he made there. He recalls:

"As long as I was stuck at Republic, I thought I might as well try to get Jack to come out there too. I knew that Yates was worried about television taking the audience away from 'B' pictures. I knew he wanted to start making 'A' pictures. I went to him and told him he should get Jack Ford to come to Republic. If he got him, then the other big directors would follow.

"Yates liked the idea. He said, 'OK, what do I have to do?' I said, 'Let him make a property he owns called "The Quiet Man." Give him fifteen percent of the gross and tell him nobody checks his budgets.' Yates took out a pencil and wrote this into a three-page contract on yellow legal paper. Then he signed it and said, 'Give this to Ford the next time you see him.'

"That night I went over to play bridge with Jack, Dick Calhoun, and Grant Withers. I said, 'Coach, before we start, I've got something I want you to read.' I gave him Yates's contract. He held it an inch or so away from eye and read it, then wadded it into a ball and threw it into the fireplace. He never answered me. He never said, 'Jesus, Duke, that's a hell of a deal, but I don't trust that bastard Yates.' He never said another word. I thought he was mad at me for buttin' into his personal affairs where I had no business. But the next thing I knew he had made a deal with Yates to make 'The Quiet Man' and had moved into an office next to mine."

The deal Argosy negotiated with Yates was strikingly similiar to the one John and Merian Cooper had made with RKO three years before. Argosy was to make three pictures for Republic. They would split the financing, and after Republic deducted 15 percent for overhead, they would split the gross profits 50–50. John could make anything he wanted for the first picture. If it made money, and only if it made money, he could go ahead and make *The Quiet Man*.

For the first project John decided to stick with a proven money-making formula and film another Bellah short story. In February 1950, Argosy bought one called "Mission With No Record." It was the story of a steel-hearted perfect soldier named

Colonel Massarne, whose son has enlisted in the regular army after flunking out of West Point. He turns up in his father's regiment in the west, but Massarne is so dedicated to duty, so afraid of being accused of favoritism, that he refuses to recognize the boy as his son.

"Mission With No Record" was adapted by John's old friend James Kevin McGuinness, who had recently fallen from favor at MGM. (According to Wayne, the conservative McGuinness was the victim of a "liberal blacklist" because of his political activity.) McGuinness expanded, complicated, and added love interest to Bellah's story, which in the film version became *Rio Grande*.

With Wayne as Massarne (the name was changed to Kirby Yorke in the script) and Maureen O'Hara as his wife, John shot *Rio Grande* in Moab, Utah, in June and July of 1950. The picture is notable for several things, among them because it marks the beginning of a long and successful casting match between Wayne and Maureen O'Hara. John himself got along exceptionally well with Maureen O'Hara, whom he had used on *How Green Was My Valley*. They had their "Irish connection" working for them, and they frequently held long conversations in Gaelic—which must have sounded awfully strange in the middle of the Utah desert.

Rio Grande also marks the beginning of John's turbulent, quarrelsome relationship with Republic chief Herb Yates. Republic was a second-class operation that operated on niggardly, penny-pinching principles, the kind that John hadn't seen since his Universal days. Even though John had trimmed *Rio Grande's* budget down to a paltry $1,238,000 (compared to $2.5 million for *Fort Apache* and $1.8 million for *She Wore a Yellow Ribbon*), Yates kept picking away at this figure until the day shooting began. At the last minute he got John to cut the salaries of both Ben Johnson and Harry Carey, Jr. He also got John to promise to pick up time and save another $28,000 in the below-the-line costs.

When shooting began, John learned that in addition to all his other faults Herb Yates was a meddlesome executive, the kind that was always slipping onto the set to offer his opinion on a prop, a camera angle, or a wardrobe detail. One day, after John had come back to Republic for interiors, Yates and a group of his lieutenants came onto the set. They were standing off in a dark corner of the sound stage watching John shoot a scene. When John saw them, he stopped the action and gathered the entire company around him.

"What's going on, Jack?" Yates wanted to know.

"Herb, when I go to your office the phone doesn't ring and nobody barges in. You always give me your undivided attention." He flicked the ash off his cigar. "Well, now you're in *my* office, and I'm returning the courtesy. You have my undivided attention. What is it that you wanted?"

When the dust from their fights had settled, Yates could see that John had made him a nugget of a film. *Rio Grande* was filled with banners and bugles and John Ford cavalrymen riding along a western skyline. It had action, drama, excitement, and romance. Even Herb Yates liked it. After he screened it for a group of Republic's distributors he wired John that he thought it would be one of the great pictures of the year. Yates was so delighted with *Rio Grande* that he gave John the go-ahead on "The Quiet Man" even before it was released.

But John wasn't able to move directly on to "The Quiet Man." In October 1950, the navy asked him to make a propaganda film about the war which had broken out in Korea. John had been following the conflict with great interest and talked about it constantly to Merian Cooper, John Wayne, and anyone else who would listen. He was disturbed by the deteriorating military situation and by the American public's lack of enthusiasm for the war.

After talking Herb Yates into distributing the film, John reactivated Mark Armistead and two of his best combat photographers from the last war: Charlie Bohuy and Bob Rhea. The day after Christmas 1950, they left for Korea, where they arrived on New Year's Day 1951.

After six days of filming in and around Pusan, John was surprised when he received orders to fly to Japan. He was even more surprised when he found out why: General Douglas MacArthur had personally sent for him. He wanted to meet his favorite director.

Leaving the enlisted men behind, John and Mark Armistead were flown to Tokyo, and for a day they luxuriated in the old Imperial Hotel. Armistead remembers, "Jack Ford's personal habits were bad enough, but you should have seem him after a week in Korea. He hadn't shaved or changed his uniform in a week, and he was a mess. It took him about twenty minutes to turn the hotel room into a disaster area of mud-encrusted clothes, cigar butts, and

Hershey bar wrappers. I rummaged all over Tokyo and stole a clean set of navy blues with captain's stripes on them. Then I got Jack cleaned up enough for his appointment with MacArthur."

On the evening of January 8, a limousine picked John up and took him to MacArthur's headquarters in the American Embassy. He was greeted by General Charles Willoughby, MacArthur's G-2 officer, and taken in to meet the Great Man. John had never been in awe of Douglas MacArthur in the way that many people he knew were. As an O.S.S. man, John knew of the bitter fights that had gone on between MacArthur and Bill Donovan, and about the General's high-handed refusal to work with the O.S.S. during the war.

Somehow John had expected someone heavier and more regal than the long, lean, almost spare man that greeted him. The general was dressed in creased suntans and the jaunty gold-braided hat was conspicuously absent. The two men sat, smoked their pipes, and talked. John was amazed to learn that MacArthur was familiar with all his pictures, and even more amazed to learn that he knew every detail of his war record. MacArthur told John that he had grown up on the frontier posts of the southwest, and that he considered John's cavalry pictures an authentic reproduction of life on a frontier outpost. The general went on to say that he considered them among the best films ever made. John was elated and stunned.

The next day John and Armistead flew back to Korea, where they still had a film to make. Not surprisingly, John's feelings about MacArthur had changed completely, and he spent the entire flight talking about the general, calling him "a great American."

Back in Korea, John and his men reported aboard the aircraft carrier U.S.S. *Philippine Sea*, to photograph carrier operations. John himself flew enough missions off the *Philippine Sea* to earn an Air Medal. It would prove to be an important decoration.

While John was still aboard the *Philippine Sea*, Mark Armistead went over to the battleship *Missouri*, the flagship of Vice-Admiral Struble. He recalls,

"On the *Missouri* I told Admiral Struble that Ford's birthday was coming up on February 1 and asked if we could do something for him. He said, 'OK I'll send for him.' He sent a destroyer over to the *Philippine Sea* and picked Jack up. They brought him over and transferred him by breeches buoy. When Jack was suspended over the water between the two ships, the *Missouri* rolled way over in the swell, and he got dunked. He was wet and kind of mad when they brought him on board. Apparently they had caught him by surprise. He had an Army field jacket and a pair of Japanese boots on, and he hadn't shaved in about four days. Struble had the ship's band out in full dress uniform playing 'Happy Birthday' for him.

"It was pretty cold, and I had to find some dry clothes for him. The only uniform I could find that fit him belonged to a lieutenant in the Chaplain's Corps. He wore it the whole time he was aboard the *Missouri*.

"I'd been flying in the helicopter that had been spotting the *Missouri*'s shells. I had noticed that they would only fire three guns at a time. At Ford's birthday party I asked Admiral Struble if he would fire a nine-gun salvo. 'It would look spectacular on film,' I said. There was a dead silence around the room. They looked at me as though I were some kind of an idiot. They told me that no battleship ever fired all nine guns at the same time. They were afraid that the ship would roll over. Finally Struble said, 'What the hell, I'm due for retirement. I've often wondered what would happen myself. Let's find out tomorrow.' The next day they fired a nine-gun salvo. The *Missouri* rolled over about forty-five degrees. Ford was in a helicopter and photographed the whole thing."

On February 3, John and his men were flown back to Pusan. John wanted to get some ground-combat footage, so they commandeered a jeep and drove to Andong, the forward position of the First Marine Division. They stayed there for the next five days photographing sporadic action at the forward positions.

On February 10, they flew home via Tokyo, where they spent four days waiting for air transportation. John was drinking heavily in Tokyo, and Armistead and the two enlisted men spent the better part of their layover taking care of him.

Back at Republic by the end of February, John began breaking down and organizing his Korean film. He screened it for Jim Bellah and asked him to write the narration. Then, without mentioning Bellah, John showed his film to Frank Nugent, and also asked him to write a script. Nugent's narration was more cinematic and logical, but it lacked the emotion and the intensity of Bellah's. As he had done with the *Battle of Midway*, John took the best of both versions, edited them together, and had John Ireland speak the narration.

This Is Korea as the film was called, was released by Republic in August 1951. The film was so poorly received that the studio had a great deal of difficulty getting theater owners to book it. Most of those who agreed did so only for patriotic reasons.

The navy wanted the film's profits to go to its own and the Marine Corps' relief funds, but Herb Yates wanted to keep the profits himself. It was a moot point; *This Is Korea* never recovered its costs.

This Is Korea was a commercial and artistic failure, but it did bring John something he wanted very badly. The Air Medal he had earned flying off the *Philippine Sea* was a combat decoration, and in those years reserve officers could retire one grade above the last rank held if they had a combat decoration. As a captain in the naval reserve, John could now retire as an admiral. In March 1951, the naval chapter on his life officially closed, and he became Admiral John Ford, United States Naval Reserve, Retired. Had he waited three more years he would have had a full twenty years in the reserves and would have qualified for a significant pension. But John opted for early retirement and waived the pension so he could become an admiral that much sooner. John didn't care about the money. Being an admiral was a dream fulfilled. The two stars on his collar meant more than all the Oscars on his mantel.

This Is Korea was an important landmark for John. He had freely given his time and his talents and was rewarded, if indirectly, with his admiral's star. But there is an irony here: he had tried to glorify an unpopular war and had made a bad picture as a result. He had miscalculated his audience.

America was changing, even if John wasn't. He was the American Kipling, but the country was starting to turn away from his call.

19

The
Quiet Man

The Quiet Man was John Ford's most cherished personal project and, quite possibly, his most beloved film. A love story set in a pastoral Ireland almost too beautiful to believe, it was a completely different kind of picture from John's postwar westerns and represents another side of his nature altogether. The story, the characters, its setting in the west of Ireland, make *The Quiet Man* the most autobiographical film he ever made.

Based on a short story by Maurice Walsh that John had owned since 1936, "The Quiet Man" was the tale of Shawn Kelvin, who, at twenty, left his native Ireland and went to America to toil in the steel mills of Pittsburgh and fight as a professional boxer. Now, at thirty-five, he returns home, buys a small farm and begins to work it and tries to forget about his life of hardship and violence in America.

Shawn meets and begins courting beautiful Ellen O'Grady, but her brother and guardian, big Liam, doesn't like Shawn and threatens to withhold his sister's dowry. Shawn marries her anyway, and they settle into a fine and comfortable life in Shawn's cottage. Their marriage ripens into a deep and lasting love, but there is one sore point in this union—the dowry Ellen feels she's entitled to it and which she wants Shawn to get, even if he has to fight for it.

John had tried for fifteen years to find backing for this story. Now, in February 1951, Herb Yates gave him the go-ahead. Yates himself saw no merit in "The Quiet Man"; he was convinced that John had tricked him into making a "phony art-house picture." John Wayne remembers Yates calling him into his office. "He sat there with his boots on his desk, spitting tobacco juice into an ashtray, told me that *The Quiet Man* was going to hurt my career. He wanted me to know that he had nothing to do with it and refused to take any responsibility for it."

Adapting "The Quiet Man" was a long and difficult task. Maurice Walsh's short story was a mood piece, more dependent on feeling and warm sentiment than on character or plot, and it needed much preliminary work. Before leaving for Korea, John had turned it over to Richard Llewellyn, the Welsh novelist who had written *How Green Was My Valley*, to expand it into a novella. John had told Llewellyn to set the story in 1922, at the time of "The Troubles," and to tie Shawn's homecoming in with his desire to help his family.

In March 1951, John and Frank Nugent dove into Llewellyn's novella. They began by changing the names of all the major characters: Shawn Kelvin became Sean Thornton, Ellen O'Grady became Mary Kate Danaher, and her brother, big Liam, became Red Will. They called their fictional village Innisfree, taking the name from Yeats's famous poem, and added three principal characters who act as catalysts and keep the story moving: Father Lonergan, a preposterously profane and unsaintly priest; the Reverend Cyril Playfair, an Anglican priest without a parish; and a village busybody named Michaeleen Og Flynn.

All the early drafts of *The Quiet Man* were full of references to The Troubles and contained scenes in which the village of Innisfree was being harassed by British Black and Tans. But as the story began to take shape, it became obvious to John that these scenes didn't fit. *The Quiet Man* was a love story and a comedy, and these scenes of violence and harsh repression destroyed its mood. For the good of the story, John eliminated them. This helped the mood, but it made the story much weaker; if *The Quiet Man* was going to work, it would have to be as a director's picture.

About casting the film there had never been any question. The part of Sean Thornton had been written for John Wayne and that of Mary Kate had been written for Maureen O'Hara. Victor McLaglen was set as Red Will Danaher; the unsaintly Ward Bond, as the unsaintly Father Lonergan; Barry Fitzgerald as the "stage Irish" Michaeleen Og Flynn; and his brother, Arthur Shields, as the Reverend Cyril Playfair.

The Quiet Man was to be filmed in Ireland. While John was working on the script, Lord Killanin was busy working on the production details. With the exception of cinematographer Winnie Hoch, assistant director Wingate Smith, art director Frank Hotaling, and prop man Ace Holmes, *The Quiet Man* was to have an all-British crew. Although such international productions were common by 1951, this was to be the first picture Republic had ever made outside the United States, and Herb Yates, who had little faith in the project anyway, was nervous. To make matters worse, with a budget of $1,750,000 *The Quiet Man* was one of the most expensive pictures Republic had ever made. Yates, who had almost suffered from heart failure at the prospect of spending $1.2 million on *Rio Grande*, was beside himself at the thought of spending $1.7

million on *The Quiet Man*. True to form, he told John that this was too much money and demanded that he trim the budget.

But John had already cut the budget down to the bone; there was simply nothing left to trim. In desperation he turned to John Wayne. After years of struggling, Wayne had recently succeeded in getting a percentage participation from his Republic pictures. John asked him to waive his percentage and make the picture for a flat fee of $100,000. Wayne was reluctant; he didn't want to make any financial concessions to Herb Yates. But John persisted, appealing to Wayne's sense of friendship and loyalty, and in the end the actor agreed to waive his percentage. With this concession, Yates approved the $1,750,000 budget.

The Quiet Man was so personal a statement, so autobiographical a film, that John could imagine only one place to shoot it: the west of Ireland, around Galway Bay. In April 1951, as soon as the script was completed, John, Republic production manager Lee Luthaker, and Winnie Hoch flew to Ireland to scout locations and work out the production details with Lord Killanin.

For their primary location they selected the village of Cong in County Mayo. They chose as headquarters the Ashford Castle Hotel, a concrete tower with no heat, no windows, no elevators, and no telephones. John made a side trip to Spittal, where he was reunited after an absence of thirty years with his cousin Martin Feeney and visited the cottage where his father had been born. The feeling of being in touch with his roots and John's sense of identification with *The Quiet Man* could not have been more intense.

To make *The Quiet Man* as authentically Irish as possible, John wanted to use Irish actors in the lesser parts. From Galway the survey party went to Dublin, where John auditioned actors from that city's internationally famous Abbey Theatre. He would use many of them in the picture. Shooting began in June 1951, in the village of Cong.

Despite all the planning, all the careful preparations, *The Quiet Man* proved an exceptionally difficult picture to make. The idyllic Irish countryside had a distracting effect on John's English crew, and he also had a good bit of trouble with people looking out of windows and bystanders wandering into shots.

The vagaries of Irish weather also made *The Quiet Man* difficult to photograph. Winnie Hoch says, "In the six weeks we were in Ireland we only had six days of unbroken sunshine. Most of the time clouds were moving across the sky, and the light was constantly changing. I had to light each scene three different ways: for sunshine, for clouds, or for rain. I worked out a set of signals with the gaffer, and we were ready no matter what the light was. But I'll tell you, it wasn't easy."

Fortunately for John, Herb Yates stayed in Hollywood through the making of *The Quiet Man*, but he was still able to make his presence felt. Before John began shooting, Yates told him that *The Quiet Man* couldn't be longer than 120 minutes and threatened to cut it if it ran one minute over—no matter what it did to the story line. Determined that John should stay within his budget, Yates scrutinized the daily production reports, watched where every nickel was being spent, and threatened to shut *The Quiet Man* down if John went one cent over his limit. Yates didn't even like the title. In his mind *The Quiet Man* didn't sound like a John Wayne movie, and while the company was in Ireland he tried to change it to *Unchartered Voyage* or *The Man Untamed*.

Even Winnie Hoch's beautiful color photography was a disappointment to Yates. He couldn't understand it. When the rushes were shown to him, his only comment was, "But it's all green."

John Wayne remembers *The Quiet Man* as a difficult and exhausting project for John because of his fights with Yates: "Jack had always worked at studios where people had respect for his work, where they understood that he was the brightest, sharpest director in the business. But now, here he was at Republic, where everything had always been second class, he was getting a lot of flack from Yates. The 'but-it's-all-green' thing epitomized it.

"About a third of the way through the picture it started getting to him. Even though he had spent a lot of time on the script, brought Llewellyn into it and all, he still wasn't sure of the story line. I don't think he had a lot of confidence in it. Going in he knew that the picture would depend on what he got with the camera, and the feedback he was getting from Yates was making it pretty rough. At one point he caught a cold, and he was really down. He called me into his room and said, 'Duke, I don't know what to do. I'm just not sure about the script. I don't know whether I've got a picture here or not.' In all the years that I knew and loved Jack Ford, I never saw him so down and so willing to admit his fears as he was that morning.

"I tried to cheer him up. I said, 'Look, Coach, you've got a cold. You're physically low. Why don't you stay in bed for a couple of days. We'll take the second unit out and get some action scenes and let you get some rest.' He said, 'OK, Duke, you do that.' We went out and shot some of the horse-racing sequences. A few days later he was feeling better, and the old fire was back in him. It took a hell of a lot more than Herb Yates to beat Jack Ford.

"Jack and I had only one disagreement on *The Quiet Man*. It was about a scene where Maureen goes and slams the door and locks me out. The way they had written it, I go over, pick up my boxing gloves, and throw them onto the fire. Well, shit! They had me cowdogging and saying 'Yes, Ma'am' and 'No, Ma'am' all the damn time. I was beginning to wonder if they ever were going to let me show some balls! I brought this up with Pappy and he just gave me a dirty look. But later he changed the scene and said, 'Duke, I'm going to let you do what you always do when a broad locks you out. I'm going to let you kick the fuckin' door down.'"

On July 17, after location work was completed, John flew back to Hollywood. A few days later, despite time-lag exhaustion, a lingering cold, and an unappreciative front office, he took his seat beside the camera and began shooting *The Quiet Man*'s interiors. For the next two weeks he shot quickly and efficiently, averaging eight to ten pages a day, and *The Quiet Man* "wrapped" on August 3.

Working with editor Jack Murray, John assembled the film in August and September. For all its beauty, *The Quiet Man* was a simple film that worked because of the warmth and charm that John had given it. Just as Maurice Walsh had done in the short story, John had injected enormous feeling into the film. As in *She Wore a Yellow Ribbon*, the thread that holds *The Quiet Man* together is Winnie Hoch's beautiful color photography. Ireland, with its green pastures and glistening ponds, seems a land straight out of a fairy tale.

John scored *The Quiet Man* entirely with Irish folk songs: "The Wild Colonial Boy," "The Humor Is On Me Now," "The Young May Moon," and "Galway Bay." He used a song called "The Isle at Innisfree" that had been written by a Dublin policeman named Richard Farrelly. Like the Yeats poem, it too evoked the central theme of the film: a man repudiating a life of emigrant toil and searching for a quieter, more peaceful existence. John used music to convey a feeling of time and place. More than any film he ever made, *The Quiet Man* is almost a musical.

As the film was being assembled, there was much talk around the Republic lot that *The Quiet Man* was a masterpiece. Everyone who saw it in its rough stages—musicians, editors, Republic executives—raved about it. But there was one person who remained skeptical—Herb Yates. He still thought that John had pulled a fast one and made an "egghead picture," and his only comment was that it better be kept within 120 minutes.

John trimmed it and trimmed it. He cut out entire sequences and finally got it down to 129 minutes, at which point he felt that he couldn't cut any more without destroying the picture. He appealed to Yates.

"No dice," said the studio chief. "It's got to be 120 minutes. My experience has taught me that no matter how good a picture is, audiences won't sit longer than two hours."

"But it'll upset the whole symmetry if I cut any more out."

"*You* get it down to a hundred and twenty minutes or *I* will."

"OK, OK," said John.

Not wanting to take any chances, Yates decided to screen *The Quiet Man* for a group of Republic's distributors. If they liked it, and thought it was box office, then he'd get behind it and mount a big promotional campaign. But if they didn't like it—if they thought it was as phony and "cutesy-poo Irish" as he did—he'd base an ad campaign around the fight, slip it into mass distribution, and get his costs back before word of mouth killed it.

John had meanwhile heard about Yates' plan and deliberately kept his 120-minute version away from the studio chief. On the morning the picture was to be screened, Yates still hadn't seen John's 120-minute cut.

At the screening John took a seat beside Yates. The lights went out and the picture came on. The audience, hardened, jaded picture men all, fell silent. They were completely charmed and enthralled by John Ford's never-never land of Innisfree. There could be no better sign that they were looking at a winner. John knew it. They knew it. Even Herb Yates knew it.

But Yates was getting nervous. He couldn't see a single change from John's 129-minute version.

"Jesus, Jack, are you sure it's down to 120 minutes?"

"Sure I'm sure, Herb. You'll see in a few minutes."

The picture ran unchanged right up to the point where Sean Thornton at last accepts the challenge to fight. Then the screen was washed white by the light of the projector.

"Hey, what the hell's going on? What is this, some kind of a gag? We wanna see the fight," the distributors clamored.

John looked over at Yates and said, "There you are, Herb. Exactly 120 minutes. I couldn't figure out how to cut nine minutes out without ruining it, so I figured, what the hell? Why knock myself out? I just cut out the fight and got it down to 120 minutes."

Yates decided to go with John's 129-minute version.

When Yates realized that *The Quiet Man* was probably going to make him a fortune he stopped hating the picture and began to love it. He mounted an unprecedented publicity campaign, a blaze of ballyhoo the likes of which the studio had never seen.

Republic booked *The Quiet Man* into Radio City Music Hall for a run beginning February 28, 1952. Following Cecil B. DeMille's *The Greatest Show On Earth* and preceding MGM's *Singing in the Rain*, it was the first (and last) Republic picture to play Radio City.

With the best reviews for a John Ford film since *How Green Was My Valley*, *The Quiet Man* did a land-office business all across the country. People waited in long lines to see it, and some came back four and five times. Almost everywhere it played, it was held over, sometimes for as long as eight weeks. Every screening was accompanied by gales of laughter.

Praise poured in from everyone in Hollywood. Jack Warner, Darryl Zanuck, Harry Cohn, Frank Capra, and George Sidney all wrote long letters to John. Even Sam Goldwyn praised it in his own contorted prose.

In the trade press *The Quiet Man* was being mentioned for Academy Awards for best picture, best direction, best screenplay, and best cinematography. Republic had never made a picture so widely successful, so critically acclaimed as *The Quiet Man*. Being honored as a creative genius was an entirely new experience for Herb Yates.

John meanwhile remained characteristically detached from all the excitement. Herb Yates had made *The Quiet Man* so difficult for him that he just wanted to walk away from it. Save for one New York sojourn, he granted no interviews and sought no personal publicity.

John was, of course, pleased by the success of *The Quiet Man*. The film greatly increased his interest in Ireland and things Irish. In October 1951, Lord Killanin and Brian Desmund-Hurst began forming an Irish film company called Four Provinces Productions. They wanted to build up a native Irish film industry and bring to the screen some of the classics of Irish literature, including works by James Joyce, Sean O'Casey, and Liam O'Flaherty. John was asked to serve on Four Provinces's Board of Directors. Killanin wrote him that their plan was to make a provincial town their headquarters—preferably one like Galway, which had a great variety of country within easy reach, was not on any airplane routes, and was not too far from Dublin. If their first venture went well, they would build up their facilities and equipment. Killanin felt the plan had great possibilities when one thought of the vast English-speaking world as their potential market.

John wired his reply: "Count me in."

20

Mogambo

John followed *The Quiet Man* with a film called *The Sun Shines Bright*. Set in a Kentucky town in 1905, it was everything that the timely, violent, "relevant" films of the 1950s weren't supposed to be: a lighthearted, low-budget bit of Americana, which John approached as though it were a paid vacation.

But what should have been a relaxed, easy project became the scene of a bitter falling-out between John and Herb Yates. For while John was amusing himself with *The Sun Shines Bright*, Yates was having some fun of his own—playing with Republic's books. Under the terms of the January 5, 1950, contract, the studio was to have charged Argosy 15 percent for providing offices, stage space, and administrative personnel. But Yates changed the fine print and upped the "overhead charge," as this was called, to 35 percent. He was also charging Argosy for props, wardrobe, and musicians that he was using elsewhere.

But Yates's financial manipulations on *The Sun Shines Bright* were nothing compared to what he was doing with the box-office receipts of *The Quiet Man*. The contract called for Argosy and Republic to split the gross profits 50–50. *The Quiet Man* was, of course, an enormously successful picture. But while the money should have been raining in, it was only dribbling in. Something obviously was wrong. John was reading in *Variety* that "*The Quiet Man* [was the] top Chicago grosser with $158,000 run ... smash B.O. in Detroit with $146,000," but Republic's books were showing half those amounts. Somewhere between the theaters and Republic's accounts the money was disappearing, and John had a pretty good idea where it was going: right into Herb Yates's pocket.

Knowing that a direct confrontation would get him nowhere, John turned to "Wild Bill" Donovan, who as one of Argosy's backers had a direct interest in *The Quiet Man*. Donovan brought the full weight of his law firm, Donovan, Leisure, Newton and Irvine, to bear and began an audit of all three Argosy–Republic pictures. It was a very complicated and expensive project, but millions of dollars were at stake. The dispute left John disgusted since he knew that Yates never would have made *The Quiet Man* on his own but it was instead a gift from heaven that was turning into the most profitable film Republic had ever made. John walked away vowing never to get involved with "back of the bus" operations like Republic again. He told John Wayne, who was also leaving Republic—although for different reasons—that he had "worked too long and too hard to put up with this kind of cheap poverty-row bullshit."

John's problems with Yates spilled over into his personal relationships. He blamed John Wayne for getting him involved with Republic in the first place, and their friendship went sour for several months. It also caused a rift between John and Merian Cooper, since John felt that Cooper should have been reading the fine print and watching out for this kind of chicanery. Actually, John's dissatisfaction with Cooper had been brewing for a long time: Cooper's contributions to *The Quiet Man* had been minimal, and it was actually Lord Killanin who had served as the line producer.

In May 1952, Cooper left Argosy to replace Mike Todd as head of production at Cinerama, ending their seven-year partnership. John didn't know it but Merian Cooper was going to be awfully hard to replace; in the years ahead he would go through a succession of producers looking for someone who was both personally compatible and capable of absorbing some of the detail work, the financial and legal problems, that were becoming more complex with every picture.

During the summer of 1952, while John was in the midst of his battle with Herb Yates, MGM approached him about remaking *Red Dust*, a classic safari film that the studio had made in 1936 with Mary Astor, Jean Harlow, and Clark Gable. The project had been put together by Sam Zimbalist. No refugee, like Yates, from the tobacco business, Zimbalist was a tough, no-nonsense movie man to the core; he'd been in pictures since they were nickelodeon peep shows turned with a hand crank. Zimbalist wanted to remake *Red Dust* with Ava Gardner, Grace Kelly, and, again, Gable, and had commissioned a new script by John Lee Mahin, a veteran writer who had written many of Gable's tough-talking pictures of the 30s. Mahin updated the picture, keeping the same love triangle and the same conflicts but changing the setting from French Indo-China to British East Africa. He also changed the title to *Mogambo*, which, in Swahili, means to "speak of love."

John's first reaction was that this was trite material, too much of a "popcorn eater's movie," but the more he thought about it, the more appealing *Mogambo* became. It was a big-budget studio project, an "assembly line" picture in the classic sense, and all the people involved in it—including Zimbalist, Mahin, and Gable—

were first-class professionals. After John's problems at Republic, the thought of getting some real support and not having to worry about every last detail of production was very appealing. In July 1952, John told MGM that he'd be glad to take on *Mogambo*.

In August the film started to come together. That month, Zimbalist sent Jim Havens, the veteran second-unit director with whom John had worked on *They Were Expendable*, to survey locations in East Africa. Havens approached his survey with the thoroughness of a military campaign. He spent six weeks bouncing all over East Africa in a Land Rover. Everywhere he went he made careful notes on the roads, the quality of the water, the cooperativeness of the local officials, the proximity of medical facilities, and the location of the nearest landing strips. Havens chose two principal locations: the Serengeti Plain of Tanganyika, where the grazing animals numbered in the millions, and the Kagera River of Uganda, which had spectacular rapids and waterfalls.

Havens was in Africa at the time of the Mau Mau rebellion, a campaign aimed at driving the white settlers out. Life on the remote farms had become a matter of constant tension and irritability. Every white Kenyan was armed to the teeth, and a steady stream of British troops was moving into the East African colony, Bereted Tommies, Sten guns draped over their backs, patrolled the streets of Nairobi while tanks waddled down the roads in the remote regions. But the British colonial officials seeking to minimize the threat, convinced Havens that the Mau Mau were just "bandit rabble" and "ordinary outlaws," not genuine revolutionaries.

Mogambo was to be an MGM–British production. Except for John, Wingate Smith, cinematographer Robert Surtees, and the three American stars, the entire company was to be English. In September 1952, John and the other Americans left for London, where they spent three weeks preparing the picture and casting the lesser roles. *Mogambo* was a big picture with three high-priced, temperamental stars. It was going to be shot on a remote location with a revolution going on in the background. The logistics were so complicated, the personalities so varied and volatile, that just *managing* the company was going to be an enormous accomplishment.

On October 16, John, Surtees, and Smith left for Africa and arrived at Nairobi's Eastleigh airport the next day. There they were met by Havens and a tall man with a face the color of baked Kenya

252

clay and eyes faded out to a light, watery blue by the brilliant African sunshine. His name was Norman Read, and he was to be their safari guide.

Read whisked them through customs and immigration and loaded them into a shiny black Jaguar sedan that the studio had hired. As they started through the crowded native districts outside the airport, John saw his first African sights, smelled his first African smells, and heard his first African sounds. It was an overpowering series of impressions: he saw people clustered together in mud and thatch huts with roofs made from dented and hammered petrol cans. They had dark, smoky interiors and earthen floors padded smooth by years of use. A thousand smells hung in the air: rotting meat, decaying fruit, animal dung, tangy curry, rancid cooking fat, and drifting hashish. A thousand sounds joined together and formed a veritable din: the crying of children, the bleat of goats, the wailing of an Arab song on somebody's wireless.

As the sleek car moved through the crowded native district he noticed that the shrill laughter, the talk, the animation, ceased and the Africans fixed them with a frozen stare. There was no active anger, but John sensed their animosity.

It was the most chilling thing that he had ever experienced.

Mogambo was the biggest picture ever shot in Africa; the schedule called for sixty-seven days on location, and the logistics involved were mind-boggling. MGM had organized the largest safari ever put together and had rented every safari vehicle in East Africa. Before the cast arrived, John, Havens, and Read chartered a small Cessna to scout the locations by air. They flew down the length of the Great Rift Scar and saw the cliffs made by a volcanic upheaval that had once torn Africa apart. They flew west over the Ngorongoro Crater, then south over the Serengeti Plain, which was alive with great herds of animals. The next day they headed north toward Uganda and flew over the chain of lakes—Edward, George, and Albert—pink with enormous flocks of flamingos. Everywhere, John saw great herds of animals, native villages under thatch, fishermen in dugout canoes, elephants, buffalo, and hippos on the lake shores. They spent an evening in Entebbe on the northwest shore of Lake Victoria and the next day flew over the White Nile, then along the Victoria Nile, where the river plunged over a spectacular series of waterfalls.

The cast began arriving in Nairobi in the first week of

November. *Mogambo* was a reunion of sorts for John and Clark Gable. They had known each other socially for many years and had always wanted to work together. Gable was an avid hunter and had brought a number of guns to Africa. Norman Read took him out and got him the necessary licenses.

With much hoopla in the local press, Ava Gardner and Frank Sinatra, her husband at the time, arrived in Nairobi. John had expected Sinatra to be a tough-talking, wisecracking "Here-Pal-here's-fifty-Take-a-hike" approach to Africa. Instead he found him pleasant, courteous, and supportive of his wife.

Grace Kelly, then the fastest rising actress in motion pictures, arrived at about the same time. Charming and poised, she endeared herself to John. She also endeared herself to Clark Gable.

From the first day of shooting, *Mogambo* was a picture beset with an unending stream of difficulties. There were problems with the awesome, beautiful, but often brutal land. In the wastelands of baked clay and scrubby thorn, temperatures soared to 130 degrees at midday; alkali dust got in the camera; vehicles snapped springs and burned out bearings; lenses, lights, and reflectors broke in the jolting trucks.

There were problems with the animals—screaming, yowling, jabbering, honking. One scene was delayed time and time again by a colony of curious baboons in a nearby tree, screeching their disapproval at the Hollywood way of doing things. There were scenes in which the dialogue had to be scrapped because hippos nearby were bellowing so loudly. One night hyenas sneaked into the equipment tent and ate a camera bag.

There were problems with personalities. Despite their initial enthusiasm about working together, John and Clark Gable were not getting along. The two men had many things in common—including a fondness for periodic bouts with the bottle—but as professionals their styles were very different. Gable was careful, methodical, and a notoriously slow study who didn't like spontaneity and change. If he was interrupted in the middle of a scene, he'd have to go back and start at the beginning.

Nor did John think that Gable was taking the picture seriously. At every opportunity he was off in the bush with Norman Read hunting tomi, impala, lion, and rhino. Read was a member of the White Reserve Police, and he and Gable took the studio's Cessna on reconnaissance flights over areas suspected of containing

Mau Mau. This may have endeared Gable to Read and to other white Kenyans, but it didn't endear him to John. He thought it was dangerous and unprofessional.

But the biggest problem of all was the sheer enormity of the picture and its sixty-seven-day shooting schedule. John was really feeling his age on this one. For the first time he felt a picture might be beyond him, that it might be too much. By the time he arrived in Tanganyika, he was bone-weary and fed up: tired of being hot by day and cold by night, of being wet, filthy, and bug-bitten. The African sun was wilting him like a batch of fresh-cut flowers, souring him like a pitcher of fresh milk. He yearned for the comforts of civilization, for the luxury of a hot bath, air conditioning, and the room service of a really good hotel.

Complicating matters, John was having problems with his health. His vision was blurred and strangely out of focus. The company doctor, unable to diagnose the problem, urged him to leave the picture and fly into Nairobi for an examination, but he refused.

In Tanganyika John came down with amoebic dysentery and was doubled over by stomach cramps. The dysentery took a heavy psychological toll before it was arrested. Every day his mood grew blacker, and every minor failure became a calamity. Instead of approaching the last scenes of the picture with enthusiasm, John began looking for ways to cut the location work short. He rewrote several long dialogue scenes so that they took place inside of tents and rescheduled them for London. Reasoning that they were extraneous to the story, he cut out a number of animal scenes.

Back in Hollywood, Sam Zimbalist was worried when he heard about John's changes. Not wanting John to make wholesale cuts, he began to send him telegrams to that effect. They were all very carefully worded, all very apologetic in tone ("I have no intention of advising you how to direct ... You are the general in the field ...") but their message was unmistakable: Zimbalist wanted to exploit fully the African locale, wanted a lot of animal footage, and wanted John to shoot it.

But John ignored Zimbalist's orders, and in late January 1953, he brought the company back to Nairobi. Three days later they were in London. Jim Havens stayed in Tanganyika with a second unit to shoot the animal scenes.

London's cool, wet air and damp fogs were an elixir to John

after the searing African heat. He immediately settled into Claridges, where his first order of business was to take bath after bath and soak off the caked-on layers of African dirt. In London there were reunions with Brian Desmund-Hurst and Lord Killanin; with the latter John talked fondly about *The Quiet Man*, all that picture's difficulties now forgotten. They talked about Four Provinces Productions and discussed projects that could be filmed in Ireland, including *The White Company*, Sir Arthur Conan Doyle's classic of medieval England, and several smaller, less ambitious possibilities. Lindsay Anderson, the British film critic who later became a director himself, was another frequent guest at Claridge's; he brought John a copy of *Out of Africa*, by Karen Blixen, a Dane who wrote in English under the pen name Isak Dinesen. John had shot parts of *Mogambo* near a plantation she had once owned in the Ngong Hills of Kenya.

Getting his eyes checked at last in London, John got bad news: he had cataracts in both of them. He was told that his vision would become progressively more blurred and light-sensitive until he had the cataracts removed, which he decided to do as soon as he got home.

At almost the same time John learned from Bill Donovan that the audit of Republic's books was paying off. Indications were that Herb Yates had perpetrated an enormous fraud, and he was offering to make a cash settlement. John also learned that *The Quiet Man* had been picking up awards left and right while he was in Africa.

In October it won the prestigious Venice Film Festival Award, and in February John's direction had earned him the Director's Guild Award. Although it was nosed out by *The Greatest Show on Earth* for best picture, in March John won his fourth Oscar for his direction of the film; Winnie Hoch also won for his cinematography. John was, of course, delighted about the Oscar, but he was even happier to have been off in Africa and "too busy" making yet another picture to attend the awards ceremony. In his mind being a working professional was more important than winning awards. John Wayne picked up the Oscar for him.

But even the good news about *The Quiet Man* didn't cool off the long-smoldering feud between John and Clark Gable. It exploded into the open soon after they returned to London. After shooting a love scene between Gable and Ava Gardner, John ordered it printed and started to move on to the next set up. But Gable wasn't satisfied with the scene.

"Jack, I think I can do it better," he said.

"You do, huh?"

"Yeah, I'd like to do it again."

"Well, OK, Clark. *You* can do it again."

John got the actors back into place and sat down beside the camera. "Action," he said.

Gable started the scene, but after a few seconds it occurred to him that he hadn't heard the familiar words "roll 'em" and "speed." Gable was playing the scene, but John wasn't shooting it. He stopped and looked over at John, who had a sly grin on his face. "I said *you* could play it. I didn't say *I* was going to shoot it." Gable clenched his fists and turned beet red before storming furiously off the set.

By the time John finished cutting, looping, and scoring *Mogambo* he was so exhausted that he was nearly indifferent to it. The film had been an endurance contest, and more than anything else he just wanted to get away from it. His feeling of despair was heightened by his concern over his eyes.

Sensing that he was having problems, Mary flew over and joined him in London. Before returning home they took a holiday together, hiring a car and driving along the Riviera, then down the boot of Italy to Naples, where on April 2 they boarded the *Andrea Doria* and sailed for home. In the course of the voyage John's vision grew progressively worse, and he spent the entire passage in his darkened cabin.

If John's life were to be plotted on a graph, *Mogambo* would represent an important downward turn, the point at which he left the euphoric heights of *The Quiet Man* and began a long, slow professional decline. Although his reputation within the industry had never been higher, the truth of the matter was that cracks were already beginning to show. Things that he could have dealt with easily only a few years before—demanding stars, an intransigent front office, or a too-tight shooting schedule—now posed real problems for the nearly sixty-year-old director.

When John arrived back in California his personal crisis continued to mount. Everything he loved, everything he really cared about, seemed to be falling into decay. He learned that his brother Francis had cancer, and the news was all bad: exploratory surgery showed a massive malignancy, and he was given only a few months to live.

He also learned that a severe winter storm had racked Santa Barbara, where the *Araner* was moored. She had been driven onto a sand bar, her bottom damaged and her Lyman launch destroyed. When she was dry-docked afterward, a routine insurance survey found her riddled with dry-rot. Many of her planks and most important structural members were crumbling beneath their shell of heavy paint. John spent nearly $100,000 having her repaired, but it was only an interim solution. The *Araner* was old. Her wood was soft, her machinery antiquated, her bilges foul, and her electrical system hopeless. In the years ahead, she would become a constant financial headache.

Even John's familiar and comfortable Odin Street home was not immune. The City of Los Angeles was building a parking lot for the Hollywood Bowl, and under the laws of "eminent domain" they were buying up the adjacent property and forcing the owners out. No amount of begging, pleading, or legal maneuvering could stop the impersonal gnomes of City Hall.

In May, John and Mary moved out of the house where they had lived since 1920 and into a white Colonial mansion at 125 Copa de Oro Road in the plush Bel Air section of Los Angeles. The house, designed by Paul Williams and once owned by William Wyler, was spacious and beautiful, but it lacked the feeling of having been lived in, that intangible sense of having absorbed part of John and Mary's spirit.

On June 30, 1953, John was admitted to the Good Samaritan Hospital for the removal of the cataracts in both his eyes. It was the most important operation of his life—his career was on the line. The operation was a success, but only a qualified one. The left eye was fine, but the right one would remain light-sensitive for the rest of his life. After the operation John began wearing the eye patch that would become his trademark.

John spent the summer of 1953 convalescing from the operation. It was a difficult period. Unable to read, screen films, or even watch the increasingly popular household device called television, he spent the time in his darkened bedroom pondering his own mortality and worrying about his future. Although he wouldn't have admitted it, John's problems on *Mogambo* had scared him. The picture had almost been too much, and for the first time in his life he realized that the number of his working years was finite.

Francis Ford didn't fare nearly as well. Throughout the summer, his health continued to fail. I can remember as a young child going with my grandfather to pick him up at the hospital, and the three of us riding together through the streets of Hollywood. When we got to the site of one of the giant studios, we stopped. John and Francis exchanged a look. Then Francis turned to me and said, "I used to own that studio." For a moment he smiled and the old twinkle was there in his eyes. Then it faded away.

"You know," he said, "I've really had a very wonderful life."

He died on September 6, 1953.

21

The
Career
Man

On October 5, 1953, everyone that had been connected with *The Quiet Man* gathered on the Republic lot to pay tribute to John with an awards ceremony. It was a warm reunion of co-workers and old friends. John Wayne, Maureen O'Hara, Barry Fitzgerald, Victor McLaglen, Charlie FitzSimmons, Ward Bond, Winnie Hoch, Wingate Smith, Eddie O'Fearna, Frank Beetson, Don Hatswell, Ace Holmes, Jack Murray, and Barbara Ford were there. John Wayne acted as master of ceremonies; Maureen O'Hara sang "Galway Bay" and "Wild Colonial Boy."

After dinner Ace Holmes wheeled up a table with the golden forest of awards that *The Quiet Man* had won. George Sidney, president of the Director's Guild, presented John with the large gold disc that was the Guild award, and Ward Bond presented him with his Oscar. John clutched the awards for a moment, then looked around him at his friends and co-workers, choking back a rush of emotion. Finally he spoke: "I would be untruthful—at any rate I would be a bad actor—if I pretended modesty tonight. Of course I am proud, enormously so. In fact, I am filled with conceit, if you can imagine such a trait in an Irishman." He set the awards down, and adjusted the patch on his right eye and continued: "Look here, you'll have to forgive me. This is my first appearance in the role of an award winner. The first time, for *The Informer*, I was at the bedside of our daughter at a time when the doctors thought we might lose her. The second time, for *The Grapes of Wrath*, I dressed in white tie and tails too early for the opening curtain, and on the way to the theater I was suddenly taken drunk. The third time, for *How Green Was My Valley*, I was somewhere off the shores of Japan helping the members of the junior service in one of their habitual snafus. But here I am now, and I think it's time to state my creed as a director. It is simply this: I ain't no career man. I don't chase after no medals. I simply direct [pictures], and if you're good enough, you stars and you cameramen, you supporting players and you set people, if you're good enough, then you make me look like a career man.

"Half of my friends are in those potholes in Forest Lawn because they waited until they had the perfect script, until they signed every big name in the business, until they had three million dollars to throw away, and then the lightning didn't strike 'em. But I simply direct pictures, and if I had my way, every morning of my life I'd be behind that camera at nine o'clock waiting for the boys to roll 'em, because that's the only thing I really like to do.

"It would be untruthful if I didn't say that the devotion we have for one another, the mutual respect, the willingness to work in team harness, is what put me here on this grandstand. You put me here with your talents, your skills, your affection. As for me, if I have a career, you have given it to me. And I can promise that when we work again, I ain't going to be no career man then."

In the fall of 1953, while John was still recuperating from his eye surgery, Columbia approached him with a property called *Bringing Up the Brass*, the much-romanticized autobiography of Mary Maher, an Irish immigrant who for fifty years had been an athletic instructor at the U.S. Military Academy at West Point. They had a script by Edward Hope called "The Long Gray Line."

In those years Columbia was the healthiest, most solvent studio in Hollywood. Headed by Harry Cohn, the toughest and most ruthless of all the moguls, the studio was run like a company town, a private police state. Over the years John had heard all the "Harry the Hun" stories about Cohn, but he had also heard that his word was gilt-edged, that a handshake from him was money in the bank. In John's mind Cohn represented the old guard in a Hollywood that was changing all too rapidly, and after his experiences with Herb Yates, the thought of working for him was appealing. While John realized that "The Long Gray Line" was no great work of literature, he liked the story's military traditionalism. Moreover, he was restless after his long convalescence and anxious to get back to work. He jumped at the offer.

It was a decision he was soon to regret. At almost the moment he had committed himself to the picture he was approached by Warner Brothers about directing one of the most successful plays in the history of the American theater, *Mister Roberts*. It was a dream project. With Henry Fonda in the title role, it had been running on Broadway since 1947. Set in the waning days of World War II, *Mister Roberts* was the story of a navy cargo ship moored as far from actual combat as it could be. The principal characters were the tyrannical captain, the mild-mannered ship's doctor, the bumbling, baby-faced Ensign Pulver, and the ship's executive officer, Doug

Roberts. Mister Roberts is the soul of the ship and the only man on board willing to stand up to the captain. A man of courage and integrity, Doug Roberts is afraid of only one thing—that the war will pass him by—and he fights hardest for the thing he wants most: a transfer to a combat ship.

Mister Roberts had been produced on the stage by super-agent-turned-producer Leland Hayward and directed by Josh Logan. In August 1953, Hayward sold the film rights to Warner Brothers. Part of the deal was that he should produce the film version and that Henry Fonda should play the title role. Everyone connected with *Mister Roberts*—Warner Brothers, Hayward, and most of all Fonda—felt that John was the perfect choice. They wanted him badly enough to postpone production until the summer of 1954, when he would become available.

Meanwhile there was still the *The Long Gray Line* to deal with. With a cast including Tyrone Power, Maureen O'Hara, and Donald Crisp, John began shooting at West Point in mid-March 1954. While doing so he found time to slip down to New York and take in the stage version of *Mister Roberts*. He was totally enthralled by what he saw. In John's mind Henry Fonda *was* Mr. Roberts; he thought it was the best thing the actor had done since *The Grapes of Wrath*. After the play the two men visited backstage.

On May 5, *The Long Gray Line* returned to Hollywood, where John set about shooting its interiors. A few days later a young actor wandered onto the set who was under contract to Columbia and whom John had seen recently in a picture called *It Could Happen to You*. He walked up to the actor and said, "Aren't you Jack Lemmon?"

Lemmon surveyed the gnarled figure dressed in a rumpled fatigue jacket with a baseball cap set low on his forehead. He looked vaguely familiar. Probably some grip who worked around the lot.

"Yeah," said Lemmon.

"I've been watching you. You're pretty good."

"Thank you," said Lemmon, humoring the old guy.

"You familiar with *Mister Roberts?*"

"Of course."

"You'd make a helluva good Ensign Pulver."

"Tell that to John Ford, will you?"

"I *am* John Ford, and you *are* Ensign Pulver. Shooting starts in Honolulu in September." Lemmon stood there slack-jawed as John turned around and went back to his work on *The Long Gray Line*.

John wrapped up *The Long Gray Line* in June 1954, and plunged into *Mister Roberts*. Like all projects—even dream projects—this one was having its share of hitches. The navy was refusing to support the picture because they felt the character of the captain was detrimental to its image. Navy cooperation was essential if the film was to have an authentic look, so John took the matter into his own hands. He appealed directly to the chief of naval operations, Admiral Robert Carney, and reminded him of some of the favors he had done for the navy in the past—not the least of which was the making of *They Were Expendable* and *This Is Korea*. Two weeks later the navy reversed itself and decided to support the film.

But the navy's misgivings about *Mister Roberts* was not the film's only problem. At the last minute Jack Warner decided that Henry Fonda wasn't right for the film version—that he was too old and had been away from films too long. He wanted to use a younger, more "contemporary" leading man, either William Holden or Marlon Brando. John went right to the studio chief and laid it on the line.

"Mister Roberts is Fonda's part," he said. "He's right for it on the stage, and he's right for it on the screen. If he doesn't do this picture, then I don't do it either."

Warner backed down and agreed to go with Fonda.

Another snag developed when John and Frank Nugent went to work on the script. John had definite ideas about converting *Mister Roberts* into a screenplay. He wanted to enlarge the scale and add characters, to make the humor more physical, more slapstick. This put him in conflict with Leland Hayward and Fonda, who felt that what had worked on the stage would also work in the film. Almost from the start, they were headed for a showdown. Henry Fonda says today:

"Playing Mr. Roberts on the screen started out as a dream come true for me. After all those years I would be back with Pappy. He was the right man for it for every reason that I could think of. He was a navy man, a location man, and a man's director. He was a giant in the business, and when he was on the battery nobody could touch him. I think that I can say that after all our years together we were a love story. He loved me just like he loved Duke and Ward. Still, I was uneasy about the changes he was making. As far as Leland and I were concerned, there was only one way to do things, the way we had done them in the play. I can remember laying awake at night wondering what Pappy was going to do with this property which had been so successful for so many years. How was he going to film it? What changes was he going to make? I had forgotten that Pappy was an egomaniac, an Irish egomaniac as well."

At least everyone was in agreement about the casting. Following John's wishes, Jimmy Cagney was cast as the odious captain of the U.S.S. *Reluctant*. William Powell was set as the kindly ship's doctor; and most of the other roles went to John Ford regulars, with Ward Bond in a big part as Chief Petty Officer Dowdy, and Ken Curtis and Dobe Carey also in the cast. Pat Wayne, Harry Tenbrook, Jack Pennick, and Danny Borzage all had bits. And, of course, Jack Lemmon was brilliantly cast as Ensign Pulver.

Mister Roberts was to begin shooting September 1, 1954, at locations on Midway Island and at the Kanoehoe Marine Corps Air Station in Hawaii. John had sent the *Araner*, fresh out of the yard, down to the islands and moored her in Honolulu's Ali Wai Yacht Harbor. There she would serve as his hotel suite and office, and to provide him with an impressive stage for dealing with Leland Hayward and some of the other big egos on the picture.

Most of the company went down to the islands early, and on Monday, August 23, they gathered at the Kahala home of Honolulu sports columnist Red McQueen to celebrate the wedding of Ward Bond and his girl friend of many years, Mary Lou May. Henry Fonda gave the bride away, John served as Bond's best man, and most of the people who inhabited the world of John Ford were there. It was a joyous occasion with music, hula dancing, and plenty of liquid refreshment. They were celebrating Bond's wedding and the fact that after so many years, Henry Fonda was back in the fold.

A week later the big company was flown up to Midway in a chartered DC-6. As the plane circled over the island, John could see that it had changed little since 1942. The runway was longer and freshly resurfaced to accommodate the new jets, and there was a new, more modern control tower. But basically it was still a low, sandy atoll, a military fortress in the middle of nowhere. On the island, the *Mister Roberts* company moved into navy quarters and settled into a familiar routine.

One of the funniest scenes in *Mister Roberts* is when the *Reluctant*'s long pent-up crew returns from liberty. The drunken sailors are loaded into cargo nets and hoisted aboard the ship. The script called for one of the sailors to show up gloriously smashed, riding a motorcycle; with his hat down over his eyes, he was to ride it off the end of the pier. The company had been carrying a particular stuntman through the entire picture for this one stunt, but the night John wanted to shoot the scene, the man decided that the pier was a lot higher than he had bargained for and backed out. One of the drivers the company had hired in Honolulu was standing by, watching this, and he volunteered to do the stunt. Wingate Smith told him to wait, that they'd get to him in a couple of hours. He went back to his pickup truck, where he had a bottle stashed.

Three hours later, when John was ready to shoot the stunt, the driver was so drunk that somebody had to start the motorcycle for him. He got on, cranked it up, and flew down the pier. He went way out over the water, about fifty feet farther than anyone had expected, before finally splashing down. Several anxious moments went by. Then, just as John was about to send in some lifeguards, the man popped up. He'd been holding his breath under water so he wouldn't spoil the shot.

Although *Mister Roberts* had begun as a joyful reunion of John and Henry Fonda, their conflicts over the script—never really resolved before shooting began—grew more intense every day. They were clearly headed for a showdown. Henry Fonda recalls:

"The day before shooting began, we were told that there would be a meeting of the entire cast to read through the script. There was a long hallway in the BOQ where we were staying, and we all went in and sat down on the floor. This was my eighth film with Pappy, and we had never done anything like this.

"We read through the first scene, which was between myself and Bill Powell, and that was all right. But when we got to the second scene, which is where we meet the rest of the crew—Stefanowski, Dolan, Insignia, Gerhart, and the rest—suddenly the room fell silent. Finally Unc said, 'They don't know what parts to read.' That moment I realized that Pappy had done something really incredible. He had cast the picture without telling any of the minor actors which parts they were playing. He had taken all the actors he liked, all the members of his stock company—Dobe

Carey, Ken Curtis, Pat Wayne, Shug Fisher—and just told them they'd be part of the crew. He started handing out parts right there in the BOQ.

"I guess I was just a purist about the play. Maybe it was my fault, but I had played it for seven years, and I had very strong opinions about it. I didn't like the kind of roughhouse humor that Pappy was bringing to it. I knew where the laughs were, and I knew the timing. The scene where the crew is looking through binoculars and they see the nurses taking their shower was one of the funniest in the play. But Pappy shot it all wrong. He didn't know the timing. He didn't know where the laughs were and how long to wait for them to die down. He had them all talking at once, throwing one line in on top of another. When I said something he just handed me the script and said, 'Here, you wanna direct?'

"We had spent a lot of years together, and he was sensitive enough toward me to know that I was upset. One afternoon, after we had finished shooting, I was sitting in my BOQ room when Leland came in and said, 'Pappy wants to see you.' We went into Pappy's room. He was sitting in a wicker chair chewing on a handkerchief. Leland sat down on the bed. Pappy turned to me and said, 'OK, what's the matter? I know something's eating you.' I said, 'Pappy, everybody knows you're the best director in the business. I wouldn't presume to tell you what to do, but I was in this play for seven years, and I have to be honest and say what I think. You're making some very big mistakes.' Then I told him what they were. I don't know how far into this conversation I got, but suddenly he rose up out of the chair and threw a big haymaker and *POW*, hit me right in the jaw. It knocked me over backwards, and I crashed into some furniture.

"Well, that's about all there was to it. I was more embarrassed than hurt. I just walked out of the room. Half an hour later Pappy came up to my room to apologize, not a big deal. He just said 'I'm sorry' and turned and walked out. But from then on, our relationship never was what it once had been. For the rest of the picture he would ask me, never really sarcastically, but always in a very pointed sort of way, 'Do you think this is all right?' or 'What do you think of that?' I never said anything except, 'You're the director; shoot it any way you want.'"

Mister Roberts which had begun as a dream reunion come true, now became a drudgery to be endured. John started drinking on

268

Midway. First it was just a little beer in the afternoons, but it got worse every day. In November, when the company moved back to Honolulu, John went aboard the *Araner* and drank himself into oblivion. What he had intended to be his showplace now became his hiding place. Morbid and morose, he refused to eat or to see anyone for days. Finally, Hayward closed the picture down and the company spent several idle days at the Edgewater Hotel waiting for John to sober up. After five days he pulled himself together and shooting resumed.

Almost mercifully, John never finished *Mister Roberts*. Soon after the company returned to Hollywood he suffered a ruptured gall bladder and was rushed to St. John's Hospital, where he had it removed. Hayward brought in Mervyn LeRoy to finish the picture. After a few days LeRoy had things well in hand. He made no attempt to redesign it and shot the remaining scenes the way he thought John would have done. In the finished picture it's impossible to separate his work from John's.

With John out, Hayward had a free hand in the editing. He modified John's broad humor and recut the scene where the crew returns from liberty. He eliminated the motorcycle stunt altogether, but later Jack Warner overrode him and put it back in.

Mister Roberts ended badly for John and Fonda, but amicably enough for John and Lemmon. After the actor saw a rough cut of the picture, he wrote John a letter thanking him for making possible the most worthwhile and exciting experience of his career to date.

Released in July 1955, *Mister Roberts* was generally well received critically and was very popular with audiences. Within a year after its release it had grossed $5.8 million, and Jack Lemmon's portrayal of Ensign Pulver won him an Academy Award for best supporting actor. As for John, who spent six weeks recuperating from his surgery, the fight with Fonda, added to Hayward's recutting the film, had left him soured on the entire project. In spite of its success and popularity he disassociated himself from it altogether, and his relationship with Fonda never fully recovered. As Fonda says today, "The love affair was over."

While John was finding it more difficult than in past years to make motion pictures, his old partner, Merian C. Cooper, wasn't having any problems putting deals together for new ones. After a year at

Cinerama, during which he had helped produce *Seven Wonders of the World*, Cooper talked Cornelius Vanderbilt "Sonny" Whitney, the heir to the Minnesota Mining and Manufacturing fortune, into forming a production company. A WASP aristocrat, a man of the Establishment in every sense, C.V. Whitney shared John's and Cooper's interest in military glory and their romantic notions of the American military tradition.

A great admirer of John's cavalry trilogy, Whitney wanted to make a series of films based on another series of Bellah short stories called "The Valiant Virginians," then running in *The Saturday Evening Post*. Whitney wanted John Wayne to star and John Ford to direct. But Merian Cooper knew that "The Valiant Virginians" would only work as an epic-scale motion picture, and he also knew that Sonny Whitney was his golden goose. He wanted to ease Whitney into motion pictures with a solid commercial project, one that had mass audience appeal, before he took on "The Valiant Virginians." Cooper began shopping around for a western that would be sure to work as a John Wayne–John Ford vehicle.

In April 1954, Cooper took an option on a short novel by Alan LeMay called *The Searchers*. It was the story of a man's ten-year search for the band of Comanches that have killed his brother and kidnapped his niece. The protagonist, Amos (changed in the script to Ethan) Edwards was a complex, neurotic man, a fascinating blend of warrior, hero, and antihero, who becomes so obsessed with revenge that he hovers on the brink of madness.

C.V. Whitney was surrounded by some of the shrewdest money men in the country, who were there to see that any personal crusades he got involved with were also profitable ones. They kept a close eye on Merian Cooper and made sure that he negotiated the best deal he could, one in which Whitney was exposed to the least amount of risk. As a Ford–Wayne western with partial outside financing, every major studio in Hollywood was interested in *The Searchers*. MGM offered to split the profits and the financing 50–50. Columbia offered a 65–35 split, but at the last minute Warner Brothers offered the same split and sweetened the deal by waiving the studio overhead charges. Cooper signed with Warners. John was to receive a flat fee of $125,000 plus 10 percent of the net. It was the most he had ever been paid.

While Cooper was negotiating a distribution deal for *The Searchers*, John's son, Pat, who would be working on it as an associate producer, was doing some extensive preproduction planning. *The Searchers* takes place over a seven-year period and was going to require location work all over the West—in deserts, mountains and plains. Pat very cleverly made up a schedule in which *The Searchers* would be shot as two separate pictures: a small second unit would begin shooting months in advance and travel all over the West, while the main unit would begin production in Monument Valley in June.

In January 1955, John and his favorite collaborator, Frank Nugent, began work on the script, maintaining the violence and brutality of the novel and keeping the character of Ethan Edwards the same. If *The Searchers* had a weakness as a novel, it was that it was too grim. To give it more balance, John added two comic characters not in the book: a semiretarded old man called Mose Harper and a preposterously top-hatted Texas ranger who does double duty as a preacher, named Rev. Samuel Clayton.

The part of Ethan Edwards was, of course, written for John Wayne. John cast Jeffrey Hunter as Martin Pawley and Vera Miles as Laurie Jorgensen, his faithful sweetheart. Ken Curtis was set as Martin's rival, Charlie McCorry; Natalie Wood as Debbie, the grown-up niece that Ethan at last finds; Hank Worden as Mose Harper; and Ward Bond as the Rev. Clayton. Ollie Carey and other Ford regulars filled out the cast. The photography, in Technicolor, was to be by Winnie Hoch.

As per Pat Ford's plan, *The Searchers* was shot as two separate films. In February, a small second unit began work in Aspen, Colorado.

After all the seasonal footage had been shot, and after months of careful preparation, the main unit began work in Monument Valley on June 15. Like *Fort Apache*, *The Searchers* was a summer picture, and like the earlier picture it was plagued by 115-degree temperatures, summer sandstorms, and driving winds. Yet, despite the physical hardships, making *The Searchers* was a happy experience for John. It had all the conditions that he loved: he was off at his favorite location; surrounded by a familiar troupe of actors and technicians who acquiesced to his every demand; and he was back with Merian Cooper, a compatible producer who took care of the detail work without interfering with the creative side of things.

All of John's familiar rituals were carefully observed on *The Searchers*. Every night the company gathered outside the dining room at Goulding's and waited for John to enter. Then the dinner bell was rung and everyone obediently filed in. After dinner John and a select group of actors and stuntmen adjourned to his room, where a green felt cover was spread over the table and they had their game of pitch. John even had Ward Bond to kick around.

One of the threads that binds *The Searchers* together is Winnie Hoch's beautiful Technicolor photography. Hoch says today that he and John had several bitter fights on *The Searchers*, in which John accused the meticulous Hoch of being excessively fussy. Nevertheless, the end result is nothing short of spectacular. *The Searchers* is a visual masterpiece that stands as John Ford's most beautiful western.

Another one of the ties that bound the picture together was John Wayne's performance. Wayne's Ethan Edwards is a man obsessed, oblivious to the normal desires for comfort and safety. Engaged in a heroic quest, he loses his humanity in the process.

While *The Searchers* gets some comic relief from the characters played by Hank Worden and Ward Bond, most of it comes from Ken Curtis' slow-witted, stammering Charlie McCorry. The part had originally been written as a straight part, but John changed it on location when he overheard Curtis, who had once used a hillbilly accent in radio routines, telling some stories with it.

"Ken, the accent's terrific. You're going to use it in the picture."

"But Pappy, it's a gag. I'll look like a fool," protested Curtis.

"Look, Ken, I hate to tell you this, but you've got a nothing part. You're the guy who doesn't get the girl. There's no way you're going to look good. If we can't make you look good, then let's make you look funny. Play it with that accent and you'll make it a part that people will remember."

Perhaps even more important than the humor he added to this grim, violent story, was the aura of warmth, the feeling of family and community that was always so deeply felt in his work. The violence in the daily lives of these pioneers binds them together and gives them an even greater appreciation for one another.

John used Harry Carey's widow, actress Ollie Carey, as a symbol of hearth and home, and throughout *The Searchers* he continually favors her with "plums"—little bits of business not in the script but which stand out as memorable moments in the finished picture.

The Searchers closes with a scene revered by all Ford buffs. Ollie Carey, Vera Miles, Jeff Hunter, and John Qualen gather on their front porch to welcome Ethan and Debbie back into their world. The shot favors Ollie Carey. She sobs with joy, and through her we are reminded of the depth of John's reverence for the family bond. Ethan, meanwhile, always the loner, stands framed in the doorway. He crosses his arms so that one hand touches the opposite elbow. (The gesture was an old Harry Carey gesture, and Wayne says today that he did it as a private salute to Ollie Carey.) Then, leaving the others inside, he turns and walks away. The door closes, and the screen is enveloped in blackness.

A lot of directors could have made *The Searchers*, but no one else could have captured the same unique tone and mood. Exactly *how* John was able to do this is the single most elusive thing about the man, and probably the most important. Part of it was technique, part of it was the quality of the people around him, part of it was his ability to communicate with his actors. Nevertheless, the whole was greater than the sum of its parts, and the end result was nothing less than brilliant.

John brought *The Searchers* back to Hollywood and began shooting interiors on August 1. While he was putting the finishing touches on the film, Merian Cooper began preparing *The Valiant Virginians* for production. Everyone connected with the project—including John, Cooper, and Jim Bellah—saw the film as a continuation of John's cavalry trilogy, and they were all very excited about the prospect. Some of C.V. Whitney's financial advisers, however, weren't so excited. They kept telling Whitney that movies were becoming an increasingly risky game, that the movie audience was getting smaller every year, while television was the thing of the future. They wanted him to get out of motion pictures and buy television stations instead. For better or worse, Whitney acquiesced. Even before *The Searchers* was released, he shelved *The Valiant Virginians* and closed down C.V. Whitney Productions and bought five television stations in the Midwest. They all became very profitable.

Released in May 1956, *The Searchers* was John and Merian Cooper's swan song. Age was catching up with Cooper, and for some years he had been looking for a chance to retire. In June 1956, after three years of litigation, Bill Donovan negotiated an out-of-court settlement with Republic whereby John and Cooper were each to receive $546,000 for their percentage participation in *Rio Grande*, *The Quiet Man*, and *The Sun Shines Bright*. The money was a capital gain and therefore lightly taxed. When C.V. Whitney Productions closed its doors, Cooper took his settlement money and his participation from *The Searchers* and retired. Turning his back on Hollywood, he bought a small house in Coronado, California, a military retirement community across the bay from San Diego. There he spent the rest of his days living among retired generals and admirals, some of them former classmates of his at the Naval Academy.

As with John, the military had always been Merian Cooper's first love.

For a while John talked about following Cooper's lead—of taking his settlement from Republic and getting out of the Hollywood rat race altogether. He had left the *Araner* in Honolulu after *Mister Roberts*, and he and Mary talked about moving aboard her and cruising the islands. He had been a working director for thirty-nine years, he had 128 pictures to his credit, and had received six Academy Awards. There were no more surprises in moviemaking for him, no more thrills. Moviemaking was becoming more complex, more of a young man's game. Every picture he had made since *Rio Grande* had been more difficult than the one before it. Each had involved more production problems and detail work. He remembered the hard times on *Mogambo* and *Mister Roberts*, the battles with Sam Zimbalist and Leland Hayward, and knew that without Cooper it was only going to get harder. *The Searchers* was a successful picture, a good one to go out on.

But in the end all John's talk about retirement was just that: talk. Work was his life's blood, his driving force, his one true religion. He was as obsessive about it as Ethan Edwards was about his search.

Like Merian Cooper, John also turned his back on Hollywood after *The Searchers*, but instead of retiring and embracing the military, he chose something that was equally dear to him: Ireland. In the fall of 1955 he made a small, noncommercial film called *The*

Rising of the Moon. A feature-length trilogy whose segments were each introduced by Tyrone Power, it was produced by Lord Killanin, financed in Britain, and shot in Ireland. *The Rising of the Moon* was a lighthearted, low-budget Irish comedy that John made primarily for his own amusement. Released in the U.S. in 1957, *The Rising of the Moon* went largely unnoticed by critics and today stands as one of John's least-known films. Its principal importance is that it serves as a reminder that in the overall patchwork quilt of John's work, the thread of Ireland was always visible.

While John was in Ireland making *The Rising of the Moon*, MGM approached him about a picture based on the life of Spig Wead, the naval aviator turned screenwriter who had written *They Were Expendable.* This project didn't come out of thin air. The studio owed the navy a number of favors, and it had agreed to make a film that would promote naval aviation. Rather than make a big-budget war epic, they wanted to make a personal, small (that is, inexpensive) film. For years there had been talk around Hollywood about filming Spig Wead's life, and in 1953 the studio had commissioned a script by Frank Fenton and William Haines, who called their story "The Wings of Eagles."

John had mixed feelings about the project. Like John, Wead, who had died in 1947, was deeply involved in both the navy and in Hollywood. He had been John's close personal friend, and had influenced his life. But that was just it: the subject was *too* close, *too* personal. John finally agreed to make the film, but he only did so reluctantly. As he would tell Peter Bogdanovitch in an interview some time later, "I didn't want to do it, but I didn't want anyone else to do it either." In August 1956, shooting began with John Wayne, Maureen O'Hara, Ken Tobey, and Ward Bond at the Naval Aviation Training Center in Pensacola, Florida.

The Wings of Eagles is the story of a devil-may-care navy flyer who wins an around-the-world race, sets altitude and speed records and becomes famous in the world of aviation, and then, in the prime of life, falls down a flight of stairs and is crippled for life. He goes through a long period of recovery and begins a new career as a writer of magazine stories. He meets a crusty old director named John Dodge (a thinly disguised version of John Ford, played by Ward Bond) and is launched as a screenwriter. Wead finds success, security, and comfort in Hollywood, but when America enters World War II he leaves the good life he has carved for himself and finagles his way back into the navy.

Spig Wead's story was so much like John's that *The Wings of Eagles* stands as one of John's most autobiographical films. A compulsive worker, a man of great obsessions, fanatically devoted to naval aviation at the expense of everything else, like Ethan Edwards—and like John—Wead was incapable of any real home life. Women and children were distractions that kept him from his duty, and the film is full of scenes showing the tensions in Wead's marriage, which, like John's, suffered from his long absences. His return to the service after Pearl Harbor was the *coup de grace* to that relationship; after working himself to the point of exhaustion, he returned home to find that his wife had left him.

The Wings of Eagles is revealing because it is the story of a belligerent, brave, eccentric visionary, a man of fanatical dedication who, like Ethan Edwards in *The Searchers*, is doomed to be alone.

More than the story of Spig Wead, it is the story of John Ford. The story of a career man.

22

The
Waning
of the
West

As the 1950s drew to a close, it became increasingly obvious to John that the motion-picture industry in which he had spent his life was crumbling into bankrupt decay. A forest of television antennae was springing up across the land, and a new idol, a black box with a cool glass face, sat like a shrine to be worshipped in almost every living room. One by one the old studios were being swallowed up by consortiums of insurance companies and parking-lot conglomerates. One by one the old moguls, the cigar-chomping immigrants who had built the business—the Laskeys, the Mayers, the Goldwyns, the Zukors—were being replaced by business-school graduates who flew by slide rules and computers instead of by the seat of their pants. These weren't gamblers and table-stakes players like the men they replaced; they were 5- and 10-percent men who made decisions on the basis of "audience quotients" and "research analyses" instead of their gut level feelings. Rather than make more and better pictures, as the old moguls might have done, their response to the onslaught of television was to call the real-estate appraiser to get estimates on the land their studios occupied.

With the decline of these studios and the depletion of their great resources, film making became much more difficult. Independent producers had to assume responsibility for all the detail work that the studios had traditionally undertaken— everything from the hiring of electricians, propmen, and makeup artists to the designing of sets and the making up of payrolls. Pictures became complex joint ventures between corporations, and contracts became 200-page monstrosities complete with hundreds of reasons why the film *could not* be made. The dominant theme in the last phase of John Ford's working life—a time when his energy and enthusiasm were beginning to wane—was that each picture became more difficult to put together; each picture became more burdened by detail work and noncreative problems. There was more dickering with agents, bankers, and lawyers; more arguing about percentages, split fees, and commissions; and less creative energy left over for actual film making.

With the industry in decline, John was forced to spend his last working years making "safe commercial pictures," and for him that always meant westerns. Between 1958 and 1962 he made five of them: *The Horse Soldiers, Sergeant Rutledge, Two Rode Together, The Man Who Shot Liberty Valance*, and, finally, *Cheyenne Autumn*.

Although each of these films had a generous budget and a superb cast, each reflects John's declining energies. He gave less of himself, less of the special sense of hope, optimism, and the spirit of community that had always marked his films. The special "aura"— the most important, if least easily definable, part of his work—was gone.

The Horse Soldiers seemed to be a sure-fire winner. It had been put together by a man named Marty Rackin who was straight out of the pages of *What Makes Sammy Run?* Rackin had climbed up the ladder in the picture business, going from office boy to gag writer to *Wunderkind* producer with incredible zest and drive. In 1957 he went into partnership with veteran writer John Lee Mahin, and for the princely sum of one dollar they talked a history professor named Harold Sinclair into giving them an option on a book he had written called *The Horse Soldiers*. An adventure yarn based on an actual Civil War incident, it was the story of Colonel Benjamin Grierson, who in April 1863 led a brigade of Union cavalry 300 miles into the Confederacy to destroy the supply center for Vicksburg, a town called Newton Junction.

In the winter of 1958, Rackin took *The Horse Soldiers* to the Mirisch brothers, who agreed to put up $3.5 million if—and these were big ifs—Rackin could come up with a big-name director and two superstar actors. Knowing that almost any star in Hollywood would work for John Ford, Rackin went after him first, baiting his hook by offering John $200,000 plus 10 percent of the net. John took it like a hungry fish. Then, with John aboard, the package quickly began to take shape. John drafted a detailed treatment which landed the next catch, John Wayne. For the second male lead, Rackin selected William Holden.

The deal for making *The Horse Soldiers* was one of the most complicated ever put together in Hollywood. It was a joint venture between six corporations: United Artists, The Mirisch Company, Mahin-Rackin Productions, John Ford Productions, John Wayne's Batjac Productions, and William Holden Productions. Six sets of agents, lawyers, and accountants spent six months drawing up **one** of the most complex contracts ever written, haggling over completion bonds, cost overruns, and annuities, and defining such basic terms as *net*, *gross* and *producer's net*. They hammered out a contract that was a lawyer's dream; 250 pages of legalese indecipherable to anyone but themselves.

While the lawyers were doing their thing, John, Rackin, and Mahin flew down to Honolulu to do theirs. Sitting in John's "lucky spot" in the *Araner's* main saloon, they went to work on the script. For love interest they added a woman, a loyal Confederate who learns that the Yankee column plans to destroy Newton Junction. Constance Towers was later cast in this role. They also added a scene in which cadets from a local Confederate military academy, a group of ten- to twelve-year-old boys, march on the Union troops and rout them. This was based on an incident that had actually occurred in the Civil War and that James Warner Bellah had dramatized in "The Valiant Virginians."

Although *The Horse Soldiers* had many fine moments, from the very beginning John was uneasy about the project. While he genuinely liked John Lee Mahin (with whom he had worked on *Mogambo*), he was uncomfortable with Marty Rackin and didn't really trust him. For whatever reason, the script never came together. According to Mahin it was largely John's fault: "I don't think Jack ever liked *The Horse Soldiers*," he says. "He never really got into the script. He never really applied himself to it. One day we were sitting aboard the *Araner*, and he said to me, 'You know where we ought to make this picture?' 'No,' I said, 'where?' 'In Lourdes. It's going to take a miracle to pull it off.'"

Before shooting began, John's son, Pat, working on the picture as a special assistant to his father, was sent through the South to scout locations. He flew to New Orleans and looked around the swamps of southern Louisiana. From there he drove to Natchez, Mississippi, where he found the perfect place to film the scene where the cadets attack the Union column: Jefferson Military College.

The Horse Soldiers began shooting in late October 1958 in southern Louisiana, whose hot, swampy mangrove forest kept cast and crew continually wet. Wanting to get out of the swamps before the weather turned cold, John worked as quickly as he could. John Lee Mahin once recalled *The Horse Soldiers* location with wit and insight:

"Jack had a lot of problems dealing with the segregation that was still very much part of life in the South. There was a scene in the picture where the column rides past this colored church, and a couple of Reb snipers take a few shots at the Yankees and kill Connie Towers' servant girl by mistake. Jack found this black church in Louisiana to shoot the scene and hired the whole congregation as extras. Then the redneck supervisor of the local board of labor appeared and said, 'Now, Mr. Ford, you can't pay these people more than two dollars a day.' Jack said, 'Oh, I think we can do a little better than that.' 'Oh no, Mr. Ford. Two dollars a day. It's the law.'

"Then the guy had the gall to say to Jack, 'Mr. Ford, I want to warn you of one thing. These colored people, they really resent it if you keep your hat on when you walk into their church. They are liable to get real mad, maybe even violent.' Now isn't that just *awful*. Can you imagine this son of a bitch even presuming that Jack Ford would walk into a church and not take off his hat. Jack just glared at him. Then he turned on his heel and walked away.

"Jack went into the church and got the minister's permission to address the congregation. He was warm and very gracious. He said, 'I'm paying you people regular Hollywood scale, and I'm serving lunch at twelve noon. It isn't the best food in the world, but it's the best we can do. We would consider it a great honor if you would join us.' Then he said, 'I don't want any of you to feel that because you're portraying slaves we are putting you down in any way. Everything in this picture actually happened, and you are playing your grandfathers and grandmothers. You are a part of history, and you should be very proud of it. We are glad to have you as part of our picture.'"

John finished the Louisiana sequences on November 25, and the company moved to Jefferson Military College in Natchez, Mississippi. Jack Pennick had gone on ahead to drill the cadets who were to play roles as their 1865 equivalents on Civil War-era marching techniques. They were ready when John arrived.

The *Horse Soldiers* company invaded the campus much as the Yankee soldiers of a hundred years ago might have done. Bearded actors in dusty blue Yankee uniforms swarmed over the campus, while an army of technicians working with Yankee efficiency went to work setting up lights, cables, and generators.

This scene, with its rare emotional purity, is one of the highlights of *The Horse Soldiers*. It was shot the day after Thanksgiving, November 28, 1959, late in the afternoon. A column of peach-fuzzed boys marches out to face the Union cavalry—and almost certain death. The mother of one of the drummer boys, played by Anna Lee, then comes out and begs the headmaster not to take her boy; she has already lost her husband and three boys in the war, she tells him, and begs that her youngest son be spared. The boy is dismissed and is dragged kicking from the ranks. John wanted Anna Lee to be agitated and emotional in the scene. To help her get that way he resorted to a typical Ford stratagem: he instructed her driver to pick her up half an hour late, and when she arrived on the set he wouldn't listen to her excuses but bawled her out in front of everyone. It was his way of leading her into the scene.

The Horse Soldiers was a big, complex picture, but so far the shooting had gone relatively smoothly. After John shot the cadet sequences at Jefferson Military College, however, he moved the company thirty-five miles south to the Homochitto River, and there tragedy struck.

Veteran stuntman Fred Kennedy, who was being carried as a bit player, came up to John and asked if he could do a horse fall in the film. Overweight, out of shape, and an old man, as stuntmen go, Kennedy should not have attempted such a stunt. At first John told him no, but Kennedy persisted, explaining that it was almost Christmas and he needed the extra money. Finally John gave in and let him double Bill Holden in a simple saddle fall. Afterward, Connie Towers was to rush in and throw herself down on him.

John set up the camera and told Kennedy to stay on the ground until he heard him say "cut." On "action" Kennedy spurred the horse into the swamp and rolled off right on his mark. But when he hit the ground, his head snapped back and he lay there motionless in an unnaturally contorted way. John sensed something was wrong but kept the camera rolling and sent Connie Towers in. The actress ran up to Kennedy and threw herself down on him, but then, after a frozen second, she pulled back in horror. Fred Kennedy had broken his neck and was dead.

The tragedy sickened John, who blamed himself for Kennedy's death, and destroyed what little enthusiasm John had managed to summon up for *The Horse Soldiers*. Now it became something he just wanted to get through. The script called for the Union cavalry to make a triumphant return to their own lines, and the picture was supposed to end on an upbeat note, but to get away

282

sooner John scrapped that scene and let the film end with John Wayne saying good-bye to William Holden, who chooses to stay behind with the wounded even though it means certain capture.

John Lee Mahin says: "The death of Fred Kennedy took something out of Jack. Marty wanted to shoot the last scene, but Jack would have none of it. He didn't care about the picture anymore.

"*The Horse Soldiers* wasn't a good picture. I don't know why but it never seemed to work. Jack never really had any enthusiasm for it. Poor Marty is dead now, and I don't want to blame him. He was a funny, witty man, and he always had a joke for everything, but he didn't have any warmth. I think that's what the story needed. I wanted to do some scenes over again, but Marty kept saying, 'Oh the hell with it. Leave it alone. We've got Ford, we've got Wayne and Holden. We're going to make a fortune.' Well, we didn't make a fortune. We just barely got our costs back.

"If I had to do it all over again, I wouldn't have bothered."

The Horse Soldiers had been a bad experience for John. The complicated negotiations, the detail work, the battles with Marty Rackin, and finally the death of Fred Kennedy had taken their toll. In what was becoming an ominous pattern, he walked away from it in a black, irascible frame of mind and disassociated himself from it entirely. In February 1959, as soon as it had been scored and dubbed, he flew down to Honolulu to rest up aboard the *Araner*. He spent his mornings swimming in the warm waters of the Ali Wai Yacht Harbor and his afternoons sitting in the deckhouse, watching winter squalls build up in Moanoa Valley.

This was a difficult time for John. He was depressed and worried about his future. Change was in the air; there were new currents of thought blowing in over Hollywood, and John wasn't sure he understood the scent they carried. The mood of the country was changing, and Hollywood was changing with it. There was a new, more liberal, more permissive spirit in the air. Minority groups were clamoring for their piece of the American Dream, and there was a new generation of political leaders who seemed willing to give it to them. John was confused and ambivalent. He liked the new liberalism—particularly the struggle for black civil rights, which in his mind was not unlike the struggle for Irish freedom. But he also knew that he was an old warhorse with set ideas, and that his ability to respond to change was limited.

In March, John had two visitors in Honolulu: Jim Bellah and Willis Goldbeck, the latter a tall, handsome man in his mid-fifties with Old World charm and elegance. Bellah and Goldbeck had put together a script about the 9th Cavalry Regiment, the great Negro unit that had fought some of the hardest fights of the Indian Wars. The script, called *Sergeant Rutledge*, was the story of a liberated slave named Braxton Rutledge who is falsely accused of raping and murdering a white girl.

According to Bellah, John was at first enthusiastic about *Sergeant Rutledge*, partly because of his genuine sympathy with the struggle for black civil rights and partly because he was sensitive enough to the currents adrift in Hollywood to know that this was an idea with real commercial possibilities. It could be a John Ford western, complete with banners, bugles, and horses along the skyline—but with a new and timely twist. He told the two writers that he'd be delighted to take on the project, and they plunged ahead with it.

But John's enthusiasm was less than complete. According to Bellah, John didn't display anything like the level of intensity on *Sergeant Rutledge* that he had on the cavalry trilogy. "It was pretty obvious from the start that some of the old fire was missing in Jack," said Bellah. "He had always been a real tyrant in story sessions, needling and picking away at you. It was his way of making you reach in and give your best. But on *Rutledge* he was awfully mild. Whenever an important subject came up he just said, 'Whatever you think is fine' or 'Just write it as you see fit, and I'll get it on film.' This wasn't the Jack Ford that I knew."

In April, John returned to Hollywood to make a deal on *Sergeant Rutledge*. His instincts about the story's commercial possibilities had been correct: every studio in town made a bid for it. The best came from Warner Brothers, a whopping $400,000; $100,000 for the property and $300,000 for John's services as a director. Willis Goldbeck and Pat Ford would produce it for John Ford Productions. As Sergeant Braxton Rutledge, John cast Woody Strode, a former football and track star at UCLA with a shaved head, huge moonlike eyes, and an impressive physique. Jeffrey Hunter was cast as his commanding officer, and *Horse Soldiers* alumna Constance Towers was cast as the female lead. In May, John moved into offices on the Warner Brothers lot and began attending, reluctantly, to the myriad of production details: arranging for sets, transportation, locations, and wardrobe. Even before the picture began, John was calling *Sergeant Rutledge* "just another job of work."

John's "crisis in enthusiasm" was reflected in the shooting schedule he made up. Out of fifty working days he planned to spend only ten days on location; fully 80 percent of the picture was to be shot on the Warner Brothers lot. When shooting did begin, John worked quickly and impersonally, cutting corners wherever he could. Early in the picture there is a long dialogue scene between Hunter and Towers that takes place aboard a train. John didn't bother to place the set on jacks and hire extra men to rock it—the usual method for producing a sense of motion. The result is a dull and static scene.

But *Sergeant Rutledge* did have its pluses, one of which was Woody Strode. As an actor, Strode had a lot in common with Victor McLaglen: he was big, expressive, spectacular-looking, but largely untrained. As with McLaglen, John felt it necessary to trick a performance out of him.

Strode's climactic scene is the one in which he stands up to the prosecuting attorney, full of anguish and emotion, and tells him why he came back to his regiment after deserting. "Because the Ninth Cavalry was my home, my real freedom and my self-respect. The way I was deserting it, I was nothin' but a swamp-running nigger, and I ain't that. Do you hear me? I'm a man!" The night before John shot this scene he pulled an old trick on Strode. "Woody," he said, "I've changed the schedule. You're not working tomorrow. Go out and relax tonight."

John had his daughter, Barbara, and Ken Curtis give a party for the actor. The music played, the wine flowed, and Strode, relaxing from the awful tensions of making a movie, proceeded to get good and lubricated. At 6:00 the next morning, Wingate Smith was on the phone. "Woody, Jack's changed the schedule. Be in make up in an hour. We're shooting your courtroom scene."

As McLaglen had done in *The Informer*, Strode faced his on-screen accusers with a blinding hangover; like McLaglen's, Strode's anguish was genuine.

John finished *Sergeant Rutledge* in mid-September and went to work assembling the picture with his favorite editor, Jack Murray.

285

Warner Brothers, sensitive about possible criticism from the black community, screened the picture for a number of civil rights leaders at various stages of its completion. Their reactions were almost unanimously positive. But when *Sergeant Rutledge* was released the following spring, it was poorly received by critics both black and white.

Sergeant Rutledge was followed by a long dry spell for John. The studios were in retrenchment, and the industry was in decline. There just wasn't the work there once had been, and John had to take his turn in the growing line of the Hollywood unemployed. In the nine months between September 1959 and June 1960 John was involved with no major films and, more ominously, he had no projects in development. This was the longest idle stretch of his career—one that would have been unthinkable only a few years before.

Unemployment was new to John, and he didn't handle it well. For the first time in his life he had the opportunity to relax, to develop new interests, to travel, and to spend some time with his family. But such things were always secondary to John. Instead of enjoying himself he became depressed, spending long periods in bed. Days would go by and he wouldn't leave his room. He ignored his personal hygiene; his beard, hair, and fingernails grew long and his teeth and fingers were yellowed by nicotine. Worst of all, he refused to exercise, and his muscles lost their tone.

But if John was idle, his two great friends, John Wayne and Ward Bond, were both deeply immersed in projects of their own. Wayne was producing, directing, and starring in *The Alamo*, and Bond was starring in his popular *Wagon Train* TV series.

The Alamo was John Wayne's greatest personal project. He saw the story of this beleaguered garrison as much more than a simple action picture. Politically conservative and fervently anti-Communist, Wayne believed that it could serve as a lesson to American youth and show America's moral fiber to the rest of the world. He had been working on it since 1952, and at various times he had had every studio in Hollywood interested in it. They always backed down, however, when he insisted on producing and directing it himself. "Get Ford, Hawks, or Hathaway and you've got a deal," he was told. But *The Alamo* was Wayne's baby, and he stuck by his guns, pursuing it with singleminded determination. Finally, in the summer of 1959, he talked United Artists into making it on his terms.

With a $7.5 million budget, *The Alamo* was the most expensive picture that had ever been made up to that time. But then this was no mere movie—*The Alamo* was to be an American epic, and Wayne wanted everything to be *perfect*. No expense was spared for the sake of authenticity: 400 construction workers had built an exact replica of the Alamo mission on J.T. "Happy" Shahan's ranch in Bracket-ville, Texas. They used real adobe and real Spanish tiles, bulldozed airstrips and rivers, and hired thousands of extras.

John's own feelings about *The Alamo* were mixed. While he wanted Wayne to succeed, in his mind it seemed "out of the natural order of things" for an actor (and particularly for "that big oaf Wayne") to produce, direct, and star in his own picture. Though he tried to put these feelings aside, John couldn't help but resent Wayne's ability to pull together such an enormous project.

Then, too, John was becoming more liberal, more sympathetic to the plight of America's minorities. The social consciousness that had lain dormant in him since the late thirties was coming alive. By 1959 he was actively following the presidential aspirations of the young Irish-American senator, John F. Kennedy, who in John's mind symbolized the new liberal spirit and his own acceptance into the American mainstream. Wayne, on the other hand, seemed to be growing more and more conservative. Politics seemed to touch every aspect of his life. Wayne couldn't talk about anything—horses, boats, pictures, or his alimony payments—without politics coming into it. While John thought that *The Alamo* was a good story, he didn't think it was America's epic poem and he thought Wayne's approach was too self-consciously political.

In the fall of 1959, John made several trips to the *Alamo* location, ostensibly only to watch Wayne work. Once he arrived on the set, however, he began asserting himself, and a natural tropism drew him to the camera. Instinctively he began giving orders to Wayne, second-unit director Cliff Lyons, and cinematographer Bill Clothier. Time and time again John stepped in front of the camera and said, "Goddammit, Duke, that's no way to play it. Here, try this." This put Wayne in an awkward position. *The Alamo* was his picture. He had raised the money, struggled with the project for years, and whether it was good, bad, or indifferent, he would sink or swim with it. He didn't want his detractors saying that John Ford had directed all the key scenes.

A massive production with a lot of action, *The Alamo* had all the stuntmen from the John Ford stock company in it—Cliff Lyons, Chuck Hayward, Chuck Roberson, and Slim Hightower, among others. Wayne placated John by letting him take the second unit and shoot some action scenes. Determined to prove to Wayne—and to himself—that he still had his touch, John worked the stuntment relentlessly: he had them riding, shooting, and falling until they were blistered and saddlesore. One of John's scenes is a wide shot of Santa Ana's army making its initial approach on the Alamo mission; another is a magnificent shot of a column of Mexican soldiers crossing a river. Although these were only a small part of the finished picture, John's hand is evident in both of them.

While Wayne was making *The Alamo*, John's other great friend and protégé, Ward Bond, was busy too. In 1959 *Wagon Train* was the number-one television show in America, and Bond, besides being its star, had a hand in every facet of production from casting to cutting. Though John had picked on Bond for thirty years and had made him the butt of thousands of practical jokes, he was delighted with his friend's success. But John was also worried about Bond's health and thought he might be pushing himself too hard. Despite his hearty manner and robust appearance, Bond was not a healthy man. He had high blood pressure and was an epileptic. John noticed that he was smoking heavily, drinking more than he should, and was badly overweight. Worst of all, to control his weight and get him through the long *Wagon Train* days, Bond was taking amphetamines as if they were candy. It was a very dangerous combination. Whenever John asked Bond about his health, the actor brushed his questions aside and said, "I've never felt better in my life." But John wasn't so sure.

In this slack period John was a frequent visitor on the *Wagon Train* set. After the day's shooting, John would sit with Bond, Terri Wilson, and Frankie McGrath and discuss the day's work. For years John had wanted to do something on the life of General Ulysses S. Grant, and during one of these afternoon sessions he asked Bond if he could sketch out his life in a *Wagon Train* episode. He explained his approach, and Bond cleared the way.

Working with a writer named Tony Paulson, John got a script together in ten days called "The Colter Craven Story." It was the story of a doctor on the wagon train whose experiences in the Civil

War had left him an alcoholic wreck. A young girl needs an emergency operation, and wagonmaster Bond sobers him up and tries to convince him that he can perform the surgery. To build up his confidence, he tells him the story of General Grant, an alcoholic who nevertheless became the Commanding General of the Union Armies and finally President of the United States.

Wagon Train was an hour-long series, but with commercials, shows actually lasted only forty-eight minutes each. They were normally shot in six days. Owned by M.C.A., *Wagon Train* was produced by a trio of young executives who were used to young television directors who did what they were told. They were not used to the likes of John Ford.

John shot "The Colter Craven Story" faster than anyone had ever shot a *Wagon Train* episode. In six days he shot eighty-two minutes of usable film, almost enough to make it a two-part episode. John not only shot faster, he shot better. "The Colter Craven Story," which was aired on November 23, 1959, is full of beautiful and very "Fordian" shots. *Wagon Train* was a relaxed, enjoyable project for John. He even got John Wayne to do a brief walk-on as a tribute to Bond's success.

In June 1960, John's long dry spell was broken when he was asked to film a novel called *Comanche Captives*, the story of two men—a cynical sheriff and an idealistic army lieutenant—searching for a group of white children who had been captured by Indians years before. When they are found, the children, more Indian than white, must be taken and held by force. Finally, in an escape attempt, one of them kills his own mother.

John's first impulse was to turn down this grim, violent story, but the more he thought about it, the more appealing it seemed. Its producer, Stan Shpetner, had a commitment from Jimmy Stewart to play the sheriff and from Richard Widmark to play the lieutenant. He was offering John $225,000 plus 25 percent of the net and, as producer, Shpetner would take care of all the production details.

John told Shpetner that he'd consider directing *Comanche Captives* if he could rewrite the script, add some humor, and end on a more upbeat note.

Shpetner agreed with John's suggestions and contracts were signed in July. The picture, to be called *Two Rode Together*, would be produced as a joint venture between John Ford Productions and

Stan Shpetner Productions, and would be released by Columbia. The script would be written by John and Frank Nugent.

In August, John and Nugent flew down to Honolulu, and sitting in the "lucky spot," they went to work on the script. But again John lacked enthusiasm for the story. The more John worked on *Two Rode Together*, the less he liked it, and before it was finished he was calling it "the worst piece of crap I've done in twenty years."

John's enthusiasm didn't increase when shooting began. Most of those I have spoken to who were familiar with his working methods—Wingate Smith, Dobe Carey, and Ken Curtis, among others—referred to John's "lackadaisical attitude," his "indifference toward the material" on this picture. He cut corners whenever he could and chose his locations for their ease and accessibility. "He didn't seem to have any stamina and by early afternoon he was completely wilted," Wingate Smith said.

On November 13, 1960, while John was at work in Bracket-ville, Texas, on *Two Rode Together*, word came that Ward Bond, while in Dallas to attend a football game, had suffered a heart attack and died.

Bond's death was a stunning, bitter blow to John. Too depressed to work, he shut down *Two Rode Together* and flew back to Los Angeles, where he made arrangements for a funeral at the Field Photo Home. Bond's body was placed in a flag-draped casket in the chapel, where a uniformed honor guard stood by while flags flew at half-staff. The mourners—Bond's friends and colleagues over many years—filed by to pay their respects. John hadn't intended the Farm to be a place of mourning, but by 1960 funerals seemed to be the only occasions that brought the old group together anymore.

On the day of the funeral the casket was placed on the parade ground, with huge floral wreaths at either side. The Sons of the Pioneers sang "The Song of the Wagonmaster" and John Wayne, his voice cracking and his eyes filled with tears, spoke the eulogy. Then the casket was placed in a hearse and driven down the tree-lined driveway.

John finished *Two Rode Together* late in November, then flew down to Honolulu to spend the holidays aboard the *Araner*. He started drinking heavily in the islands and spent almost twenty days in an alcoholic fog. He refused to eat or to see anyone, and he drank until his eyes grew cloudy and distant, until his cheeks looked shrunken and hollow. Finally Mary got him to check into Queen's

Hospital in Honolulu. He was suffering from alcoholic dehydration.

After two weeks, still depressed but physically improved, John was released from the hospital, and he and Mary boarded a United Airlines DC-7 bound for Los Angeles. After an uneventful seven hour flight, they went into a holding pattern over the Los Angeles airport for what seemed like an unusually long time. An hour went by, and John began to suspect that something was wrong. Finally the pilot's voice came over the P.A. system and announced calmly that they were having problems with the plane's hydraulic system; the landing gear wouldn't go down. The pilot said they were going to land at Edwards Air Force Base, where there were facilities for such emergencies.

As the plane circled over Los Angeles to use up its excess fuel, John and Mary choked back their fears and tried to face the landing bravely. After the Air Force had covered a runway with fire-retardant foam, the pilot began his approach. The DC-7 hit belly-first, bounced up in the air, then went into a long skid. When the plan came to rest, the passengers were hustled down the emergency chutes. Mary landed on all fours and was alright, but John tried to land standing up and badly twisted his ankle.

Although John had hurt himself and been badly scared by the crash landing, the mishap was not without positive effect: it shook him out of the depression into which he had sunk after Ward Bond's death. Soon some of the old michievous twinkle was back in his eye, and by the middle of February he was talking about going back to work.

The Man Who Shot Liberty Valance was both a western and a murder mystery. Based on a short story by Dorothy Johnson, it was the tale of Senator Ransom Stoddard, who, as a young man, follows Horace Greeley's advice and goes west—to a lawless town run by a vicious gunman named Liberty Valance. With help from his friend Tom Doniphon, Stoddard kills Valance in a classic western shoot-out and becomes a local folk hero. He gets elected to the territorial assembly and, eventually, to the U.S. Senate.

The Man Who Shot Liberty Valance was an *auteur* project all the way. John found the property, developed the script with Willis Goldbeck and Jim Bellah, and raised half the proposed $3.2 million budget. He brought together an all-star cast, perhaps the best he ever had: John Wayne, Jimmy Stewart, Lee Marvin, Vera Miles, Ken Murray, Woody Strode, plus veteran heavies Strother Martin and Lee Van Cleef.

Because Wayne had just signed a ten-picture deal at Paramount (for which he was paid $6 million *in advance*), John took his package there and presented the Paramount heads with what was surely one of the best writer-director-actor packages ever assembled. John thought he had a sure-fire winner. All Paramount had to do was to provide half the financing and guarantee distribution.

But John was about to find out that things moved slowly in the corporate circles of the new Hollywood. Paramount told him that they would take his package "under consideration." Weeks went by while meetings were held and memos were written. Executives with fat expense accounts and skinny girl friends flew out from New York to sit around the pool at the Beverly Hills Hotel. Weeks turned into months. John, meanwhile, legally, financially, and emotionally committed, sat and waited. All the while his own expenses—for his office, staff, secretaries, interest on the loan— kept mounting, and time was running out. Both Wayne and Stewart were being presented with other offers, and their agents wrote polite notes suggesting that unless the dates were firmed up now, "they would regrettably have to move on to other commitments."

Finally, in August, after five months of having the picture "under consideration," Paramount gave John the green light. But for John the decision was anticlimactic. The careful preproduction, the financial concerns, the detail work, had already sapped most of his energy and interest. He was fed up with *Liberty Valance* even before he began it.

When shooting started in September, John worked quickly and efficiently—too quickly and too efficiently. He shot with a lack of concern that bordered on indifference, cut corners whenever possible and filmed almost entirely on a sound stage. Everyone that I talked to spoke of John's "lack of energy," of his complete disregard for background effects, for extras, for smoke and commotion. When Wingate Smith complained that the set didn't look lived in, John said curtly, "If they notice it, then we'll give 'em their nickel back."

Released in April 1962, *The Man Who Shot Liberty Valance* opened to a poor critical reception. Most dismissed it as just another horse opera. Others objected to its many shortcuts and lack of production values. *The New York Times* found the story unconvincing and said that "it fell short of its potential." But in the years since its release, *The Man Who Shot Liberty Valance* has enjoyed a very rich critical history and has attracted on enormous amount of attention from writers, critics, and film buffs.

The Man Who Shot Liberty Valance is interesting because it is so different. It doesn't really look like he made it. There is none of that special quality that was uniquely his. Nowhere is there the equivalent of the Sunday morning sequence in *My Darling Clementine*, where Wyatt Earp and Clementine Carter dance on the floor of the unbuilt church. Nowhere is there the equivalent of Nathan Brittles choking back his tears as he accepts the watch from the men of his troupe. Nowhere is there the equivalent of Ollie Carey sobbing on the front porch as Ethan Edwards brings Debbie home.

Without exception, students of John Ford's work have pointed out that over the years John's vision of the west grew progressively darker, that there was less of the spirit of hope and optimism that had characterized his earlier work. In 1971, a writer named David Borwell compared *The Man Who Shot Liberty Valance* with *The Iron Horse* to see how John's vision had changed over the span of his career. He noted that the tone of *The Iron Horse* was one of heroic optimism, of personal happiness linked with progress, a celebration of the glorious legend of a country stretching to its full length. *The Man Who Shot Liberty Valance*, on the other hand, reveals a darker side of that legend. It begins, says Borwell, with the west already closed, and stands as an autopsy of the myth of the west, a somber meditation of the dream that *The Iron Horse* celebrated.

23
Autumn

J ohn's problems on *The Man Who Shot Liberty Valance* scared him more than he cared to admit. Moviemaking was becoming more difficult all the time, and he walked away from the picture convinced that if he was going to save his professional life, he needed a partner, someone to take care of the production details and leave him free to concentrate on creative matters. In September, he formed a joint venture partnership with a veteran producer named Bernard Smith. Smith was a tough, no-nonsense, self-made man. A former editor-in-chief at a major New York publishing house, he had come to Hollywood as Sam Goldwyn's story editor and had recently produced the epic western *How the West Was Won*.

John Ford and Bernard Smith were strange bedfellows. Smith was a calculating businessman and a tough negotiator. Extremely well connected, he moved among Hollywood's elite like a Medici prince. Although John didn't particularly like the man, he knew that he needed him, and hoped to recreate something like the relationship he'd had with Merian Cooper.

For their first project Ford-Smith Productions, as the partnership was called, decided to film a book by Mari Sandoz entitled *Cheyenne Autumn*, the historical account of one of the saddest moments in the history of the American West: the 1878 flight of the Northern Cheyenne from the old Indian Territory, now the state of Oklahoma, to their ancestral lands in the Dakotas. A western with a different slant, its politics were exactly the opposite of those in the stories of James Warner Bellah. Far from romanticizing the expansion of the American empire, *Cheyenne Autumn* told of the victims of that expansion, the American Indians. John had long been intrigued with this book. When it was first published in 1957, he and Dudley Nichols had developed a screen treatment but he had never been able to generate any interest in it. Now in 1962, with young John Kennedy in the White House and the country in a more liberal frame of mind, John thought the time might be right for it.

Bernard Smith, a shrewd and calculating man, knew just how to sell *Cheyenne Autumn*. He took the property to Warner Brothers, which had recently bought the great Broadway musical *My Fair Lady* and was turning it into a $10 million spectacle—the most expensive picture that had ever been made in the United States. Smith outlined his project to Jack Warner, then made his pitch: "You're taking the biggest gamble in the history of Hollywood," he told Warner. "You've committed too much money to *My Fair Lady*.

If it flops, you just might go under. What you need is an insurance picture, a picture that has a guaranteed audience." Jack Warner chomped on his cigar and listened intently. Then Bernie Smith leaned in for the close. "What better insurance could you have than a John Ford western, particularly a John Ford western in tune with today's social issues?"

Warner bought it. *Cheyenne Autumn* was assigned a $4.2 million budget. John would receive a $200,000 salary and the Ford-Smith venture, which shared in the financing, would keep 65 percent of the net profits. By Christmas 1962, the deal was set, and John, Mary, Barbara, and Ken Curtis flew down to Hawaii to spend the holidays with Pat Ford, who was then living on the island of Kauai. But even Christmas was, for John, a time to work. While the others explored the island's beaches and relaxed in the warm Hawaiian sunshine, John and Pat worked at reconstructing the 1957 screen treatment. Pat took notes and sent them to Bernard Smith, as follows:

"The basic premise of *Cheyenne Autumn* is to dramatize the Indian side of the conflict. The Cheyenne are not to be presented as heavies, nor are they to be ignorant misguided savages without plan or purpose to their warmaking. Their motives must be expressed early in the picture. If there is to be a heavy, it must be the distant United States Government, a government blind to the plight of the Indians. The Army is to be portrayed as an underpaid, under-manned force all but forgotten on a distant frontier; a group of dedicated professionals trying to keep the peace despite Washington's mismanagement. The 'Penny Dreadful' press of the period is no help with its stories of 'Savage Red Men' and of 'Buckskin Knights Errant' to inflame the imagination of a semi-literate public.

"My father and I are agreed that the Cheyenne should not speak English in the picture. They should serve, in his words, as a 'Greek Chorus.' Since lack of communication was one of their chief causes of trouble it would be ridiculous to show them speaking the national language. Red Shirt and Little Wolf should speak some English but in a rather stilted, traditionally Indian manner. The Indians as a people are to be portrayed as Indians, unable to speak English or to communicate their thoughts to whites, but magnificent in their stoical dignity."

John and Pat took many liberties with the Sandoz book, among them the addition of a new character—Carl Schurz, a little-known historical figure who had long fascinated John. An honest and dedicated public servant, Schurz had become Secretary of the Interior during the Republican administrations of the Reconstruction era and had fought an uphill battle for Indian rights. For love interest they introduced a Quaker schoolteacher who sides with the Cheyenne and accompanies them on their flight. To lighten up the story, they added an interlude with a comical Wyatt Earp. In the Sandoz book the Indians are pursued by many scattered cavalry units, but to give the story dramatic unity John had a single cavalry company, commanded by a captain he called Thomas Archer, pursue them.

After John returned to the mainland, Pat assembled their notes into a ninety-page treatment, which he sent off to Bernard Smith. Smith then turned Pat's notes over to Jimmy Webb, a prominent screenwriter who had written *How the West Was Won*.

An important conflict developed early on this picture between Pat and Bernard Smith. Part of it was a matter of personal styles. To begin with, Pat and his father were light years apart. They were completely different human beings. Pat had a lot of his father's brilliance, all his wit and insight, but he had none of his obsessive drive. Although he had had some success, he wasn't exactly tearing up the movie business. Bernie Smith, on the other hand, was a poor boy who had made it; a tough intense man who felt that Pat's approach to his work was too relaxed, too casual. He was convinced that Pat, who was on the picture as an "executive assistant" to his father, was nothing but dead weight.

But the conflict between Pat and Bernie Smith was much more than a matter of personal styles. The real root of their conflict was money. Jimmy Webb was getting $60,000 for his screenplay, which was only a refinement of Pat's material. Pat, meanwhile, received nothing for his writing chores and only $10,000 for the picture. Worse, he didn't go on salary until shooting began. The writing and preproduction research on *Cheyenne Autumn* was taking a lot more time than he had expected; he was working very hard for no credit and very little money. He felt that he was being shortchanged.

The year 1963 began well for John. He had his teeth into a big commercial picture, and his star in Hollywood was shining brightly. When he returned to the mainland he was approached by two neophyte producers, Robert Graff and Robert Emmett Ginna, about filming an adaptation of Sean O'Casey's enormous, thirteen-volume autobiography, *Mirror in My House*. The script, called *Young Cassidy*, was an attractive project to John. O'Casey was a giant of Irish literature, a revolutionary, a national hero who had fascinated John for years. It was a small, noncommercial project that was to be shot in Ireland, and John was to receive only $50,000 for directing it. Nevertheless, he jumped at the chance.

But meanwhile there was still *Cheyenne Autumn* to be done. In January, John moved into offices at Warner Brothers and set about the tasks of preproduction, working relentlessly, day and night. He wanted to prove that he could still perform the old John Ford alchemy.

To give *Cheyenne Autumn* box-office clout, Warner Brothers wanted to use superstars in the relatively small roles of Carl Schurz and Wyatt Earp. They signed Spencer Tracy and James Stewart, but before shooting began, Tracy was forced to back out because of ill health and was replaced by Edward G. Robinson. As Captain Archer, John cast Richard Widmark, who, like him, was a real fire-breather. Carroll Baker was set as the Quaker girl who goes along with the Indians. Ricardo Montalban and teenage heart-throb Sal Mineo were cast as the two Indian leaders, Little Wolf and Red Shirt. John Ford regulars rounded out the cast.

Publicly John was optimistic about how *Cheyenne Autumn* was shaping up, but the truth was that the film was running into problems. The story sessions, the nuts-and-bolts work, the painstaking preproduction—all were taking a toll on John's energies and interest. Bernie Smith helped him out as much as he could, but not enough, and John simply didn't apply himself as he should have. He gave Jimmy Webb a free hand with the script. After reading one of the writer's early drafts, John wrote Smith that he was "vague as to the chronology after the Fort Robinson sequence, but I'm sure that Jim has it firmly in mind." *Vague as to the chronology!* This just wasn't the same man of even a few years ago. Something clearly was missing.

John's waning enthusiasm was evident in the finished script, which just wasn't what it might have been. Even the title had somehow gotten lost; for reasons of his own, Jim Webb had changed *Cheyenne Autumn* to *The Long Flight*, and John didn't immediately challenge him on it.

Although it had its pleasant moments, *Cheyenne Autumn* was in general an exceptionally difficult picture for John. There were problems with the weather: September was late in the year to be shooting in Monument Valley; skies were overcast; the light was flat and dull. There were unseasonable squalls and windstorms, and the picture fell seriously behind schedule.

There were problems with money and logistics. John had planned to re-use some second-unit footage from the *The Searchers* but was prevented from doing so by C. V. Whitney, who still owned 50 percent of the film and wouldn't release it. After shooting began, John had to hire another second unit to shoot the same footage Pat Ford and Brick Marquard had shot in 1955.

There were problems between John and his actors. He was not getting along with Ricardo Montalban. An elegant Latin aristocrat, Montalban found John's badgering style difficult to take. John's relationship with Sal Mineo wasn't much better. The young actor was intimidated by John's gruffness, and his performance wasn't what it might have been. The personality conflict between Pat Ford and Bernie Smith, which had been smoldering for months, finally flamed into open hostility, and if John didn't have enough to worry about, now he had to act as mediator between his son and his partner.

But the biggest problem of all was, once again, with John himself. *Cheyenne Autumn* was an enormous undertaking for a man who would be sixty-nine years old before its scheduled completion. He just didn't have the stamina that he had once had, and although he wouldn't have admitted it, *Cheyenne Autumn* was too much for him to handle. After thirty days—thirty grueling, windblown, eighteen-hour days—he began to tire to the point of despondency. He became morbid and morose, and in the words of Wingate Smith, developed "a defeatist attitude toward the picture."

The situation worsened when John came down with a nagging cold accompanied by fever and chills. At one point John became so downcast that he turned the picture over to second-unit director Ray Kellogg and went into his room at Goulding's Lodge, refusing to get out of bed for five days. Word was passed among the company that he had the flu, but most of the people who were close to him knew that his problems were largely psychological. George O'Brien, who had a small part in *Cheyenne Autumn*, came in and sat with John, and the two men reminisced about their years together.

O'Brien talked about *The Iron Horse, 3 Bad Men*, and about their trip to the Far East in 1932. He tried to cheer John up, but it was no use. Every time he mentioned *Cheyenne Autumn* John grew sullen and withdrawn and simply said, "It's just no fun anymore."

When John finally did go back to work he shot mechanically and without feeling, glossing over whole sections and shooting them with a single camera set-up. Instead of going after the best possible locations, he set up whenever possible right in front of Goulding's.

On November 22, 1963, President Kennedy was assassinated in Dallas. To John, a great admirer of the young President, the news was a shocking blow. Too upset to work, he shut the picture down and once again retreated to his room.

The following day, November 23, was declared a national day of mourning. To pay his respects to the fallen president, John assembled the huge *Cheyenne Autumn* company at Goulding's Lodge. It was like a scene out of one of his pictures. John had a bugler sound taps, and the flag was lowered to half-staff. Then, like Nathan Brittles addressing the men of his troop, John stood up before the company. He was wearing an old fatigue jacket with a China-Burma-India patch and the two stars of a rear admiral on it. His eyes were clouded, his cheeks shrunken and hollow. A few years before, John would have risen to the occasion with a major speech, but the effort that would have required was now beyond him. Instead, in a weak and barely audible voice he told the company that America had lost a great leader, but that the republic was sound and things would go on. Then he led the cast and crew in a reading of the Lord's Prayer. When it was over, Dobe Carey sang "The Battle Hymn of the Republic." Then John dismissed the company. There was no filming in Monument Valley that day.

John brought *Cheyenne Autumn* back to Warner Brothers early in December. There he shot the Wyatt Earp comedy vignette with James Stewart, Ken Curtis, and Arthur Kennedy. Curtis, a low-life trailhand, has just murdered an Indian. He comes to Dodge City and, when Wyatt Earp is winning big from him at the poker table, has the audacity to challenge the famous lawman to a gunfight.

Wyatt shoots the intruder in the foot with his pocket derringer. Then he plies him with whiskey, puts him on the bar, and cuts the bullet out with his pocketknife.

A peculiar incident happened the day John shot this scene. During a lunch break he was resting outside the stage, studying his script, when a studio employee approached, sweeping up the droppings of the fifty-odd horses milling around. The man didn't recognize John, despite the black patch over his eye, and swept up to him.

"Hey, buddy, pick up your feet," he said.

John picked up his feet.

"Say, what's the name of this picture?"

"*The Long Flight*," said John absently.

"That's funny. I don't see any airplanes." The man swept on.

John looked up from the script for the first time and said, "You know something, you've really got a hell of a point there." The exchange convinced him that *The Long Flight* was a misleading title, and he changed it back to *Cheyenne Autumn*.

John finished *Cheyenne Autumn* in January 1964 and immediately went to work assembling the picture with editor Otho Lovering. In its rough form, *Cheyenne Autumn* looked like a great picture. It was being talked up around Warner Brothers as a likely smash hit, the perfect "insurance" for *My Fair Lady*. John Ford was being praised as a master of the western genre, and his name was spoken in hushed tones. But John himself and the others close to the picture weren't quite so sure. Though it had a visual magnificence, *Cheyenne Autumn* seemed to be missing something intangible but of great importance. John was plagued by a fear that he had laid a $4.2 million egg, and he worked frantically trying to pull the picture together.

When he finished his rough cut, John flew down to Honolulu. He was tired, depressed, and badly in need of rest. He wanted some time to regroup and get ready for *Young Cassidy*. He performed the usual vacation rituals of swimming in the Ali Wai and lounging in the *Araner's* deckhouse, but John was older now, and didn't bounce back as he used to. The push to finish the picture and the pressure to pull off a miracle in the cutting room had taken their toll. *Cheyenne Autumn* had drained him, and the juices didn't flow back as they used to. The cloud of depression that had been hanging over his head for the last several months would not go away.

Problems on the home front did nothing to help his mood. His marriage to Mary was in one of its periodic slumps. John knew that his days as a working director were numbered; he was thinking about making *Young Cassidy* his last picture and retiring. But to do so would mean a change in life-style. It would mean selling the Bel Air house and the *Araner*—which had become phenomenally expensive in recent years—and living on a more modest scale. Mary, however, refused to move or let John sell the *Araner*. Never particularly sympathetic to John's Irish preoccupations, she chastised him for getting involved with *Young Cassidy* when he could be taking on a high-paying commercial project that would relieve the financial pressure.

But the biggest problem of all was with his son. Pat's relationship with Bernard Smith had become so strained on *Cheyenne Autumn* that when the picture was finished, the producer put his foot down and excluded Pat from any future projects. When Pat went to his father for financial assistance, John was upset, disappointed, and finally enraged. He had given Pat an education, money, and professional advantages, but he just didn't seem to be able to make it.

While John was in Honolulu, Robert Graff and Robert Ginna were in London gearing up for *Young Cassidy*. They assembled an all-star English cast that included Dame Edith Evans, Michael Redgrave, Maggie Smith, Flora Robson, and Julie Christie. As young Sean O'Casey, Ginna and Graff cast a then-unknown Scotsman named Sean Connery. Both producers were wildly enthusiastic about him. But before the picture began, Connery was asked to play secret agent James Bond in *Dr. No*, and he was on his way to becoming an international superstar. He was replaced on *Young Cassidy* by the Australian-born Rod Taylor.

In March, after two frustrating months in Honolulu, John left for Dublin, where he was to meet with Ginna and Graff and spend a week scouting locations. John stopped over in New York and enjoyed a boisterous reunion with Ole Doering, Bill Donovan's partner and his colleague from the O.S.S. John barely managed to pull himself together enough to get on board a Pan American flight to London. Once on the plane, he began drinking in earnest: the first-class cabin attendants couldn't believe that the unshaven, red-eyed, drunken old man in their midst was Hollywood's greatest director.

After landing at Heathrow, Pan American officials hustled John off the plane in a wheelchair and got him aboard a connecting Aer Lingus flight to Dublin, where he was greeted by Ginna, Graff, and Lord Killanin. Neither Ginna nor Graff had ever met John in the flesh, and they were unprepared for the figure that reeled off the plane. His clothes were rumpled and covered with cigar ashes. His shoelaces were untied, and his eyes were red and vague. While John's appearance didn't surprise Killanin, whom John had brought onto the picture and who was used to his eccentricities, it caught Ginna and Graff completely off guard. They wondered if this was the *real* John Ford, or if it wasn't some kind of a preposterous joke. The two producers never completely got over their first impression of John, and he never enjoyed their complete confidence after that first meeting.

The Dublin survey trip started out badly and quickly got worse. John had only one week to spend in the Irish capital before he had to return to California for a major preview of *Cheyenne Autumn*—one week to look over all the locations and attend to a thousand and one details. Ginna and Graff were upset when they learned how little time John had to give them. When they protested, John growled, "What do you expect for a lousy fifty grand?"

Ginna and Graff were disappointed with John, but he was disappointed with them too. In his mind they were neophytes, inexperienced upstarts who knew little about Ireland and less about filmmaking. Convinced that they would be no help whatsoever, he began to have second thoughts about *Young Cassidy*.

To make matters worse, John and the two producers had very different ideas on how to approach the film. Because the Dublin of 1964 bore little resemblance to that of 1911, they wanted to work in a less-developed provincial town. John thought this was ridiculous. "If we're not going to shoot in Dublin, then what the hell's the point of making it in Ireland at all? We could make the goddamn thing in London or Culver City."

John accomplished little on his Dublin survey except to start off on the wrong foot with the two producers. After a week of frantic production meetings he was on a plane flying back to Los Angeles. When he arrived home he went directly to the Loyola Theater in Westchester to attend a preview of *Cheyenne Autumn*. The screening was a disaster. People coughed, talked, or simply walked out on it. John, Bernard Smith, and a platoon of Warner Brothers executives exchanged nervous glances all through it. After the screening their worst suspicions were confirmed when the audience turned in disastrous preview cards. The only sequence that received any positive comment was the comic Wyatt Earp interlude.

The next day, fighting jet lag, fatigue, depression, and self-doubt, John locked himself in a cutting room and went to work on *Cheyenne Autumn*. He cut twenty minutes out of his original version and tried to pick up the pace and give the picture some verve. But John had little hope that his efforts would succeed. He knew *Cheyenne Autumn* was a bomb and would remain so however he recut it.

After eight days of intense and frantic work, John was back in an airplane, jetting across the world on his way to Ireland to begin *Young Cassidy*. This time he planned to lay over in London and get over his jet lag before he faced "the Bobs," as he called Ginna and Graff. London was enjoying a warm spring, and the smell of English greensward reminded John of the summer of 1942, which he had spent in London preparing for the North African invasion. He met Rod Taylor for the first time and hit it off immediately with the gruff Australian actor.

A few days later John flew to Dublin, was met by Lord Killanin, and taken to the Shelbourne Hotel. Killanin was disturbed to notice that John looked much worse than he had even a few weeks before: he seemed thin and very frail. When Killanin asked him how he felt, John blustered, "I've never felt better in my life." But the truth was he had never felt worse.

Young Cassidy began shooting in mid-July 1964 at the King's Inn on Henrietta Street, Dublin. On July 28, after thirteen working days, John came down with viral pneumonia. Lord Killanin took him to his home on Landsdowne Road, where his wife, Sheila, looked after him. Jack Cardiff took over *Young Cassidy*. A few days later John was packed aboard a plane to Los Angeles.

John's illness during *Young Cassidy* had one positive side-effect: it convinced him that he had to slow down and get a proper rest. He knew he couldn't do pictures back to back anymore. After recuperating in Los Angeles for a few weeks, he flew down to Honolulu to join Mary, who was waiting for him aboard the *Araner*. The *Araner*'s captain, Rip Yeager, who hadn't seen his boss in several months, was appalled by his appearance. He seemed to have aged ten years. He looked as Killanin had noticed, frail; his cheeks were shrunken and his arm muscles were flaccid. Behind the patch and the thick glasses his eyes were clouded. This was not the robust, dynamic "skipper" he was used to.

Nor was John in a particularly good humor. Still squabbling with Mary about retirement, he took every opportunity to bully and browbeat her. One night, while walking on deck, Mary tripped on one of the *Araner*'s running backstays and badly twisted her ankle. She now became the butt of his cruel humor. He ridiculed her limping, implied that her ankle wasn't really hurt, and accused her of doing her "martyr act."

But a few evenings later the gods got back at John. One evening, after removing his glasses, he dove into the water for a short swim. After a few minutes in the water he suddenly realized that he could see only a few feet in the darkness. He didn't know where he was. Panic seized him as he treaded the inky water, but he fought it back. He had been in many worse situations. The water was warm, and if he conserved his energy he could swim about almost indefinitely. After doing so for some thirty minutes, John finally made it to the guest dock at the Hawaii Yacht Club. He pulled himself out of the water, went dripping wet into the bar, and called Rip Yeager, who came over in the *Araner*'s launch and picked him up. Yeager was discreet enough not to say anything, but he quietly rigged a bright light on the dock by the swimming ladder, one that John could see without his glasses.

While John was resting in Honolulu, Ginna and Graff wrote from London to tell him that *Young Cassidy* was coming along well. "Jack Cardiff has made an enormous effort, and a fine one, we feel, for a man plunged headfirst into an ambitious film for which he should have had weeks, even months of preparation. We'll miss the touches we had always counted on your giving the film but think the spirit you instilled in Rod and the entire unit has been kept." While "the Bobs" praised John's abbreviated efforts, they were in truth glad to be rid of him. He had always been too irascible, too opinionated, and too set in his ways for their tastes.

In Honolulu, John relaxed through the last weeks of August and into September, trying not to think about the forthcoming release of *Cheyenne Autumn*. He swam four or five times a day, and his appetite came back with a vengeance. Soon he was eating like a horse and gaining weight. John Wayne was in the islands making *In Harm's Way* for Otto Preminger and was a frequent guest aboard the *Araner*. The two men sat in the deckhouse for hours on end playing cards, cheating each other whenever possible and arguing fiercely over pennies. John noticed that Wayne looked pale and tired, and was racked by a persistent cough. When John asked him about his health the actor brushed aside his inquiries, saying that he had "some kind of a flu bug." When Wayne left for the mainland, he sent John a bottle of wine with a friendly note that ended "P.S. Stay aboard as long as you want."

When Wayne returned to Los Angeles his wife, Pilar, also noticed that he didn't look well, and she talked him into checking into the Scripps Clinic in La Jolla for a complete checkup. The examination revealed that he had something a lot more serious than the "flu bug" he thought was bothering him. He had lung cancer.

John was stunned by the news. He immediately flew home to sit at Wayne's bedside and to comfort Pilar. His heart reached out to the man who had been his closest friend for thirty years. With Ward Bond gone, Wayne was the last of the old crowd, and the thought of losing him was too much to even think about.

On September 16, 1964, Wayne was admitted to the Good Samaritan Hospital in Los Angeles, where a malignant growth was removed from his left lung. That operation, performed by Dr. John C. Jones, was completely successful. Wayne's recovery was phenomenal and John was overjoyed. Wayne had apparently licked the big C.

John's concern for his friend kept his mind off the disastrous reception *Cheyenne Autumn* was receiving. The picture had opened October 5 to a blaze of ballyhoo. Warner Brothers publicists had a field day trumpeting John's reputation as the master of the western genre. But all the publicity in the world couldn't hide the fact that the picture just didn't work. One major review spoke of the film as one of John's "biggest disappointments," and another called it "far and away the most boring picture of 1964." It appeared, as Peter Bogdanovich had observed (to John's annoyance) in an article in *Esquire*, that *Cheyenne Autumn* was the autumn of John Ford.

But if it was his autumn, it was not quite his finale. He was a tough old warhorse, and if his physical and creative energies had diminished, his ego was too sound to admit defeat. Even as he was recovering from "the bitch of a year" he was calling 1964, John was mulling over another project that Bernie Smith wanted to do: a story by Norah Lofts called "Chinese Finale." Set on the Chinese-Mongolian border in 1935, it was the story of seven missionary women in conflict with marauding warlords and each other. One of the women, a strong-willed doctor named Dorothy Cartwright, becomes the concubine of a warlord named Tunga Khan and later commits suicide.

Grim and violent as this story was, it is difficult to believe that John approached it with much enthusiasm. Its principal attraction was the deal Bernie Smith had put together. MGM was willing to put up $2.5 million and John would receive $250,000 for directing it, in addition to which the Ford-Smith partnership would retain 50 percent of the net. The failure of *Cheyenne Autumn*, and his illness in Ireland, had shaken John. He wasn't sure he could keep working much longer. Better take the money while he could still command it.

When the deal was set, Bernie Smith flew to the south of France to work on the script with a Europe-based husband-and-wife writer team, Janet Green and John McCormick. When they finished the first draft, which they now called *7 Women*, they sent it to John in Honolulu. John wrote to Smith urging him to come to Hawaii with the two writers so that they could all go over the script in his "lucky spot"—the *Araner*'s main saloon:

"I should tell you that I have greatly improved in health, I'm eating like a horse, swimming two or three times a day and sleeping well. This brings up a point. I think we should all meet, the McCormicks, you and I, for a week or ten days for the final polish. I wish it could be here in Honolulu as it is doing me so much good. TWA has a deluxe Trans-Polar flight from Paris to L.A. A couple of days' rest while you visit MGM, and then it's a lovely five-hour flight to Honolulu. What do you think, Bernie? Can you stand the gaff? Remember our latest hobby, superstitions? The main cabin of the *Araner* is lucky. Scripts on *The Informer*, *Stagecoach*, *The Long Voyage Home*, *The Grapes of Wrath*, *How Green Was My Valley*, were written or finalized here. Think it over."

But personal commitments kept the McCormicks and Smith in Europe, and John never did involve himself in the script.

He was also indifferent to the casting, letting Bernie Smith take complete charge. The producer chose Patricia Neal for the role of Dr. Cartwright, and Margaret Leighton, Flora Robson, Sue Lyon, Mildred Dunnock, and Betty Field for the other missionaries. So far, *7 Women* was a John Ford picture in name only.

In January, John moved into offices at MGM and began the preproduction work. On February 1, 1965, MGM observed his seventieth birthday with a special luncheon in the studio commissary that was attended by the studio brass and the Hollywood press corps. John told Bob Thomas of the Associated Press, "It has been a wonderful day. The lunch was charming, and I've had calls from just about everyone I know." When Thomas asked him how it felt to be seventy, John blustered, "I can still lick anyone around."

A few days after the picture began shooting, its star, Patricia Neal, suffered a severe stroke that left her paralyzed, blind, and unable to speak. In the few days they had spent together John had become very fond of her, and he was greatly concerned for her recovery. But even without her, he had to keep the picture going. He juggled the shooting schedule and shot around the Dr. Cartwright character, all the while working frantically to cast a replacement. John and Bernie Smith finally settled on Anne Bancroft, who proved to be a fine choice. Happily, Patricia Neal made a remarkable recovery from her stroke. Six weeks later she had regained her sight and was walking with the help of braces. She had to learn to speak all over again, and it's a testament to her courage that she not only did so, but a few years later resumed her acting career.

7 Women has its moments, but they are few and far between. John's lack of enthusiasm is again very obvious. The production values are exceptionally weak. At a time when the whole trend in film making was toward location shooting, *7 Women* has a musty, claustrophobic, "made on the lot" feel. The mission is a stale, drab world, and the women who inhabit it have no spiritual substance; instead of being presented as women with real complexities and real emotions, they seem caricatures of what they are supposed to be.

John wrapped up *7 Women* in April and flew down to Honolulu to rest aboard the *Araner*. He didn't have to wait for this one to be released to know that it was a failure. Already in a black mood, he began drinking in Hawaii. Sitting propped up in his "lucky spot," he went on a binge that lasted for weeks. He drank as though he were trying to do much more than blur the edges; he drank as though he were trying to find real oblivion. I was on board the *Araner* at the time and I remember him sitting there amid the hand-rubbed mahogany and the silver. He was lathering on about *7 Women*, saying that it had been a mistake to make it and that it would probably finish him. I had seen him drunk before, but never so depressed.

One evening he was up on deck leaning over the rail in helpless defeat. I walked up to him. He stirred as I approached.

"Are you all right, Gramps?" I asked.

"No," he said. "At least I don't mind telling you I'm not." His voice was thick and slurred, and I didn't know how to respond. Without waiting for me to say anything, he turned and lurched toward the deckhouse. After a moment there was a thud and the sound of broken glass. I found him lying facedown on the cabin floor. He looked dead to the world.

"You poor old bastard," I mumbled, half to myself. "I guess you've just about had enough, haven't you? I can't get you to bed like you deserve, but I'll make you as comfortable as I can." I picked him up and wrestled his dead weight into a comfortable position on the settee. I took off his shoes and loosened his belt. "You're the best there ever was. Nobody's ever going to come close," I said as I turned out the light. I was already out the door when he stirred.

"I heard that," he said.

"I meant every word of it."

I went out on deck. It was so quiet that it was like being in outer space. I stood there for a minute thinking about him: about his fantastic life and his magnificent work. Then I went down below, opened up his liquor cabinet, and got a bottle. Following what I thought was an excellent example, I sat down in the saloon and got drunk myself.

24

Yesterday's Soup

J ohn never planned or formally announced his retirement. Rather, he gradually slid into it. After *7 Women* the offers stopped coming. Hollywood had stopped making his kind of picture, and he was never able to get another project off the ground. In time he accepted the fact of his retirement, and in his later years John become increasingly reclusive, spending more and more time in bed, locked up with his books and his television set. It was as if he were shutting himself off from a world in which he no longer belonged.

John was approached by scores of writers who wanted to write his biography but he always put them off, saying that his work was "yesterday's soup" and nobody was interested in it anymore. Peter Bogdanovich was one of the few that he did talk to, and among the most important. In 1968 Bogdanovich expanded the *Esquire* article he had written, "The Autumn of John Ford," into a book that contained the article, a filmography, a critical assessment, and an extensive interview—by far the most detailed John ever gave. Later Bogdanovich made a documentary, *Directed by John Ford*, for the American Film Institute. Narrated by Orson Welles, it consisted of filmed interviews with John Wayne, Jimmy Stewart, and Henry Fonda, intercut with clips from John's pictures. The film was presented in 1971 and was widely acclaimed. John, however, wasn't too impressed. "I thought it was long" he told *Time* magazine.

There was another documentary, *The American West of John Ford*, which I co-produced and which appeared on CBS in December 1971. Similar to the Bogdanovich film, it also featured interviews with Wayne, Stewart, and Fonda, and footage of John in Monument Valley. Although it had better production values, *The American West of John Ford* was limited to westerns and didn't represent the full spectrum of John's work.

John was also approached by any number of scholars wanting to write critical assessments. But he had never liked critical analysis, and he was not known for being cooperative. In 1970 he was interviewed by Joseph McBride, who with Michael Wilmington had written a number of critical pieces that were eventually published in a book called *John Ford* (Da Capo, 1975). McBride found John irascible, evasive, and completely delightful. In one section of the interview McBride observed that John had treated the cavalry in an unusual way in *Fort Apache*.

"I don't remember what the hell it's all about," said John.

"It's kind of a Custer's-last-stand with Henry Fonda."

"Oh, that's right. Yeah, it's all right."

"I understand that John Wayne felt uneasy about being in *Fort Apache* because he thinks Custer was a disgrace to the cavalry."

"Oh, that's a lot of crap. I don't think he's ever heard of Custer."

"What do you think about Wayne finally getting the Oscar after so many years?"

"Isn't that a rather useless question?"

"When you started your career, why did you only direct westerns?"

"Because the pay was good. I still enjoy doing a western. If a story came along, I'd go out and do it now, but hell, they're not coming. I get two or three scripts a week, but they're remakes or rewrites of pictures I've already done. Or they're all filthy and sexy, and that would be against my nature, my religion, and my cultural inclinations."

"Are there any other projects you'd like to make?"

"No."

"I'm sorry I asked such silly questions."

"Well, it isn't that, but everybody asks the same questions, all you people, and I'm sick and tired of trying to answer them, because I don't know the answers. I'm just a hard-nosed, hard-working ex-director, and I'm trying to retire gracefully."

Although John was no multimillionaire, he was financially well off. In 1965 his net worth was approximately $1.7 million. The bulk of his money was in blue-chip stocks: he owned 30,000 shares of American Telephone & Telegraph, plus big blocks of General Motors and Southern California Edison. His income in 1965 was just over $100,000; not bad for a man in retirement.

His main financial worry was the *Araner*. In July 1966, she was listed in "fair" condition by a Honolulu marine surveyor, and given a market value of $175,000 and a replacement value of $450,000. But these weren't realistic figures. As beautiful as the *Araner* was, she was old, slow, and required too much maintenance. There just wasn't a market for that kind of a boat anymore. John couldn't afford her, and he couldn't sell her either. The few people who could afford a boat that size wanted something more modern. In 1968, John finally sold her to a Hawaiian hotel developer. He got $25,000 cash and an interest in a resort complex, and considered himself lucky.

The Field Photo Home had likewise become a financial burden. In the years since the war, the Farm had more than served its purpose. All the original members had long since returned to civilian life and they now only seemed to gather there for funerals. In 1961, John had sold off half the land to keep the Farm from going under, but by 1965 it was in the red again. The buildings were run-down and the grounds were unkept. With no other choice, John sold the remaining land to a San Fernando real-estate developer for $300,000 and gave the money to the Motion Picture Relief Fund. The Farm's chapel was moved to the Woodland Hills Country Home, where it stands to this day

John's relationship with his son remained strained for the rest of his life. Pat drifted out of the picture business, and they saw little of each other. But John's relationship with Mary righted itself when she at last accepted the idea of his retirement. The two of them had vacillated back and forth through good years and bad. While they had suffered many lows, they had also enjoyed many highs. One of them came on July 3, 1970, when they celebrated their fiftieth wedding anniversary with a party attended by all their friends.

But the outings were becoming increasingly rare, and John's reclusiveness became habitual. He seldom left his room, and as the years went by he tended to badly neglect himself. He exercised little and ignored his appearance—his teeth, hair, and fingernails—as well as his health. Friends who had not seen him in years were appalled at his appearance.

One of the last events that he attended was the Venice Film Festival in August 1971, at which he was presented with the Grand Lion of Venice award. John received hordes of reporters in his suite at the Gritti Palace Hotel and told them that he "worked out" every day in his swimming pool, that he "was never feeling better," and had a "half dozen projects in the works." None of it was true.

A few months later John told his doctor, Maynard Brandsma, that he had sporadic abdominal pains and didn't know what to make of them. Recognizing the potential seriousness of John's symptoms, Brandsma hustled John into a hospital for a complete series of tests. The news was not good. John had cancer. Exploratory surgery revealed a massive malignancy too large to remove. John's illness was terminal.

He returned home and accepted his fate.

But even illness didn't dim John's sharp acerbic wit. A few weeks later, he attended a luncheon honoring Spanish director Luis Buñuel. Most of Hollywood's major film makers were there: William Wyler, Robert Wise, Billy Wilder, George Stevens, and Alfred Hitchcock, among others. After the luncheon they all gathered for a group portrait—all, that is, except John. He had had to leave early because of his health, so he was photographed separately. When the accompanying piece appeared the next day, Charles Champlin, the entertainment editor of the *Los Angeles Times*, called to say he was sorry that John wasn't in the group portrait, but John saw the humor in it. "What do you mean?" he snapped. "I got the close-up, didn't I?"

In December 1972, John sold his Bel Air home and bought a spacious house in Palm Desert, a vacation and retirement community 140 miles from Los Angeles. Many of his contemporaries, including Howard Hawks, Henry Hathaway, and Frank Capra, lived nearby. The house had two wings off the living room; John took one of them, and Mary the other. I began working on this book in March 1973, assembling the papers that make up its core. They may have been "yesterday's soup" to my grandfather, but they were yesterday's treasure to me.

Scores of friends and old colleagues came to see John in Palm Desert: John Wayne, Lee Marvin, Bob Parrish, Al Wedemeyer, Peter Bogdanovich, Elizabeth Allen, Howard Hawks, and Frank Capra were all frequent visitors. But the most important guest was Kate Hepburn, who came out from New York to spend a week with John. They talked about old times for hours on end. John turned on the blarney and tried to present a stiff upper lip, but in the end he had to say good-bye to her.

John's last hurrah came on March 31, 1973, when he was presented with the first annual Lifetime Achievement Award by the American Film Institute. Richard Nixon chose the occasion to present John with the Medal of Freedom, the country's highest civilian award. It was a gala affair, held at the Beverly Hilton Hotel, and whatever its political implications, it was a lovely, emotional moment. John sat on the dais with Nixon and Ronald Reagan, while John Wayne, Jimmy Stewart, Maureen O'Hara, and Danny Kaye shared duties as hosts.

In the months that followed, John grew progressively weaker. Fully aware of his condition, he avoided doctors as much as possible and solaced himself in an Irish way, with his rosary and Guinness Stout. His basic religious feeling, his simple faith in Jesus Christ, was a comfort to him in his last days. His room had big windows that looked out onto the desert; light poured in and formed little pools on the floor. He seldom opened the windows and, despite the air conditioning, the room soon smelled as dank as a grave. He lost weight and became extremely gaunt. His eyes became more clouded, the look behind them more distant. As the searing summer heat settled in over the desert, the visitors became few.

On August 31, 1973, after receiving the last rites, John Ford passed away.

Index

318

320